Abraham Lincoln's stature as an American cultural figure grows from his political legacy. In today's milieu, the speeches he delivered as the sixteenth president of the United States have become synonymous with American progress, values, and exceptionalism. What makes Lincoln's language so effective? Highlighting matters of style, affect, nationalism, and history in nineteenth-century America, this collection examines the rhetorical power of Lincoln's prose – from the earliest legal decisions, stump speeches, anecdotes, and letters to the Gettysburg Address and the lingering power of the Second Inaugural Address. Through careful analysis of his correspondence with Civil War generals and his early poetry, the contributors, all literary and cultural critics, give readers a unique look into Lincoln's private life. Their essays also examine Lincoln's language in a larger sphere, including that of the Caribbean and Latin America, as well as Europe. Such a collection enables teachers, students, and readers of American history to assess the impact of this extraordinary writer – and rare politician – on the world's stage.

Shirley Samuels works with the American Studies program and the Feminist, Gender, and Sexuality Studies Program at Cornell University. She has taught at Princeton, Brandeis, and the University of Delaware. She has had fellowships from the American Council of Learned Societies, the Huntington Library, and the Library Company of Philadelphia. In addition to journal articles and chapters in books, she is author of *Reading the American Novel: 1780–1865* (2012); *Facing America: Iconography and the Civil War* (2004); and *Romances of the Republic: Women, the Family, and Violence in the Literature of the Early American Nation* (1996). She is editor of the *Companion to American Fiction, 1780–1865* (2004) and *The Culture of Sentiment: Race, Gender, and Sentimentality in Nineteenth-Century America* (1992).

CAMBRIDGE
COMPANIONS TO
AMERICAN STUDIES

This series of Companions to key figures in American history and culture is aimed at students of American studies, history, and literature. Each volume features newly commissioned essays by experts in the field, with a chronology and guide to further reading.

VOLUMES PUBLISHED

THE CAMBRIDGE COMPANION TO
ABRAHAM LINCOLN

EDITED BY
SHIRLEY SAMUELS
Cornell University

CAMBRIDGE
UNIVERSITY PRESS

CAMBRIDGE UNIVERSITY PRESS
Cambridge, New York, Melbourne, Madrid, Cape Town,
Singapore, São Paulo, Delhi, Mexico City

Cambridge University Press
32 Avenue of the Americas, New York, NY 10013-2473, USA

www.cambridge.org
Information on this title: www.cambridge.org/9780521145732

First published 2012

Printed in the United States of America

A catalog record for this publication is available from the British Library.

Library of Congress Cataloging in Publication data
The Cambridge companion to Abraham Lincoln / [edited by] Shirley Samuels.
p. cm. – (Cambridge companions to American studies)
Includes bibliographical references and index.
ISBN 978-0-521-19316-0 (hardback : alk. paper) –
ISBN 978-0-521-14573-2 (pbk. : alk. paper)
1. Lincoln, Abraham, 1809–1865 – Language. 2. Lincoln, Abraham, 1809–1865 –
Oratory. 3. Lincoln, Abraham, 1809–1865 – Correspondence. 4. Presidents – United
States – Biography. 5. Rhetoric – Political aspects – United States – Case studies.
6. United States – Politics and government – 1861–1865. I. Samuels, Shirley.
II. Title: Abraham Lincoln.
E457.2.C245   2012
973.7092–dc23   2012009107

ISBN 978-0-521-19316-0 Hardback
ISBN 978-0-521-14573-2 Paperback

CONTENTS

CONTENTS

ILLUSTRATIONS

CONTRIBUTORS

FAITH BARRETT, Lawrence University, has written *"To Fight Aloud Is Very Brave": American Poetry and the Civil War*.

HAROLD K. BUSH, JR., Professor of English at St. Louis University, is the author of *Mark Twain and the Spiritual Crisis of His Age* and *Lincoln in His Own Time*.

STEPHEN CUSHMAN, Robert C. Taylor Professor of English, University of Virginia, is the author of *Bloody Promenade: Reflections on a Civil War Battle*.

BETSY ERKKILA, Henry Sanborn Noyes Professor of Literature, Northwestern University, has written several books including *Mixed Bloods and Other Crosses: Whitman the Political Poet* and *Walt Whitman Among the French: Poet and Myth*.

ROBERT FANUZZI, English and American Studies at St. John's University, has written *Abolition's Public Sphere*.

PAUL GILES, Challis Professor of English, University of Sydney, is author of, among other books, *Transatlantic Insurrections: British Culture and the Formation of American Literature, 1730–1860*; *Atlantic Republic: The American Tradition in English Literature*; and *The Global Remapping of American Literature*.

DEAK NABERS, Brown University, has written *Victory of Law: The Fourteenth Amendment, The Civil War, and American Literature, 1852–1867*.

ANNE NORTON, Political Science, University of Pennsylvania, has written *Alternative Americas: A Reading of Antebellum Political Culture*; *Reflections on Political Identity*; and *Republic of Signs*.

CAROL PAYNE, History of Art, Carleton University, has co-edited (with Andrea Kunard) *The Cultural Work of Photography in Canada*.

CONTRIBUTORS

BETHANY SCHNEIDER, Bryn Mawr College, has written a forthcoming book, *Indian Intertexts: Between Native Literatures, 1820–1932*.

TIMOTHY SWEET, West Virginia University, wrote *Traces of War: Photography, Poetry, and the Crisis of the Union* and *American Georgics: Economy and Environment in Early American Literature*.

IVY G. WILSON, Northwestern University, is the author of *Specters of Democracy: Blackness and the Aesthetics of Politics in the Antebellum U.S.*

1809	Born February 12 in a one-room cabin in Hardin County, Kentucky, to Thomas Lincoln and Nancy Hanks Lincoln.
1818	Nancy Lincoln dies.
1819	Thomas Lincoln marries Sarah Bush Johnston.
1830	Lincoln family settles in Illinois.
1831	Hired to take goods by boat to New Orleans, where he witnesses slavery firsthand.
1832	Buys a general store. Begins his political career by running for the Illinois General Assembly, an election he loses. Briefly serves as a captain in the Illinois militia during the Black Hawk War.
1834	Elected to the Illinois General Assembly as a Whig. Begins studying law.
1837	Moves to Springfield, Illinois, and practices law with John T. Stuart.
1842	Marries Mary Todd, member of a slaveholding Kentucky family, on November 4. They have four sons: Robert Todd Lincoln (1843–1926), Edward Baker Lincoln (1846–1850), William Wallace Lincoln (1850–1862), and Thomas Lincoln (1853–1871).
1846	Elected to a two-year term in the U.S. House of Representatives as a Whig.
1848–1854	Returns to Springfield to practice law. Lincoln's most famous case occurs in 1858 when he defends accused murderer William "Duff" Armstrong.

1854   Returns to politics in response to the Kansas-Nebraska Act, signed into law on May 30, which allowed settlers to determine whether to allow slavery. On October 16, he delivers the "Peoria Speech," declaring he is against slavery; late in the year he decides to run for the U.S. Senate. After losing, he helps form the new Republican Party.

1858   Nominated for the U.S. Senate at the Illinois state Republican Convention, where he delivers the "House Divided" speech on June 16. Later in the year he engages in a series of famous debates with opponent Stephen A. Douglas, who eventually received the legislature's vote for the seat.

1860   Invited by the New York Republican Party to deliver a speech at Cooper Union on February 27, in which he argues against popular sovereignty. At the party convention on May 18, Lincoln receives the nomination for president. On November 6, he is elected president over Douglas, John C. Breckinridge, and John Bell. On December 20, South Carolina secedes from the Union, followed by a string of Southern states.

1861   The Civil War begins on April 12, when Confederate troops fire on Fort Sumter, South Carolina. As commander-in-chief, Lincoln imposes a blockade, suspends the writ of habeas corpus, and dispenses funds before appropriation by Congress.

1862   After the Union victory at Antietam in September, Lincoln announces that he will issue an Emancipation Proclamation to free slaves in states not under Union control. The Emancipation Proclamation goes into effect on January 1, 1863.

1863   Union troops defeat the Confederates at the Battle of Gettysburg in July. On November 19, Lincoln delivers the Gettysburg Address at the dedication of the national cemetery on the battlefield. After the Battle of Chattanooga later in the year, Lincoln names Ulysses S. Grant commander of the Union army.

1864   Wins a landslide reelection over Democratic candidate George B. McClellan. Grant wears down Confederate

General Robert E. Lee's troops in a series of campaigns in Virginia. Further south, Sherman and Sheridan destroy Confederate infrastructure.

1865   Delivers his Second Inaugural speech on March 4. Lee surrenders to Grant on April 9 at Appomattox, Virginia, effectively ending the war. On April 15, Lincoln dies after being shot the night before by Confederate sympathizer John Wilkes Booth while attending a play at Ford's Theater in Washington, DC. Lincoln's body leaves Washington, DC, on April 21 and is taken to Springfield, Illinois. Millions of Americans are estimated to have seen the train along its route. Lincoln is buried in Springfield on May 3.

Introduction

Abraham Lincoln has appeared so extraordinarily present in the cultural and political imagination of the United States during the almost 150 years since his assassination that it has become impossible to imagine how anyone could have celebrated his sudden death at the close of the Civil War. As an image of American political life, Lincoln's face seems ubiquitous. That face also circulates in currency, appearing not only on pennies but also on five-dollar bills, the only president other than George Washington to be minted more than once. The association with George Washington is significant because during the nineteenth century they were understood to be joined in a kind of national genealogy, a linked parentage for a country torn apart by Civil War.

There are now more books, articles, Web sites, and conversations than any person could take on at once concerning Abraham Lincoln. Public interest seems inexhaustible. The political ideas that his speeches generated have been succeeded by inevitable attention to his sexuality (especially given his intimate relationship with Joshua Speed), his marriage (especially given the involuntary commitment of his widow, Mary Todd, by his oldest son Robert), his attitudes toward race (in a countermove to the celebrations still associated with the Emancipation Proclamation), and his attention to the tactics of the Civil War (especially in a country where physical reenactments of battles are more popular than ever). Books on his photographed image sit next to books on his life.

To address the words and the image of Lincoln must mean inevitably to participate in renegotiating his language, his image, and his political place in history. The statue of Lincoln enshrined in concrete above the fray of politics in the middle of the mall in the United States capital always returns the viewer's gaze, even as tourists stand reading his words on the marble walls. Such words as those of his Second Inaugural Address appear there, as Lincoln pleaded for "malice toward none, charity for all." As tourists read these words carved in stone, they look at the enormous statue gazing out at the nation's capital. But what kind of gaze is that, after more than 150 years of interpretations of those words?

However many historical and biographical accounts of Lincoln have appeared, the difference made by this collection emerges from the new attention paid here by literary critics who have specialized in matters of style, affect, nationalism, and history in the nineteenth-century United States. Their essays here examine the rhetorical power of Lincoln's prose – from the earliest legal decisions, stump speeches, anecdotes, and letters to the Gettysburg Address and the lingering power of the Second Inaugural Address. What made this language so effective? Succinct in an era when political speeches often lasted for hours, Lincoln could be witty and precise in the face of bombast, as in the debates with Stephen Douglas. Pithy and even vulgar on occasion, although capable of dignified distance, Lincoln performed galvanizing transformations on restless audiences, from the backwoods of Illinois, where he crusaded as a traveling lawyer, to the Cooper Union address in New York City, where he began his run for the presidency, to the dangerous streets of Washington, DC that he traversed on his route to a refuge in the Soldier's Home during the most violent days of the war.

In addition to crucial public statements such as the Emancipation Proclamation, in this collection attention is given to the private words of Lincoln, his relation to the Black Hawk War along the Mississippi River, his correspondence with Civil War generals, the early poems that displayed his dreams and fears, and his attention to theater – in short, the private and the public man. The essays also challenge an interpretation of Lincoln specific to the United States by looking at the influence of Lincoln's language in a larger sphere, that of the Caribbean and Latin America as well as that of relations with Europe. Such a collection of essays enables teachers and students in classrooms around the world to return to the impact of this extraordinary writer – and rare politician – and to consider the impact on the world's stage of his moral vision of human possibility.

For a reader to encounter Abraham Lincoln in the twenty-first century must inevitably mean that his assassination overshadows his life. The difficult matter of interpreting his life as other than momentous set in immediately after its precipitous conclusion on April 14, 1865. The coincidence of the Easter weekend when the nation began to mourn spurred famous poems, stirring oratory, religious analogies, and gilded memories.

In the immediate aftermath of the American Civil War, mourning for lost family members preoccupied inhabitants of the United States. Lincoln's death proved cathartic for such mourners as well as for onlookers around the world, many of whom poured out testimonials. Lincoln's words are, instead, silenced at the moment of his passing. Whereas Lincoln's leading general,

Ulysses S. Grant, could spend his declining years on an autobiography, and Jefferson Davis, the ex-president of the Confederacy's lost cause, could entertain visitors with stories on his southern plantation, Lincoln, dying, left the last words of eulogies and the distorting fame of his assassination in a frozen account.

These words of loss obscure two dynamic possibilities for considering the resonance of Lincoln's language. The first is comic, the oral traditions that came to be characterized as southwest humor. Such traditions link Lincoln's patterns of speech not only to the frontier tall tales that reached their fullest resonance in the writings of Mark Twain but also to the cultural echoes in the oral traditions associated with slavery. Born in the slave state of Kentucky, Lincoln grew up on the margins of slave culture. His attention to the fraught legal matter of how the United States might endorse the expansion of slavery into newly acquired territories must be read against his intimate witnessing of its consequences during travel on the Mississippi River.

Second, the cadences of Lincoln's language drew on classical traditions of oratory. Whether declaiming or debating, Lincoln appeared before audiences whose ears already rang with the oscillations between the bawdy insult of the political arena and the rhetorical flourish of training in classical rhetorical modes. Lincoln's debates with Stephen Douglas remain famous, but contemporary accounts punctuate them with thrown cabbages and tomatoes, approving cries, raucous shouts, and jeering comments.

In this volume, the cacophony of such a crowd cannot appear. We can, however, work at hearing the voices of Lincoln's friends and colleagues as they remembered him as well as when they challenged him. The derision that greeted his notoriously ungainly appearance follows a North/South divide about race as well as invoking an East/West quarrel about class. The presumption so early bandied about that Lincoln's racial ancestry was suspect blurs the uneasy relation that his "log cabin" origin had to the anxious resistance of a still-emerging aristocracy in America.

The very repetition of arguments based on the presumed intentions of the founding fathers to exchanges with Karl Marx makes Lincoln's language both relevant and rich. Biographical attention to Lincoln has included close scrutiny of his courtship and marriage as well as debate over his political stands, notably with respect to the abolition of slavery. For almost 200 years, readers have recounted the reactions to speeches heard in the public squares of small towns in Illinois as well as reactions to the repeated memorizing and memorializing combined in recitations of the Gettysburg Address.

The Abraham Lincoln who galvanized cultural memory in the years after his tragic assassination remains for students as an iconic figure in large part through his enigmatic language. Such pithy sayings as "'Tis better to be silent and be thought a fool, than to speak and remove all doubt" are a lasting legacy of a president who enjoyed presenting aphorisms about wisdom in that language of the folk. The vividness of Lincoln's language lies at the surface of a deep strategy that this famed politician used to draw attention toward a moral vision of the United States.

Lincoln's sacred document was the Declaration of Independence. The strongest declaration of his reliance on the founders of his nation came in the Gettysburg Address when he declared, "Four score and seven years ago our fathers brought forth on this continent a new nation, conceived in liberty and dedicated to the principle that all men are created equal." The dedication of the cemetery at Gettysburg that was the occasion for the address has been overshadowed by the power of Lincoln's words as he sought, there and elsewhere, to bring together a nation divided by a bloody Civil War. Relying on a patriarchal "birthing" both makes the nation a familial space and encourages a masculine lineage of inheriting national responsibilities. Hence, Lincoln was often paired with George Washington. The ringing close of the address expresses Lincoln's heartfelt desire that "government of the people, by the people, and for the people shall not perish from the earth."

Much of our sense of Lincoln survives through such language, but Lincoln's face survives because of images. The first president to be photographed and the first to be recorded as responding to his public image, Lincoln repeatedly visited the photography studios of Mathew Brady in Washington, DC, and tried to tame his stiff wiry hair for the camera lens. Growing a beard in response to comments about his appearance, Lincoln shaped the face that now appears in countless presentations about the nineteenth-century United States. He was also the first president, indeed the first world leader, to be shown on the battlefield in conversation with his generals.

The image of Abraham Lincoln persists through anecdote as well as elegy. Lincoln was shot on April 14, 1865, only five days after the war ended, while attending the satirical play *Our American Cousin* at the Ford Theater in Washington, DC. The Reverend Henry Ward Beecher, brother to Harriet Beecher Stowe, memorialized Lincoln in a sermon a week after the assassination, declaring, "This nation has dissolved – but in tears only!" The tears that the nation was imagined to shed collectively became a way to unify not only the nation but also the memory of Lincoln.

Although Lincoln has been strongly associated with the American Civil War, his speeches also reflect his pained resistance to war. The first chapter of this collection addresses the effect of Lincoln's language on the formulations that came to define the United States. Such expressions as "A House Divided cannot stand" have become so powerfully identified with Lincoln that the lively context of his campaign speeches and the debates with Stephen

Douglas has almost dropped away. Here the effect of such oratorical traditions, especially in language that establishes a sense of national division and possible reconciliation, appears in analyses of the speeches about the Kansas-Nebraska Act and the Fugitive Slave Law in which Lincoln made some of his most powerful arguments.

The second chapter considers how, as a lifelong reader of poetry, Abraham Lincoln's literary taste reflected both the wide range of his aesthetic and intellectual interests and the versatility of this literary genre in the nineteenth century. A master of comic storytelling, Lincoln read and wrote satirical doggerel with pleasure, penning poems that mocked his neighbors even as they also mocked their speakers' rough-hewn vocabularies and outsized postures. Lincoln read and memorized literary poetry as well: his courtship with Mary Todd was fueled in part by their shared love of poetry. Not surprisingly, poems about Lincoln abounded both during and after the Civil War. Chapter 2 examines the poetry that Lincoln read and the poetry that he wrote; it also considers some of the many poetic representations of Lincoln written by northern and southern writers in the Civil War era. The third chapter turns from literary tactics to explore imaging tactics used from the earliest days of political photography, when an engraving of the photograph of Abraham Lincoln as clean shaven prompted a letter from a young viewer to suggest that he grow a beard. Chapter 3 also addresses the political cartoons that presented Lincoln as always telling jokes while finding himself in precarious scenarios of political risk taking.

Books have been written about Lincoln's short account in the Gettysburg Address of the terrible business of reclaiming national identity through bloody sacrifice. The fourth chapter looks at the language he used for this consolidation out of tragedy – a consolidation carried further in the Second Inaugural Address – and it treats Lincoln's style of political mourning at a time when mourning rituals convulsed the United States, North and South, as it reeled from the impact of more than 600,000 Civil War deaths. The fifth chapter analyzes the production of national identity and the translation of the violence of war into political meaning. In his wartime speeches, Lincoln drew on four contemporarily available figures of nationhood – territory, common ancestry, social contract, and embodied actor – to counter the challenge of secession. While Lincoln countered the logic of territorial nationalism by appealing to the American pastoral image of a "national homestead," increasing death tolls urged the question of what conception of nationhood Union and Confederate soldiers could draw on. Using the figure of the "body politic," Lincoln integrated the questions of nationhood and violence.

The sixth chapter concentrates on Native Americans and political questions. During Lincoln's lifetime, the diverse populations of the emerging

United States included populations along the frontier that involved themselves in land disputes. Lincoln saw military service in the armed conflict that came to be known as the Black Hawk War. The legal construction of land disputes during the late eighteenth and early nineteenth centuries forms the background of the discussion. Although he continues to be associated with the Emancipation Proclamation, the earlier public writings of Lincoln addressed racial discrimination in rather more hesitant ways. Responding to the implication of extending the practice of slavery within the United States (an implication contained in the proposed Kansas-Nebraska Act) during his debates with Stephen Douglas, Lincoln wonders with honest trepidation whether slavery can be ended as a matter of legal practice. The seventh chapter examines Lincoln's conception of race in the decades leading up to the Civil War by looking at the role of the constitution and legal decisions in these famous debates.

The Civil War greatly exacerbated the ongoing spiritual crises of a republic nearly torn apart by opposing accounts of belief, doctrinal authority, and national narrative. These struggles over the nature, meaning, and religious elements of the American idea are documented in the debates about Lincoln's personal spirituality during his White House years. The eighth chapter considers what we should make of the long and passionate accounts of Lincoln's religious practice and orthodoxy. It also considers how Lincoln's religious vision greatly deepened from 1862 onward. Highlighted by such themes as fatalism, reliance on Providence, and the continuing bonds with the dead, this is depicted in the major speeches and other writings.

The South relied on the need for cotton in the industrialized Midlands even as the politicians in London tried to maintain a neutral stand with respect to the Civil War. The ninth chapter looks at the language of Lincoln's exchanges with London as well as considering what impact the war had on attitudes about the United States. The effect is to consider the transatlantic view of Lincoln as well as to look at Lincoln's legacy in Victorian Britain. The revolutions of 1848 had excited a great deal of interest in the United States. Attention to the heroes of Poland, for example, affected the concepts of democracy bound up with the United States. France had come to the aid of the United States during the American Revolution, and large numbers of emigrants from countries such as Germany, Ireland, and Poland had changed the political landscape, so there were direct appeals to Europeans to join in as allies during the war. At the same time, anxieties about European immigrants seem at odds with such appeals. The tenth chapter considers how Lincoln, who began as a backwoods lawyer, became an international president.

Lincoln's Union, like the nineteenth-century United States, was both a national and hemispheric construct, deeply intertwined with the fates of colonial possessions throughout the Caribbean and vitally linked to the national interests of Mexico. The eleventh chapter revises our understanding of Lincoln by positing him as a protagonist – and antagonist – of trans-American literary and political history. His enduring link to Latin American counterparts like President Benito Juarez of Mexico is perhaps the strongest evidence that the history of the North-South conflict and the Civil War is also a history of trans-American relations.

The impact of an assassination that took place on Good Friday and was widely known by Easter Sunday was to produce a widespread hagiography about Abraham Lincoln. The effect of enshrining a political figure was also to produce language about Lincoln that drew on legends that go back thousands of years. Because politicians in the early republic tended to have classical training, the purpose of the last chapter is at once to look at how such classical images entered into Lincoln's language and to consider the after-image of his assassination.

Throughout the collection Lincoln's voice emerges in conversation with artists, writers, and politicians whose alternating astonishment and admiration reveal perhaps the most vividly present president of the nineteenth-century United States. As a contemporary observer told the story, when pleading to have one of her sons spared from battle, a troubled mother stood running her fingers through the president's hair, tears streaming down her face.[1] The mother's presumption of intimacy reveals her feeling that the White House contains a president whose head can be touched as well as his heart. However legitimate the story, the tears that started from Lincoln's eyes on that occasion speak to the great grief he felt over losing his own sons as well as to the great empathy he felt for the sons and daughters of the nation over which he so briefly and powerfully presided. I want to acknowledge the help of three wonderful graduate students at Cornell: Alex Black, Jill Spivey, and Xine Yao.

NOTES

1 Francis Bicknell Carpenter, *Six Months at the White House with Abraham Lincoln: The Story of a Picture* (New York: Hurd and Houghton, 1867), 338.

I

IVY G. WILSON

Rhetorically Lincoln:
Abraham Lincoln and
Oratorical Culture

In a November 1884 issue of *The Christian Recorder*, one of the leading nineteenth-century African-American periodicals, the Reverend R. G. Mortimer recounted an anecdote about a visit from Abraham Lincoln to a prominent Sunday school. With all the excitement that might be expected from such a visit, the students anticipated a long and profound speech. Instead, Lincoln offered only a simple statement: "My dear young friends, do not chew, do not smoke, do not swear."[1] Mortimer, a former professor of Latin, Greek, and exegesis at Wilberforce University, used the moment less as an illustration of the children's disappointment than as a didactic tool of instruction. He implored his readers to heed Lincoln's example, noting that "the address deserves to be held up as worthy the imitations of public speakers generally."[2] Underlining the address's "brief, plain, sensible, timely" delivery, Mortimer accentuated the succinct economy of Lincoln's mode of rhetoric as ideal.[3]

Mortimer's assessment of Lincoln's address is a reminder of Lincoln's significance as a rhetorician and orator. Remembered now for political phrases like "A house divided against itself cannot stand" and a "government of the people, by the people, for the people, shall not perish from the earth," Lincoln is also identified with popular adages such as "Better to remain silent and be thought a fool than to speak and remove all doubt." Lincoln's "House Divided" speech is one of his most identifiable and iconographic, but like most speeches it has been rendered recognizable primarily through one or two encapsulated key phrases. Beginning with George Washington, Americans have been especially enamored of presidential speeches and, even more so, with their figures of speech. From Thomas Jefferson's "That government is best which governs least, because its people discipline themselves" in the nineteenth century to John F. Kennedy's "And so my fellow Americans, ask not what your country can do for you; ask what you can do for your country" in the twentieth century, Americans have remained fond of presidential maxims.

However recognizable these phrases remain as forms of synecdochic representation, they are often excised from the larger, more complex social narratives of their historical moment even as they point to the wider command of their speaker's oratorical range. Many of Lincoln's most well-known phrases are associated with the impending crisis of the Civil War. Lincoln's speeches, however, were articulated not only during a particular political era but also at a particular cultural moment in the history of performative speaking in the United States, one that was influenced by reprinted speeches revoiced in public forums to the declamatory, recitative poetry delivered in living room parlors. Rather than turn to Lincoln's speeches as a way to trace his political discourse, this essay turns to his political discourse as a way to examine his understanding of rhetoric and mid-nineteenth-century oratorical culture.

Lincoln's Oratorical Style

One early site where Lincoln rendered his understanding of rhetoric was his 1852 "Eulogy on Henry Clay." As part of the Great Triumvirate, which also included South Carolina's John C. Calhoun and Massachusetts's Daniel J. Webster, the Kentuckian Clay was one of the most important orators of the 1830s and 1840s. If Clay's ability to broker compromises on the slavery issue became increasingly untenable to Lincoln by the early 1850s, Lincoln nonetheless appreciated Clay's service as a statesman. As Lincoln reminded the audience before him at an Episcopalian church in Springfield, Illinois, Clay was involved with seemingly all the major political events of the day, including the War of 1812, the formation of the American Colonization Society, the Nullification Crisis, the Missouri Compromise of 1820, and the Compromise of 1850. Lincoln's eulogy praised Clay's congressional accomplishments and traced the political biography of Clay with the political history of the nation, waxing that "the infant nation, and the infant child began the race of life together. For three quarters of a century they have traveled hand in hand."[4] However, as a type of speech itself, Lincoln's eulogy was less than remarkable, a sentiment that was expressed by his law partner William Herndon, who surmised that "if his address in 1852, over the death of Clay, proved that he was no eulogist, then this last effort ... demonstrated that he was no lecturer."[5]

Beyond Clay's political feats, Lincoln's encomium of Clay's speeches also intimates his own understanding of oratory.

> Mr. Clay's eloquence did not consist, as many fine specimens of eloquence do, of types and figures – of antithesis, and elegant arrangement of words and sentences; but rather of that deeply earnest and impassioned tone, and manner,

which can proceed only from great sincerity and a thorough conviction, in the speaker of the justice and importance of his cause. This it is, that truly touches the chords of sympathy; and those who heard Mr. Clay never failed to be moved by it, or ever afterwards, forgot the impression. All his efforts were made for practical effect. He never spoke merely to be heard. He never delivered a Fourth of July oration, or an eulogy on an occasion like this.[6]

If there is a distinction between oration, whereby oratory is the art of speaking eloquently, and rhetoric, whereby rhetoric is the art of logical argumentation, Lincoln underscores Clay's achievement as an orator who is masterfully adroit at engaging emotion and sensation. In Lincoln's assessment, Clay's oratorical subtleties exploited affect, tapping "the chords of sympathy" of his listeners. Lincoln's understanding of oratory, in this respect, accentuated its affective dimensionality and its sensory capacity. As an illustration of this understanding, Lincoln cites one of Clay's speeches on the War of 1812 in which, "during its delivery the reporters forgot their vocations, dropped their pens, and sat enchanted from the beginning to quite the close."[7] Yet, insofar as Clay did not regularly offer ceremonial deliveries, his speeches could indeed be said to have a "practical effect"; that is, they could simultaneously be examples of oratory in their style and delivery as well as examples of rhetoric in their design and functionality.

While Lincoln praised Clay for his use of affect and sensation, his own "A House Divided" speech manipulated both affect and a kind of austere formulaic method in deploying his mode of persuasion. Late in the evening on June 16, 1858, Lincoln took to the stage to deliver an address as part of his campaign to secure the Republican nomination for U.S. Senate. In the speech, Lincoln rehearsed many of the ideas that he would rearticulate in his debates with the Democratic nominee Stephen A. Douglas later that year. In substance, Lincoln's speech before the Hall of Representatives was not much different from other recent speeches in which he critiqued the Kansas-Nebraska Act of 1854 and the threat of expanding slavery. The Kansas-Nebraska Act, Lincoln maintained, was joined by the recent Dred Scott decision to form a new kind of "machinery."[8] He excoriated Douglas's advocacy of "popular sovereignty," which proposed that residents of a territory should decide whether or not slavery would be allowed, and ridiculed his "care-not" policy as a feigned indifference that was actually a political, if not moral, threat to the nation.[9] Perhaps most importantly, Lincoln opened his speech with a paraphrase from Matthew 12:25 as a metaphor for the current state of the nation, cautioning his audience, "A house divided against itself cannot stand."[10]

As an example of rhetoric, the speech is noteworthy less for its invocation of biblical verse than for how Lincoln deftly parsed the quoted aphorism to selectively situate the key words "house" and "divided" into the specific history of the contemporary moment. In so doing, Lincoln contested the political claims of southern Democrats and Copperheads who argued the country could continue to exist half slave and half free – "I do not expect the Union to be *dissolved* – I do not expect the house to *fall* – but I *do* expect it will cease to be divided."[11] Strategically rearranging these key words, Lincoln deploys a form of interpolation that produces a sonic reverberation to underscore his central message.

More specifically, Lincoln utilized the aphorism's latent visual correlative to have it function as an ideogram. As an example of discourse, the political efficacy of the speech is engendered less by its verbal cadence than by its graphic resonance as a pictorial illustration. In a later part of the speech that is much less quoted than the famous aphorism, Lincoln continues with the symbolism of the house to depict how Douglas, Franklin Pierce, Roger Taney, and James Buchanan formed a mismatched, but nonetheless reforti-fied, home as a political bloc.

> [W]hen we see a lot of framed timbers, different portions of which we know have been gotten out at different times and places, and by different workmen – ... and when we see these timbers joined together, and see they exactly matte the frame of a house or a mill ... we feel it impossible not to believe that [they] all understood one another from the beginning and all worked upon a common plan or draft drawn before the first blow was struck.[12]

Critical of how a number of questions from "different times and places" were inappropriately superimposed onto the Dred Scott decision, Lincoln transmuted the earlier aphorism with its image of a single partitioned house into a metaphor where there are at least two opposing houses.

If Lincoln's "A House Divided" speech was a veritable example of both the affective and the austere, his "Cooper Union Address" was essentially all austere. After initially accepting an invitation to address Henry Ward Beecher's church in Brooklyn, New York, Lincoln's later visit was moved to the Cooper Institute where it was sponsored by the Young Men's Republican Union. An unofficial presidential hopeful, Lincoln offered his address before an audience of 1,500 in a speech that is commonly understood now to have secured Lincoln's position as the Republican nominee on February 27, 1860.

Notwithstanding its importance as a turning point in his political career en route to the presidency, the "Cooper Union Address" is also important because it displays a mode of Lincoln's rhetoric that was relentlessly methodical and systematic. Informed by his experience as a debater and lawyer, his "Cooper Union Address" approximates a form of forensic rhetoric. In it, he fastened onto one of Douglas's most significant claims that "our fathers, when they framed the Government under which we live, understood this question just as well, and even better, than we do now."[13] Conceding that he agrees with the logic of Douglas's line from the outset of his address, Lincoln spent the remainder of it illustrating how Douglas's claim should be understood not to prohibit but rather to allow federal control over slavery in territories (not states). The most fundamental tactic that Lincoln deployed in the speech is to parse Douglas's line clause by clause. In strategic maneuvers that are less philological than archeological, Lincoln delineates an argumentative position that exemplifies how the majority of the original thirty-nine signers of the Constitution believed that the federal government held the authority to regulate slavery in the territories.

> Here, then, we have twenty-three out of our thirty-nine fathers "who framed the government under which we live," who have, upon their official responsibility and their corporal oaths, acted upon the very question which the text affirms they "understood just as well, and even better than we do now;" and twenty-one of them – a clear majority of the whole of "thirty-nine" .... Thus the twenty-one acted; and, as actions speak louder than words, so actions, under such responsibility, speak still louder.[14]

Politically, Lincoln inverts the strict constitutionalism commonly invoked by the contemporaneous Democratic party to arrive at something ostensibly closer to the original intent – and, importantly, deeds – of the founding fathers. Lincoln redirects the phrase "even better than we do now" such that it turns on Douglas, becoming a veritable ad hominem attack on him that is seemingly voiced not with Lincoln's tongue but rather with Douglas's and, in essence, makes the statement rhetorical.

Whereas his "Cooper Union Address" interrogated a specific issue about the expansion of slavery into territories, Lincoln had outlined his general position against slavery six years earlier in his "Peoria Speech" on the repeal of the Missouri Compromise. Delivered on October 16, 1854, only months after the passage of the Kansas-Nebraska Act, Lincoln declared in this speech that he loathed slavery for a number of reasons: It was a monstrosity of justice; it disallowed the United States from being a republican example to the rest of the world; it enabled enemies of free institutions to label Americans hypocrites; it compelled Americans into "an open war with the very fundamental principles of civil liberty" embodied in the Declaration of Independence.[15] Among these reasons, neither the subjugation of blacks nor violence done to the idea of the human was part of Lincoln's public declaration of his hatred of slavery.

Although Lincoln turned to the history of the constitutional convention in both the "Peoria Speech" and the "Cooper Union Address" to formulate his argument, the "Peoria Speech" is different in that it contains a degree of self-awareness that reveals his rhetorical programmatic for the speech itself. Calling it the "sheet anchor of American republicanism," Lincoln cites the passage from the Declaration of Independence about deriving just powers from the consent of the governed.[16]

> I have quoted so much at this time merely to show that according to our ancient faith, the just powers of governments are derived from the consent of the governed. Now the relation of masters and slaves is, PRO TANTO, a total violation of this principle.[17]

Here, as throughout the "Peoria Speech," Lincoln quotes the founding fathers to construct a figurative orchestra of voices. There is a sense that Lincoln himself recognizes that his own voice should, and perhaps even needs to, be supplemented with others. The quotes are invoked as much for their forensic utility as evidence as they are for their sonic utility as a chorus.

If Lincoln's speeches only nominally approach a degree of musicality in their sonic register, his "First Inaugural Address" demonstrates that his speeches could possess a degree of the poetic. Lincoln's election was seen as an ominous sign by many, and he sought to allay Democratic fears that he threatened the existence of slavery in Southern states when he delivered his address on March 4, 1861. Although the political atmosphere was bleak, Lincoln's first inaugural address was epideictic. Emphasizing the necessity of maintaining the Union, the speech is, for the most part, perfunctory in its attempt to placate his detractors. But it closes with one of Lincoln's most poetic lines – "The mystic chords of memory, stretching from every battlefield, and patriot grave, to every living heart and hearth-stone, all over this broad land, will yet swell the chorus of the Union, when again touched, as surely they will be, by the better angels of our nature."[18] In culminating his "First Inaugural Address," Lincoln employs music as metaphor for the nation where a set of recombinant notes will more fully develop into a grand chorus.

However, whereas Lincoln's "First Inaugural Address" concluded with an element of the poetic, the central discursive message of the speech itself was ambivalent about anything more than the preservation of the Union. African Americans like Frederick Douglass were disappointed that Lincoln circumvented the issue of the extension of slavery. In the first issue of his monthly periodical after Lincoln's "First Inaugural Address," Frederick Douglass derided Lincoln for avoiding such an important issue, something that he registered as both a political mistake and a transgression of effective rhetoric – "Mr. L[incoln] knew this, and the South has known it all along; and yet this subject only gets the faintest allusion, while others, never

seriously in dispute, are dwelt upon at length."[19] As one of the nation's preeminent orators himself, Douglass's evaluation intimates that he felt Lincoln
violated the conventions of rhetoric by reversing the relationship between
the primary and the subordinate in the proper arrangement of his speech.
What Douglass wants from Lincoln is something closer to his "Cooper
Union Address," but to do so would have changed Lincoln's speech from
the epideictic to the dialectic. Douglass acknowledges nearly as much when
he condemns Lincoln's language for being more "honied" than direct.

> Whatever may be the honied phrases employed by Mr. L[incoln] when con-
> fronted by actual disunion; however silvery and beautiful may be the rhetoric
> of his long-headed Secretary of State, when wishing to hold the Government
> together until its management should fall into other hands.[20]

Here, Douglass conceptualizes "rhetoric" less in the classical sense of the
word but in the sense of being gloss, glib, and inauthentic.

In addition to being one of the nation's preeminent orators, Douglass was
also the most recognized African-American public figure and was keen about
introducing Lincoln's words and political discourse to black America.[21]
Douglass republished large portions (if not *in toto*) from the speeches
Lincoln delivered on the train ride from Springfield, Illinois, to Washington,
DC. In addition to the passages where Lincoln expresses his faith in the aid
of divine providence (in Springfield), his plea that the country follow the
example of George Washington and Thomas Jefferson (in Cincinnati), and
his commitment to the Constitution (in Cleveland), the March 1861 issue
of *Douglass' Monthly* included a key passage from the Indianapolis speech
that addresses Lincoln's views both on politics and rhetoric.

> Solomon says, "There is a time to keep silence," and when men wrangle by the
> month with no certainty that they mean the same thing while using the same
> word, it perhaps were as well if they would keep silence. The words coercion
> and invasion are much used in these days, and often with much temper and
> hot blood. Let us make sure, if we can, that we do not misunderstand the
> meaning of those who use them. Let us get the exact definition of these words,
> not from dictionaries, but from the men themselves, who certainly deprecate
> the things they would represent by the use of the words.[22]

In this quote from his February 12, 1861 "Address to the Legislature of
Indiana at Indianapolis," Lincoln invokes the proverbial wisdom from
Ecclesiastes 3:7. However, Lincoln bifurcates the statement by only providing the first half of the parallelism, thereby rendering explicit the need for
his detractors to remain silent while implicitly maintaining the necessity of
this being his time to speak. The second half of the adage of "A time to keep
silence, And a time to speak" would have particular appeal to free northern

African Americans who felt it was their duty to speak for themselves as well as on behalf of their enslaved brethren in the South.

If Douglass scrutinized the smallest turns of phrases in Lincoln's "First Inaugural Address," he was less exacting with the Emancipation Proclamation, even projecting putatively positive charges where there were ostensibly little. The Emancipation Proclamation granted freedom to all slaves in the Confederate States that did not return to Union control by January 1, 1863. It was criticized almost immediately by Radical Republicans for its conservatism in that it did not free slaves in states where the Union already held control. Douglass did not extol the proclamation for its rhetorical value, but he did extol the decree for its political value. Delivering a rousing speech at the Cooper Institute, the same venue where Lincoln essentially secured the Republican nomination for president three years earlier, Douglass asserted that the proclamation would rank with the Fourth of July as a national act that became a universal principle and submitted that it would stand in the history of civilization with Catholic Emancipation, the British Reform Bill, the repeal of the Corn Laws, and the release of millions of Russian serfs from servitude. Douglass felt the Emancipation Proclamation liberated the entire nation, pushing it closer to the "amazing approximation toward the sacred truth of human liberty."[23] Lincoln would express nearly as much, although admittedly with much more caution, in "The Gettysburg Address" when he spoke of "a new birth of freedom."[24]

"The Gettysburg Address" is Lincoln's most well-known and perhaps his most symbolic speech. Lincoln delivered it in the midst of the Civil War on November 19, 1863, at the site of a costly Union victory in Pennsylvania. David Wills invited Lincoln for largely ceremonial reasons: "It is the desire that, after the Oration, you, as Chief Executive of the nation, formally set apart these grounds to their sacred use by a few appropriate remarks."[25] The address itself was relatively short; Lincoln's few minutes paled in comparison to Edward Everett's two-hour oration. It opens and closes with two of the most resonant lines now latent in the U.S. collective imagination: "Four score and seven years ago our fathers brought forth on this continent, a new nation, conceived in Liberty, and dedicated to the proposition that all men are created equal" and "that we here highly resolve that these dead shall not have died in vain – that his nation, under God, shall have a new birth of freedom – and that government of the people, by the people, for the people, shall not perish from the earth."[26] Whereas there was evidence that he could approach this kind of sublimity, notably in the conclusion of the "First Inaugural Address," Lincoln stylized a veritable prose poem in "The Gettysburg Address." H. L. Mencken, the iconoclastic arbiter of American speech and letters in the early twentieth century, said, somewhat disparagingly, the address was "poetry, not logic; beauty, not sense."[27]

The initial reception of "The Gettysburg Address," however, was divided.[28] The two major Chicago newspapers had contrary assessments: The *Chicago Tribune* found the address noteworthy, whereas the *Chicago Times* found it glib. The *New York Times* was fairly gracious in its report and reprinted Lincoln's address but offered nothing by way of commentary. Instead, the *New York Times* offered a few words about Everett's oration – "So quiet were the people that every word uttered by the orator of the day must have been heard by them all, notwithstanding the immensity of the concours[e]."[29] African-American newspapers like the *Christian Recorder* hailed the moment for its gravity and importance but had little to say about Lincoln's address itself beyond simply reprinting it.[30] By contrast, the *Springfield* (Massachusetts) *Republican* lauded Lincoln's oratorical skill.

> Surprisingly fine as Mr. Everett's oration was in the Gettysburg consecration, the rhetorical honors of the occasion were won by President Lincoln. His little speech is a perfect gem; deep in feeling, compact in thought and expression, and tasteful and elegant in every word and comma. Then it has the merit of unexpectedness in its verbal perfection and beauty…. Turn back and read it over, it will repay study as a model speech.[31]

Given that most accounts focused on the political meaning of Lincoln's address, it is noteworthy that the *Springfield Republican* took particular notice of his verbal stylistics. Of the different aspects that the newspaper details, its mentioning of Lincoln's use of commas is significant insofar as it conveys a recognition of his control of rhythm generated by his regulation of relative and subordinate clauses and caesuras. The *Springfield Republican*'s declaration that "The Gettysburg Address" will serve as "a model speech" seems especially prescient given that Lincoln's speech was commonly taught in both civics and rhetoric classes throughout the first half of the twentieth century.

Importantly, the address also illuminated Lincoln's continued reinterpretation of the relationship between the Constitution and the Declaration of Independence. Lincoln had been insistent about underscoring the law and order of the Constitution, and, by comparison, the Declaration of Independence surfaced relatively little in his speeches. From David Walker, William Wells Brown, and Frederick Douglass, the early African-American protest tradition continually referred to the Declaration. Walker's *Appeal* (1829) implored white America to revisit the Declaration's political and rhetorical tenor – "See your Declaration Americans!!! Do you understand your own language? Hear your language, proclaimed to the world."[32] Two and a half months after the Dred Scott decision in March 1857, Lincoln asserted that the sentiments of Chief Justice Taney and Stephen A. Douglas violated the "plain unmistakable language of the Declaration."[33] Lincoln believed in the Declaration's phrase that "all men were created equal," but he did not believe, as he put it, "all men equal in all respects."[34] The most symbolic aspect of Lincoln's speech on the Dred Scott decision was his statement that the "all men were created equal" phrase was placed in the Declaration for future use, implying that the phrase was an ontologically proleptic political idiom, the meaning of which would only materialize in later years. His invocation of the Declaration's quintessential line six years later for "The Gettysburg Address" perhaps suggests that one such future moment had arrived, intimating that the Civil War was about something more than saving the Union alone. By staging the reference to the Declaration in the opening line, Lincoln was able to culminate the address with a pronounced image of a government "of the people, by the people, for the people," amplifying a form of direct democracy in degrees that perhaps Jefferson himself had not imagined.

Lincoln's Echo

Well beyond the context of the Civil War, Lincoln's rhetoric has continued to resonate in the United States, especially in the African-American cultural imagination. During the early years of the Harlem Renaissance, W. E. B. DuBois published two editorials in the *Crisis* in which he quoted one of Lincoln's most damaging statements about African Americans as evidence of his political transformation in the crucible of the impending crisis and Civil War. DuBois used the editorials to remind his readers that iconographic figures need to be appreciated for their complexities rather than simply for their virtues and that the historical record on Lincoln should not be obfuscated by accentuating only one train of his speeches.[35] Even when Lincoln's actual words were not quoted, his presence has been summoned by Langston Hughes in "The Negro Speaks of Rivers" (1921) and Suzan Lori-Parks's play *Topdog/Underdog* (2001).

But the two African Americans who have most conspicuously appealed to – and extended – Lincoln's rhetoric are Martin Luther King and Barack Obama.[36] Standing on the steps of the Lincoln Memorial leading the March on Washington for Jobs and Freedom, King delivered his "I Have a Dream Speech" in August 1963. King opened his speech with a reference to Lincoln – "Five score years ago, a great American, in whose symbolic shadow we stand today, signed the Emancipation Proclamation" – creating a kind of sonic reverb with Lincoln's voice.[37] Whereas Frederick Douglass apotheosized the proclamation as a promise, King reminded his audience that the promise had not yet been fulfilled. If the "all men were created" phrase was put into the Declaration for later use, as Lincoln stated it had been, then King's emphasis on the "fierce urgency of Now" insisted that this was such a moment.[38] By alluding to Lincoln's Gettysburg Address, King was able to transfigure the Emancipation Proclamation into something more than strictly a strategic military decree; King essentially transposed the latent poetic impulse of "The Gettysburg Address" onto the colorless prose of the Emancipation Proclamation edict.

Whereas King alluded to Lincoln's "better angels" without explicitly articulating it as such, Obama returned directly to it nearly fifty years later. The similarities between Lincoln and Obama are numerous; beyond both establishing their political careers in Illinois, they are also regarded as exceptional orators.[39] In his February 2007 speech before the Old State Capitol in Springfield, Illinois, announcing his run for the Democratic nomination for the presidency, Obama referenced Lincoln's "house divided" phrase. Nearly two years later as president-elect in 2009, Obama retraced part of Lincoln's 1861 train ride to Washington, DC. On the Philadelphia portion, Obama directly referenced Lincoln's "better angels" concept – "What is required is a new declaration of independence, not just in our nation, but in our own lives – from ideology and small thinking, prejudice and bigotry – an appeal not to our easy instincts but to our better angels."[40] Captivated by what he has called Lincoln's "ultimate mastery of language," Obama has confessed his admiration for and affinity with Lincoln.[41]

In a larger sense, the African-American response to Lincoln is as much about their particular reaction as it is the proleptic nature of his idiomatic language itself. What seems remarkable about Lincoln's language is how it transcended the conventions of nineteenth-century U.S. oratory in ways that distinguished it from other famous orators of the day such as Henry Clay, Daniel Webster, and Edward Everett. Much of this can be attributed to the mid-nineteenth-century moment of national crisis, which have made his words salient at subsequent moments in U.S. history. However, Lincoln's language also remains salient because of what one could call his theory of oratory. Lincoln's assessment of Jefferson's inclusion of the "all men are created equal" phrase might also be understood as a strategy for his own practice of oratory – words and expressions that gain their fuller political meaning in the future. Lincoln, in this respect, was self-aware that his words might be taken up and reinterpreted. Hence, in an antiphonal relationship between Lincoln and his interlocutors, past and present, the call gets ventriloquized through the response. The continued resonance of Lincoln as a public speaker is that he deftly embedded elements of the oratorical into his rhetoric, reminding his listeners that moments of beauty and democratic promise remained latent in both the quotidian and cataclysmic episodes of national life.

NOTES

1 R. G. Mortimer, "Abraham Lincoln's Model Speech," *Christian Recorder*, November 6, 1884.

2 Ibid.

3 Ibid.

4 Abraham Lincoln, "Eulogy on Henry Clay Delivered in the State House at Springfield, Illinois, July 6, 1852," in Roy Prentice Basler, ed., *Abraham Lincoln: His Speeches and Writings* (New York: De Capo Press, 2001), 265.

5 Quoted in John Channing Briggs's *Lincoln's Speeches Reconsidered* (Baltimore: Johns Hopkins University Press, 2005), 192.

6 Abraham Lincoln, "Eulogy on Henry Clay Delivered in the State House at Springfield, Illinois, July 6, 1852," in *Speeches and Writings*, 269.

7 Ibid., 271.

8 Abraham Lincoln, "The Dred Scott Decision: Speech at Springfield, Illinois, June 26, 1857," in *Speeches and Writings*, 373, 375.

9 Ibid., 375.

10 Abraham Lincoln, "A House Divided: Speech Delivered at Springfield, Illinois, at the Close of the Republican State Convention, June 16, 1858," in *Speeches and Writings*, 372.

11 Ibid.

12 Ibid., 377.

13 Abraham Lincoln, "Address at Cooper Institute, New York, February 27, 1860," in *Speeches and Writings*, 517.

14 Ibid., 522.

15 Abraham Lincoln, "The Repeal of the Missouri Compromise and the Propriety of Its Restoration: Speech at Peoria, Illinois, in Reply to Senator Douglas, October 16, 1854," in *Speeches and Writings*, 291.

16 Ibid., 304.

17 Ibid.

18 Abraham Lincoln, "First Inaugural Address, March 4, 1861," in *Speeches and Writings*, 589.

19 Frederick Douglass, "Inaugural Address" in Philip S. Foner and Yuval Taylor, eds., *Frederick Douglass: Selected Speeches and Writings* (Chicago: Lawrence Hill Books, 2000), 433.

20 Abraham Lincoln, "First Inaugural Address, March 4, 1861," in *Speeches and Writings*, 589.

21 On the lives of Lincoln and Douglass, see David W. Blight, *Frederick Douglass and Abraham Lincoln: A Relationship in Language, Politics, and Memory* (Milwaukee, WI: Marquette University Press, 2001); James Oakes, *The Radical and the Republican: Frederick Douglass, Abraham Lincoln, and the Triumph of Antislavery Politics* (New York: W. W. Norton, 2007); and John Stauffer, *Giants: The Parallel Lives of Frederick Douglass and Abraham Lincoln* (New York: Twelve, 2008).

22 Douglass, "The President Elect," *Douglass' Monthly*, March 1861.

23 "Frederick Douglass at the Cooper Institute. The Proclamation and a Negro Army," *Douglass' Monthly*, March 1863.

24 Abraham Lincoln, "Address Delivered at the Dedication of the Cemetery at Gettysburg, November 19, 1863," in *Speeches and Writings*, 734.

25 Quoted in Douglas L. Wilson's *Lincoln's Sword: The Presidency and the Power of Words* (New York: Knopf, 2006), 210.

26 Abraham Lincoln, "Address Delivered at the Dedication of the Cemetery at Gettysburg, November 19, 1863," in *Speeches and Writings*, 734.

27 Mencken found the speech "genuinely stupendous" ("Five Men at Random," in H. L. Mencken's *Prejudices: Third Series* [New York: Knopf, 1922], 174–175).

28 See Hans L. Trefousse's "The Role of the Press," in Harold Holzer and Sara Vaughn Gabbard, eds., *Lincoln and Freedom: Slavery, Emancipation, and the Thirteenth Amendment* (Carbondale: Southern Illinois University Press, 2007), 107.

29 "THE HEROES OF JULY.; A Solemn and Imposing Event. Dedication of the National Cemetery at Gettysburgh [sic]. IMMENSE NUMBERS OF VISITORS. Oration by Hon. Edward Everett—Speeches of President Lincoln, Mr. Seward and Governor Seymour. THE PROGRAMME SUCCESSFULLY CARRIED OUT," *New York Times*, November 20, 1863.

30 The *Christian Recorder* took special note of Reverend T. H. Stockton's prayer ("Our Great National Cemetery – Its Dedication and Consecration," *Christian Recorder*, November 28, 1863).

31 Josiah G. Holland, *Springfield Republican*, November 20, 1863. Holland was also an early biographer of Lincoln, publishing *The Life of Abraham Lincoln* in 1866. For more on the Gettysburg Address, see also *Lincoln's Sword*, 230.

32 David Walker, Appeal in Four Articles; Together with a Preamble, To the Colored Citizens of the World, But in Particular, and Very Expressly, To Those of the United States of America, Third and Last Edition (1829. Boston: David Walker, 1830), 85.

33 Lincoln, "The Dred Scott Decision," 360.

34 Ibid.

35 DuBois writes: "Do my colored friends really believe the picture would be fairer and finer if we forgot Lincoln's unfortunate speech at Charleston, Illinois, in 1858?" Abraham Lincoln said that "there is a physical difference between the white and black races which I believe will forever forbid the two races living together on terms of social and political equality." (DuBois, "Again, Lincoln," *Crisis*, September 1922).

36 Ivy G. Wilson, *Specters of Democracy: Blackness and the Aesthetics of Politics in the Antebellum U.S.* (New York: Oxford University Press, 2011), 172.

37 Martin Luther King, Jr., "I Have a Dream," in Drew D. Hansen's *The Dream: Martin Luther King, Jr. and the Speech That Inspired a Nation* (New York: Harper Collins, 2005), 72.

38 Ibid., 74.

39 See Phil Hirschkorn, "The Obama-Lincoln Parallel: A Closer Look," *CBS News*, January 17, 2009). See also Gerard Baker on the "self-conscious echo .... of the speeches of his hero and fellow Illinoisan, Abraham Lincoln" (Gerard Baker, "Realistic If Not Soaring: President Obama's Inauguration Speech," *The Times*, January 21, 2009).

40 Quoted in Tim Shipman, "Barack Obama Calls on Americans to Rediscover Their 'Better Angels' and Rebuild Their County," *Telegraph* (UK), January 17, 2009.

41 Obama asks, "What is it about this man that can move us so profoundly?" For him, it is "Lincoln's humble beginnings, which often speak to our own [and] that allowed a child born in the backwoods of Kentucky with less than a year of formal education to end up as Illinois' greatest citizen and our nation's greatest President" (Barack Obama, "What I See in Lincoln's Eyes," *Time*, June 26, 2005).

2

FAITH BARRETT

Abraham Lincoln and Poetry

In the margins of his arithmetic notebook, an adolescent Abraham Lincoln scrawled a few lines of doggerel that may or may not be original but that signal the self-deprecating wit that would become a trademark of the mature Lincoln's self-presentation as a politician:

> Abraham Lincoln
> his hand and pen
> he will be good
> but god knows When[1]

Although they have been preserved because of Lincoln's iconic stature, these juvenile verses offer a new angle onto the cultural position of poetry in the United States during Lincoln's lifetime. Read as an exemplar of poetry's crucial role in the schoolroom, these lines underline the centrality of poetry to Lincoln's education and to his development as a writer and speaker, a topic that this essay will explore by considering both the poetry that Lincoln read and the poems that he wrote over the course of his life.

Lincoln's love of poetry is widely documented in the scholarship about him. Biographers almost invariably mention his fondness for Shakespeare and Robert Burns, as well as favorite poems such as William Knox's "Mortality," Thomas Gray's "Elegy Written in a Country Churchyard," and Oliver Wendell Holmes's "The Last Leaf."[2] Lincoln's skill at storytelling and his love of folk idiom are also frequently noted. The connections between his love of poetry and his love of oral folk culture receive far less mention, however. In nineteenth-century America, poetry was a literary genre that was embedded in popular culture and that often circulated via oral means: The memorization, recitation, and reading aloud of poetry were integral components of schoolroom pedagogy, and although Lincoln had only scattershot experience with formal schooling, already as a boy he had developed a life-long habit of memorizing favorite poems, slipping excerpts from his store of memorized work into both conversation and written pieces (Armenti).

Lincoln's strong connections to popular and oral culture thus worked hand in glove with his fondness for poetry.

Moreover, although Lincoln's love of poetry seems exceptional when viewed in relation to the lives of recent American presidents, it seems far less so when read in relation to mid-nineteenth-century American culture. Although it is true that Lincoln was an individual who responded deeply to literature, it is also the case that the genre of poetry was central to American culture and identity in the nineteenth century. In other words, Lincoln's love of poetry tells us as much about the commitments of the deeply divided nation he led as it does about his own aesthetic and intellectual tastes. The list of poets whom Lincoln admired is both long and varied, reflecting the extraordinary versatility of the genre of poetry in this era as well as the wide range of work being read by the American public. In addition to Shakespeare, Burns, Gray, and Holmes, Lincoln liked work by Fitz-Greene Halleck, Byron, Edgar Allan Poe, and John Greenleaf Whittier (Kaplan, Armenti). As the inclusion of both Holmes and Halleck on this list makes clear, Lincoln enjoyed not only literary poetry but also lighter and wittier verse. A witness to his own apotheosis in literature, he also read many of the poems written for and about him by both professional and amateur writers while he was in the White House. Hannibal Cox, an African-American soldier and a former slave, sent Lincoln a poem in praise of the flag of the Union in March of 1864, while Oliver Gibbs sent Lincoln a comic poem titled "The Presidential Cow" in May of that same year. We know that Lincoln read at least some of these pieces: When Frank Wells sent a poem in praise of Lincoln in June of 1864, Lincoln noted on the piece – perhaps with some self-mocking irony intended – that it was "pretty fair poetry." The many parodies and satires of Lincoln that appeared in the popular press in the form of both cartoons and jokes would have served as counterweight to the poetic effusions of his well-wishers and admirers. As these examples suggest, nineteenth-century American poetry was extraordinarily versatile both generically and rhetorically. The brevity of the genre and the lack of copyright protections meant that poems could be quickly read, recopied, and printed widely. Moreover, poetry also gave writers the possibility of combining different registers of diction and tone in one piece; the permeable boundary between poetry and popular song made poems highly portable and sped their circulation throughout the country. For example, while Julia Ward Howe's "Battle Hymn of the Republic" first appeared on the pages of the prestigious *Atlantic Monthly* in February of 1862, it soon became a favorite with Union troops and was widely sung in the North by both soldiers and civilians.

Like many Americans of his day, Lincoln wrote poems, both comic and serious, on several occasions throughout his life. Because of the cultural centrality of poetry both in educational settings and in print, many literate

Americans tried their hand at writing poetry in the nineteenth century, penning Valentines for sweethearts or a few lines of verse for a friend's album.
In this era, poetry was culturally ubiquitous: poems were widely printed
in newspapers and magazines and also distributed in the form of broadsides and song sheets at campaign events, school programs, political rallies,
and recruitment events for soldiers. Many Americans kept scrapbooks or
albums of favorite poems, recopying them for inclusion in letters to family
and friends. In his twenties and thirties, Lincoln wrote a number of poems,
publishing at least one of them in a regional newspaper. As a political candidate in his fifties, he wrote souvenir verses in the autograph books of two
young women he met while campaigning. And as president in the summer
of 1863, Lincoln penned several lines of comic doggerel on Lee's defeat at
Gettysburg, a seemingly improbable counterpoint to the gravity and dignity
of the Gettysburg Address he would write in November of that same year.

Lincoln displayed remarkable range as a reader and writer over the course
of his political career; in the genre of poetry he found a capaciousness and
versatility of stance that would allow him to give voice to some of that
extraordinary range of thought and feeling. Both his personal and his political life were shaped by his interest in poetry: Lincoln's relationship with
Mary Todd was fueled in part by their shared love of poetry – Robert Burns
was a favorite with both – and reminiscences about Lincoln's years in the
White House return again and again to his reading aloud of poetry.[3] Lincoln
would frequently open cabinet meetings with readings from humorous stories or verse, much to the irritation of some members, and during the war
years, he read poetry both for diversion and for consolation.[4] Traveling by
steamboat to visit Union troops in 1862, Lincoln read aloud from Fitz-
Greene Halleck's "Marco Bozzaris," a contemporary poem that celebrated
the heroism of a Greek soldier in the war against Turkey. Poetry's flexibility in adapting itself to both high literary and popular purposes would
have only added to its appeal for Lincoln. Indeed the generic flexibility of
poetry made it particularly well-suited to the American literary marketplace
because poems could be multilayered and comic simultaneously, drawing in
growing numbers of literate Americans as enthusiasts of the genre.

Two often-cited descriptions of Lincoln's style of thinking underline the
reasons why poetry might have had such a strong appeal for him. Emerson
writes: "He is the author of a multitude of good sayings, so disguised as
pleasantries that it is certain they had no reputation at first but as jests; and
only later by the very acceptance and adoption they find in the mouths of
millions, turn out to be the wisdom of the hour."[5] The aphoristic compression and semantic polyvalence of poetry would certainly have attracted him.
In his eulogy for Lincoln, Charles Sumner notes that his ideas "moved as the

beasts entered Noah's ark, in pairs."[6] Poetry's focus on metaphor and ana-logical thinking would also have appealed to Lincoln's mind.

Moreover, Lincoln's literary tastes underline the relationship between the stances of the poetic speaker and the stances of political identity. Lincoln's fondness for the Scottish poets Knox and Burns likely resulted from the fore-grounding of both class issues and nationalist pride in their work; Burns's commitment to writing in dialect would have appealed to Lincoln's interest in both rural and oral culture.[7] As an American reader of both European and American work, Lincoln found in poetry some of the freedoms of per-spective that the Declaration of Independence promised in proposing that all Americans had the right not only to life and liberty but also to the pur-suit of happiness. Praised for his talents at storytelling and mimicry, Lincoln loved poetry because poetry enabled him to inhabit imaginatively the lives and voices of other speakers. Civil War-era poems by northern writers often present Lincoln as a living saint, even as they also underline that his life tra-jectory – from rural poverty to the office of the presidency – is an archetypal American story. In view of its generic versatility, it is not surprising that poetry played a central role in conversations about American national iden-tity during the Civil War era; poetic representations of the life of Abraham Lincoln were an important component of that dialogue.

The poetry Lincoln read as an adolescent and the earliest poems he wrote illuminate both the means by which he gained literacy and his pride in that achievement.[8] His father was not literate; his mother could read but not write. Apart from the Bible, one of the first books Lincoln encountered would have been Thomas Dilworth's *New Guide to the English Tongue*, which included a small selection of Aesop's fables and some poems; in the *New Guide*, literacy skills and Christian morality were taught to new readers simultaneously. A representative poem titled "Life Is Short and Miserable" admonishes its readers to remember that life is fleeting, an idea that Lincoln's life experience confirmed, especially with the sudden death of his mother in the fall of 1818. When Lincoln's father remarried in the winter of 1819, his stepmother's arrival brought him access to several new books, among them William Scott's *Lessons in Elocution*, a reader that would introduce Lincoln to thirty pages of selections from Shakespeare as well as some English poetry, including Thomas Gray's "Elegy Written in a Country Churchyard." Fred Kaplan notes that Lincoln was reading poetry regularly by the age of twelve, and that poetry had become an important focus of his reading by the time he turned sixteen.

It is easy to imagine that Gray's poem would have struck a powerful chord in Lincoln's imagination. First published in 1751, Gray's elegy was a career-making poem.[9] The picture that closes the poem of the disillusioned young man who dies before living up to his own promise would surely have had a powerful pull for a young Abraham Lincoln, who felt the stirrings of ambition and intellect within him and who was eager to reach beyond the aspirations of his immediate circle of family and friends in Indiana. Like William Knox's "Mortality," Gray's elegy is a *memento mori*, urging its readers to remember that they too must die. Lincoln's fondness for the genre foregrounds its cultural dominance in nineteenth-century America.

Gray's "Elegy" opens with images of a pastoral world that is full of harmonious splendor even though the speaker's voice is from the start of the poem tinged with melancholy for the dead. The second stanza sets the tone for the speaker's intimate and pleasurable relationship to nature:

> Now fades the glimm'ring landscape on the sight,
>> And all the air a solemn stillness holds,
> Save where the beetle wheels his droning flight,
>> And drowsy tinklings lull the distant folds;[10]

Gray's speaker goes on to contrast the pleasures the dead enjoyed when they were alive with the immobility of death. In life they enjoyed the freedom to move through this harmonious natural world and the pleasures both of family and of agricultural labor.

> The breezy call of incense-breathing morn,
>> The swallow twitt'ring from the straw-built shed,
> The cock's shrill clarion, or the echoing horn,
>> No more shall rouse them from their lowly bed.

> For them no more the blazing hearth shall burn,
>> Or busy housewife ply her evening care:
> No children run to lisp their sire's return,
>> Or climb his knees the envied kiss to share.

Growing up in a community where agricultural labor was central to daily life, Lincoln would likely have found particular power in this description. The image of the disrupted parent-child relationship would also have resonated for Lincoln as he mourned his mother's death.

In the latter half of the poem, Gray introduces its central argument: namely that the lives of working men and women are worthy of honor and celebration, even though those lives were never recorded in the book of history. This argument is first made explicit in stanza eight:

> Let not ambition mock their useful toil,
>> Their homely joys, and destiny obscure;
> Nor grandeur hear with a disdainful smile
>> The short and simple annals of the poor.

The poem's last several stanzas offer an extended description of a young man, who as a poet attempts to honor these lives but whose fate is somewhat ambivalent. Although the poem offers closure through its insistence on the young man's union with God in the afterlife, it also points implicitly toward his unrealized potential. With its emphasis on the young man's unrecognized gifts and on his struggles with melancholy, Lincoln would surely have recognized a figure for himself in the poet at the end of Gray's "Elegy." Hovering on the margin between the Enlightenment ideals of classicism and the political consciousness of the English romantics, Gray's poem reflects two intellectual traditions to which Lincoln responded strongly. While Gray's "Elegy" laments the reified class hierarchies of England, Lincoln's life experience would have already suggested to him that Americans might have greater opportunities for advancement.

Whereas Gray's "Elegy" likely had powerful resonances for the adolescent Lincoln, the extant poetry by Lincoln from these early years strikes an altogether different tone. In reading the mischievous verses cited at the opening of this essay, I suggested that they signal the self-deprecating wit that Lincoln would come to rely on in his political career; read in relation to the poetry Lincoln saw as a young man, however, these verses also offer an emphatic declaration of pride in his hard-won literacy skills. The poem revises the verse-signature inscribed in a book owned by a previous generation of Lincolns, suggesting both that Lincoln claims pride in his family name and perhaps also that a wry sense of humor ran in the family:[11]

> Abraham Lincoln
> his hand and pen
> he will be good
> but god knows When (CW 1:1)

Still another quatrain from this same era slyly puts the joke on the reader who is foolish enough to value the verses he or she reads:

> Abraham Lincoln is my nam[e]
> And with my pen I wrote the same
> I wrote it in both hast and speed
> and left it here for fools to read (CW 1:1)

Foregrounding poetry's generic versatility, Lincoln's adolescent quatrains talk back to Gray's "Elegy," suggesting that he will not, like the poet-speaker at the elegy's end, languish in a grave of unfulfilled promise: Rather, he will realize that promise by means of his access to the written word and to the genre of poetry, which serves as guarantor of his literacy.

Although Lincoln is known to have written other verse in his teens and twenties, examples survive only in the memories of his Indiana neighbors: in his 1829 "Chronicles of Reuben," Lincoln took poetic revenge on the Grigsby brothers for what Lincoln perceived as slights against his family. A bawdy narrative in doggerel, the poem represented the brothers as impotent buffoons and memorialized a double wedding day prank in which each brother was brought to the wrong bride's chamber. The writing was vivid enough that many in the community recalled the comedic impact of the poem decades later and earthy enough that a demure female neighbor insisted on relaying her memories of the poem to William Herndon through an intermediary.[12] Some scholars conjecture that the romantic poem "The Suicide's Soliloquy," published in the *Sangamo Journal* in 1838, may also have been written by Lincoln; given Lincoln's struggles with depression and his readerly fondness for romantic melancholia, it certainly seems possible that he was the poem's author, although no evidence has been found that would definitively corroborate that theory.[13] A young western lawyer with powerful political ambitions might well have taken care to ensure that neither the bawdy doggerel nor the depressive musings of his early adult years would have been directly linked to his name – either in print or in personal correspondence.

While the adolescent Lincoln used doggerel to lay claim to the power of literacy and later to take poetic revenge on the neighbors who had crossed him, as a rising lawyer and politician in his mid-thirties, Lincoln offered a more sophisticated proof of his hard-won education and middle-class status in the form of a long romantic poem titled "My Childhood Home I See Again."[14] In the fall of 1844, two years after his marriage to the well-connected Mary Todd, Lincoln visited his old haunts in Indiana while campaigning for Henry Clay: the visit inspired his most extended attempt at writing poetry. In April of 1846, he began sending his friend the editor and politician Andrew Johnston installments of the piece. Lincoln was pleased when Johnston offered to publish two of the parts in the Quincy Illinois *Whig* in the spring of 1847, sections that reflect on the mix of joy and sadness Lincoln felt as he visited Indiana. A third section, which Johnston chose not to publish, is a tonally complex narrative poem that describes the excitement of a bear hunt in the backcountry: Mixing local color stances with a remarkable empathy for the inner lives of the bear and the dogs in the hunt, the poem closes with an Aesopian gesture that comically likens the behavior of a posturing dog with his human counterparts. By printing the two-part "My Childhood Home I See Again" and omitting "The Bear Hunt," Johnston chooses to publish the more high-literary piece and also the one whose tone and central message would likely have been more appealing to a broader range of readers.[15]

Emboldened by his growing skills as a lawyer, orator, and politician, in "My Childhood Home Again I See," Lincoln steps up to the challenge of writing his own version of Gray's "Elegy." Lincoln's poem also suggests a likely familiarity with Wordsworth in the simplicity of its language, in the rural setting it evokes, and in its focus on the living contemplating the dead. Given the strong roots of romanticism in the American South, it is no accident that Lincoln's return to Indiana sparks a turn toward romanticism in his poetry. Born in Kentucky to two parents who were Virginians, Lincoln moved as a boy to a rural part of Indiana where the southern presence was dominant. His subsequent marriage to the Kentucky-born Mary Todd would only confirm the strength of his cultural ties to the South.

On the surface, Lincoln's "My Childhood Home I See Again" offers a sequence of conventional romantic stances. In part one of the poem, the speaker returns to his childhood home, is astonished by the flood of memories that wash over him, and feels a mixture of joy and sadness at the presence of the dead all around him. A fleeting reference to a "grand water-fall," part of a metaphor for the hallowing force of memory, gestures perhaps toward the natural wonders of a specifically American landscape, perhaps even toward the tourist destination of Niagara, although Lincoln would not travel there until 1857 (CW 1: 368). In the final stanza of part one, the speaker describes how the memory of those whom he has lost threatens to draw him down into the static world of the dead:

> I range the fields with pensive tread
> And pace the hollow rooms;
> And feel (companions of the dead)
> I'm living in the tombs.   (CW 1: 368)

In part two, the speaker encounters a man who was a friend in childhood but who descended into mental illness in early adulthood and never recovered his sanity. The first stanza of section two describes the young man's transformation:

> Poor Matthew! Once of genius bright, –
> A fortune-favored child –
> Now locked for aye, in mental night,
> A haggard mad-man wild.   (CW 1: 369)

The speaker recalls the extraordinary beauty of the mournful song Matthew would sing after the first onset of his illness, and nature listens compassionately to the madman's grief. Clearly the poem takes as its goal the articulation of a series of fairly standard romantic postures; it's certainly not surprising that studies of Lincoln have tended to dismiss the poem because of its loyalty to romantic conventions.[16] Read in relation to Lincoln's career

trajectory and his personal history, however, the poem offers both an archetypal American story of geographic and class mobility and remarkable – if
oblique – access to the inner feelings of this frequently private man.

Lincoln's rising professional stature enables the writing of the poem in
at least two distinct ways. First, it is Lincoln's growing success as a speaker
and politician that puts him on the campaign trail in Indiana for Henry Clay
in 1844; second, it seems likely that Lincoln would never have returned to
the home of his Indiana childhood if he had not achieved some measure
of professional and personal success in the intervening years. Just beneath
the surface of its language, the poem asks a profoundly American question
about whether it is possible to go home again – especially if great distances
of geography and education and class separate the traveler from his family and his past. It is because he has successfully extricated himself from
the poverty, obscurity, and hardscrabble farming of his Indiana childhood
that Lincoln has the luxury of traveling to Indiana and writing a polished
and competent romantic poem about the experience. In the poem's second
stanza, the speaker describes memory as a liminal space between this world
and the next:

> O memory! thou midway world
> 'Twixt Earth and Paradise,
> Where things decayed and loved ones lost
> In dreamy shadows rise.   (CW 1: 367)

Writing in his mid-thirties, as a lawyer and politician who has enjoyed some
success regionally, Lincoln is himself in "a mid-way world." He has left
behind the manual labor of his father's farm, but he has not yet fully realized his aspirations as a lawyer and politician.

What remains implicit in the poem – veiled beneath the speaker's conventional romantic melancholy – is the specificity of Lincoln's mourning for
his beloved mother Nancy who died in his childhood and his beloved sister Sarah who died when he was a young man, both of whom were buried
near the family home in Indiana. In stanza ten of part one, when Lincoln's
speaker paces "the hollow rooms" and feels he is "living in the tombs," it is
the loss of his mother and sister that Lincoln grieves (CW 1: 368). Read in
relation to Lincoln's class mobility, however, the fear of being drawn down
toward the cold and static world of the dead is surely also a fear of being
caught again in the "hollow rooms" of a childhood that never seemed to
have enough mental stimulation or enough educational opportunity to fulfill
the young Lincoln's aspirations. It is the psychological tomb of his father's
illiteracy and his subsistence farming that Lincoln's speaker fears as much
as anything else. For a man who had begun to define his identity and his

aspirations in opposition to his father's from a very young age and whose adult relationship with his father was detached and cool at best, the return to the childhood home would surely bring with it the fear of being buried alive in his father's way of life. Only in poetry could Lincoln grapple with this complex mix of emotions; only in poetry could he articulate such intensity of feeling while containing that intensity within the prescribed stances of romantic convention. By articulating his mourning for his mother's death in a conventional romantic poem, Lincoln allies himself with other literate writers and readers; he thus gains the consolations of participation in that literary community even as the generic conventions also allow him to efface the personal specificity of his own mourning. Moreover, the metaphoric versatility of poetry means that the same set of metaphors can suggest both the intensity of his mourning for his mother and sister and the intensity of his rejection of his father's identity.

The second section of the poem, the section that represents the mental breakdown of the speaker's childhood friend, provides additional support for this biographical reading: In representing Matthew's descent into madness, the poem places particular emphasis on how conflict with his parents signaled the onset of his mental illness. The speaker describes Matthew's violent conflict with his parents in the third stanza of section two of the poem:

> Poor Matthew! I have ne'er forgot
>   When first with maddened will,
> Yourself you maimed, your father fought,
>   And mother strove to kill.   (CW 1: 369)

Many scholars have noted how Matthew is an alter ego for Lincoln himself: The poem emphasizes that the young Matthew was a boy "of genius bright," and Matthew's descent into madness and violence offers an extreme version of Lincoln's own struggles with depression and suicidal impulses.[17] Beyond this standard reading of Matthew, however, the madman's violent struggles with his parents echo symbolically Lincoln's own family history. Any young child whose parent dies must grapple with the feeling of responsibility for the parent's death. Lincoln's imaginative recreation of Matthew's attempt to kill his mother allows him obliquely to express that sense of guilt. And although there is no evidence that Lincoln fought his father with physical blows, his resistance to his father's way of life and his quiet determination to gain an education in spite of his father's opposition is widely supported by neighbors' recollections. Lincoln's success as a lawyer and politician was clearly contingent on his rejection of the narrowness of his father's world. Through the figure of Matthew, Lincoln explores the imaginative consequences of the child's desire to kill his father; for Matthew, that road leads to madness and despair. For his doppelgänger Lincoln, it will eventually lead to political triumph.

Yet even as the second section of the poem reflects Lincoln's ambivalent relationship to his father, it also allows Lincoln to express his grief at his mother's death with moving eloquence. Describing the middle stages of Matthew's mental illness, the speaker recalls the extraordinarily beautiful song the madman sang, grieving the loss of his sanity, a song that the speaker often heard and frequently sought out at the break of day:

> And when at length, tho' drear and long,
>   Time soothed your fiercer woes –
> How plaintively your mournful song,
>   Upon the still night rose.
>
> I've heard it oft, as if I dreamed,
>   Far-distant, sweet, and lone;
> The funeral dirge it ever seemed
>   Of reason dead and gone.
>
> To drink its strains, I've stole away,
>   All silently and still,
> Ere yet the rising god of day
>   Had streaked the Eastern hill.   (CW 1: 369)

Then in the most luminous and transcendent passage of the poem, Lincoln describes the natural world's response to Matthew's lament:

> Air held his breath; the trees all still
>   Seem'd sorrowing angels round.
> Their swelling tears in dew-drops fell
>   Upon the list'ning ground.   (CW 1: 369)

While part one of the poem imagines a solitary speaker pacing the "hollow rooms" and "living in the tombs" of the dead when he returns to his childhood home, part two offers this extraordinary image of Lincoln's buried mother, listening responsively from within the grave. Lincoln's luminous description of nature's compassion for Matthew is thus also an image for the intimacy and reciprocity of Lincoln's relationship with his dead mother. Represented through the prism of conventional romanticism, nature listens responsively to Matthew's lament; read through the lens of Lincoln's life story, however, the image suggests that Lincoln's compassionate and beloved mother can hear and respond to her son's song of inconsolable grief. In "My Childhood Home I See Again," Lincoln finds consolation in the highly formulaic stances of romanticism, which allow for the simultaneous expression and containment of his grief, for the simultaneous revealing and concealing of his deepest feelings.

In "My Childhood Home I See Again," Lincoln uses romantic stances not only to express and contain a deeply personal grief but also to emphasize the strong ties between the poem's speaker and the natural world. Just as American writers from Emerson to Whitman to Dickinson propose that an American literature might spring from the American natural world, so too does Lincoln as amateur poet argue implicitly for the centrality of nature in the American writer's vision. In the manuscript version of "My Childhood Home I See Again," an unpublished final stanza points toward a missing or lost final section. This last dangling stanza also foregrounds the vital connection between the poem's speaker and the ground on which he walks, the Indiana fields where he worked as a child and that fed him:

> The very spot where grew the bread
>   That formed my bones, I see.
> How strange, old field, on thee to tread,
>   And feel I'm part of thee!   (CW 1: 370)

Just as this dangling stanza argues for the powerful connection between the speaker's physical development and the Indiana fields where he walks, so too will Civil War–era poems that offer hero-making portraits of Lincoln rely on romantic stances to underline the powerful connection between Lincoln's rise to political power and the western landscapes that produced him.

Lincoln's apotheosis in Civil War poetry happens with remarkable speed as northern poets seize on the image of Lincoln to represent the best and brightest aspirations of the American nation and the possibilities for upward mobility that America offers young men. Often invoked as the refrain in recruitment poems and calls to arms, Lincoln's name becomes a rallying cry for the Union Army, an incantation that underlines both Lincoln's powerful moral authority and his strong ties to the American land. In northern poems that celebrate Lincoln's rise to power – as in many poetic calls to arms – the solitary "I" of romanticism is often replaced by the celebratory nationalist "we" of the Union. In the recruitment poem "Three Hundred Thousand More," James Sloan Gibbons establishes the central image of Lincoln as the nation's moral patriarch: The "we" who speaks in the poem is the collective of newly recruited Union soldiers, soldiers who answer Lincoln's call, in July of 1862, for more troops. In its first stanza, the poem establishes Lincoln as a figure of biblical and prophetic authority:

> We are coming, Father Abraham, three hundred thousand more,
> From Mississippi's winding stream and from New England's shore;

We leave our ploughs and workshops, our wives and children dear,
With hearts too full for utterance, but with a silent tear;
We dare not look behind us, but steadfastly before:
We are coming, Father Abraham, three hundred thousand more![18]

Linking recruits from the West and the Northeast – and implicitly reminding its readers of Lincoln's western origins – Gibbons's poem converts the solitary stance of romantic mourning in poems like Lincoln's "My Childhood Home I See Again" into a collective nationalist "we." Whereas "My Childhood Home I See Again" expresses the private grief of the speaker's mourning – a mourning that is articulated by the madman's sorrowful song and assuaged by nature's responsive tears – in "Three Hundred Thousand More," private grief is transformed into the collective and active response of the nation, a nation that is symbiotically reliant on the natural world. Paradoxically – and in keeping with romantic convention – the poem gives collective voice to the emotion that individual soldiers are unable to express. They shed "a silent tear" at parting with their families; their hearts are "too full for utterance."

Stanzas two and three of the poem foreground the idea that the new recruits spring bodily from a vital American landscape, underlying the close and redemptive relationship between the American people and an American natural world. Stanza two begins: "If you look all up our valleys where the growing harvests shine, / You may see our sturdy farmer boys fast forming into line."[19] The redemptive and cyclical work of agricultural labor – the labor that Lincoln himself performed as a young man – is thus allied with a redemptive cycle of fighting and dying on the battlefield. The fourth and final stanza makes clear that the "three hundred thousand" who speak in the poem are called to action by the "six hundred thousand" who have gone before them. In the first two lines of the last stanza, the soldiers' collective voice makes explicit that they are responding both to Lincoln's call and to the sacrifices of their predecessors: "You have called us and we're coming, by Richmond's bloody tide / To lay us down, for Freedom's sake, our brothers' bones beside."[20] The poem thus establishes as its central metaphor this symmetrical pattern: that soldiers will rise up from the land to replace those who have been buried in it, thereby redeeming the nation's destiny. Enlisting and fighting are likened to the natural cycles not only of agriculture but also of human birth, death, and regeneration; in the refrain that closes each stanza ("We are coming, Father Abraham, three hundred thousand more"), Abraham Lincoln is the father of the great interconnected family that springs from the American land. The figure of the solitary son who grieves in harmony with nature in "My Childhood Home I See Again" has in "Three Hundred Thousand More" been replaced by the figure of the inspiring and generative father who can call sons forth from the bountiful land itself.

It is a testament to Lincoln's extraordinary personal modesty that frequent paeans to him seem not to have turned his head or impaired his ability to function effectively as a leader. Gibbons's poem was first published anonymously in the *Saturday Evening Post* on July 16, 1862, two weeks after Lincoln's call for additional troops, and was widely circulated both as a poem and as a song – attributed to several different authors – throughout the war. Gibbons is reported to have sung the poem to Lincoln after the December 1862 battle at Fredericksburg; the piece is a typical example of the permeable boundary between popular song and poetry in the Civil War era. The close emotional relationship that Gibbons's poem imagines between Lincoln and the Union soldiers is of course confirmed by historians' accounts of the many visits Lincoln paid to Union soldiers and the many letters of condolence he wrote to grieving family members after soldiers' deaths. Elizabeth Keckley's portrait of Lincoln's profound grief at the death of his young son Willie is also implicitly a portrait of the father of the nation grieving for the metaphorical sons he has lost on the battlefield.

Moreover, Lincoln's own wartime poetry offers an alternative kind of evidence of his strong sense of connection to the Union troops. Following the battle at Gettysburg in July of 1863, Lincoln pens eight lines of comic doggerel that signal his relief that Lee's attempt at a northern incursion has been rebuffed:

> Verse on Lee's Invasion of the North
>
> Gen. Lees invasion of the North written by himself –
>
> In eighteen sixty three, with pomp,
>   and mighty swell,
> Me and Jeff's Confederacy, went
>   forth to sack Phil-del.
>
> The Yankees they got arter us, and
>   giv us particular hell,
> And we skedaddled back again,
>   And didn't sack Phil-del. ("Lincoln as Poet")

Lincoln responds to the hero-making rhetoric of "We Are Coming, Father Abraham" with the rough humor that is characteristic of the poems written by amateur soldier-poets during the war years. Echoing the adolescent poems in which he jokingly boasted about his own literacy, Lincoln titles the poem with a phrase that insists comically on Lee's authorship and literacy ("written by himself") even as the brevity of the poem also mocks the brevity of Lee's northern incursion. In its two brisk stanzas, the poem uses working-class colloquialisms and dialect to demote Lee, a Virginia plantation owner and top graduate of West Point, to the ranks of his southern rural-born foot soldiers; in similar fashion, as the poem's speaker, Lee addresses the president of the Confederacy on a comically casual first-name basis. The poem's abundant use of commas and enjambment heightens the satire of its portrait of Lee, whose "pomp, / and mighty swell" are quickly deflated both by the military defeat at Gettysburg and by the poem's comic turns. The enjambment in particular suggests both the lurching swagger of a boastful leader and the quick reversals of fortune that can occur on the battlefield. The literary-military phrasing in the title and both stanzas ("invasion," "pomp, / and mighty swell"; "went / forth"; "sack") alternates with the comically compressed "Phil-del" and the rural and working-class phrases "they got arter us," "giv us particular hell," and "we skedaddled." In presenting a satirical version of Lee's voice, Lincoln's poem offers a cautionary tale about how easily military and political leaders can be corrupted by their own success; above all else, however, what the poem signals is Lincoln's powerful sense of identification with and affection for the Union troops, his ability to see the war imaginatively through the eyes of his own foot soldiers.

Clearly Lincoln's ability to identify imaginatively both with soldiers and civilians struck a chord with many northern supporters: For many pro-Union writers, Lincoln's life story becomes an iconic example of the possibilities for American identity and success. By the later years of the war, poetic paeans to Lincoln were mailed to the White House on a regular basis. Both published writers like Gibbons and amateurs wrote poems celebrating Lincoln's life and achievements. In many of these poems, Lincoln is himself represented as having sprung from a vital and redemptive American landscape, like the plenitude of soldiers that spring from the land in Gibbons's "Three Hundred Thousand More." In April of 1864, a young woman who identified herself as "Polly Peachblossom" wrote Lincoln asking for his autograph on a piece of silk for her wedding quilt. With this request, she included a poem of six stanzas, each eight lines in length, representing Lincoln's rise from rural poverty to the office of the presidency. The poem takes as its title and central image "The Maul," a versatile tool of country and working life, but the word gets deployed in the poem as both noun and verb, underlining its multiple layers of meaning.[21] Evoking Lincoln's political nickname the "Railsplitter," the "maul" or sledgehammer can be both a tool and a weapon; Peachblossom's poem works deliberately with this ambiguity as it traces the stages of Lincoln's life story. In "The Maul" as in "Three Hundred Thousand More," the redemptive manual labor of agriculture is linked to the violent but redemptive work done on Civil War battlefields.

Peachblossom's poem uses the metaphor of the maul to underline the connection between Lincoln's physical strength and his intellectual abilities; in its echoing of the "Railsplitter" nickname, the metaphor implicitly connects Lincoln's political success to the industrial and moral progress of the nation, as land is cleared, fences are built, rail lines laid down and – more importantly still – slaves are emancipated. Stanza one imagines a young Lincoln as "a tall lank, awkward 'figger'" who cuts through the thick wood of pro-slavery sentiment both to free "a young slave 'nigger'" and to make his own way in the world ("Till the star of Fame shines o'er me"). In stanza three, Lincoln pores over law books and declares, "I'll maul my way through the hard world still," and in stanza four, he debates and defeats Stephen Douglas by fighting him "with the maul of Truth." In stanza five, he writes the Emancipation Proclamation, using his pen as a maul. Establishing the maul as a tool of force that is vital to the building of the nation, Peachblossom writes, "And the pen he used was the heaviest maul / In this rail-mauling nation." Peachblossom's poem underlines the extent to which Northerners found in Lincoln's life story not only an archetypal model for American identity but also a vision of what the reunited nation might become in the aftermath of the Civil War. For northern supporters, Lincoln was a figure who could unify West and North, a man whose rural agricultural origins could serve as guarantor of his courage and moral authority. In the versatile genre of poetry, Peachblossom found the language to represent not only Lincoln's country roots but also his extraordinary intellectual and political achievements.

Abraham Lincoln's powerful connection to the genre of poetry illuminates poetry's centrality not only to American literary culture but also to American political culture – and in particular to Civil War–era debates about American identity. Wartime poems that lionize Lincoln emphasize both his western origins and his strong connection to the vital and redemptive American land; such poems also often foreground Lincoln's powerful emotional connection to ordinary Americans. A few years earlier, while traveling on the campaign trail in September of 1858, Lincoln had written two poems in the autograph books of the sisters Rosa and Linnie Haggard, daughters of the proprietor of a hotel that he stayed at in Winchester, Illinois. The poem for Rosa Haggard mischievously plays with the literary conventions of the *carpe diem* stance, even as the speaker mocks himself for being old and pessimistic. In the first of two verses, the speaker slyly advises the young lady:

> You are young, and I am older;
> You are hopeful, I am not –
> Enjoy life, ere it grow colder –
> Pluck the roses ere they rot.   (CW 3: 203)

The poem is both surprisingly dark and surprisingly funny in its bluntness. Whereas the poem for Rosa echoes the baudy and mischievous stances of Lincoln's youth, the poem for Linnie turns instead to the high romantic and nostalgic stances of the poetry Lincoln wrote in his thirties:

> A sweet and plaintive song did I hear,
> And I fancied that she was the singer –
> May emotions as pure as that song set a-stir
> Be the worst that the future shall bring her.   (CW 3: 204)

Written just three months after the "House Divided" speech, these two poems foreground Lincoln's ability to address the wide range of Americans he represented as a political leader. They also foreground his extraordinary versatility as a writer, the ease with which he could shift from comic to romantic stances – both within one poem and between the two poems – although both pieces were likely tossed off quickly.

Not surprisingly, Lincoln scholars have shown only a limited interest in the poetry Lincoln wrote. Lincoln himself modestly describes "My Childhood Home I See Again" as "doggerel," in spite of its polish and competence.[22] Read in relation to the cultural context in which they were produced, however, Lincoln's poems offer a rich field of inquiry insofar as they offer not only unexpected access to his emotions but also a representative instance of American poetry's rhetorical power in the mid-nineteenth century. Moreover, in examining the full range of Lincoln's poetry we can see him honing the skills that would make him one of the most powerful orators of the nineteenth century: his ability to engage with and amuse Americans from a wide range of backgrounds; his skillful imitation and use of a wide range of popular and literary stances; his dextrous switching from one literary stance to another, both within pieces and from one piece to the next; his masterful use of linguistic compression and ambiguity; his ability to create arresting and lyrical metaphors that would resonate for his listeners with multiple layers of meaning and emotion, with meanings and emotions both deeply concealed and clearly revealed. Lincoln's "poetizing" moods, as he calls them, are clearly as relevant to our discussion of his political and cultural identities as any of the other texts he produced.[23]

NOTES

1   See "Copybook Verses," in Roy P. Basler, ed., *The Collected Works of Abraham Lincoln*, vol. 1 (New Brunswick, NJ: Rutgers University Press, 1953), 1. References to this source are hereafter cited in text under the heading "CW." Lincoln's poetry also appears in an online archive from the Library of Congress: "Lincoln as Poet," *Presidents as Poets*, www.loc.gov/rr/program/bib/prespoetry/al.html

2 For Lincoln's taste in poetry, see Fred Kaplan, *Lincoln: The Biography of a Writer* (New York: Harper Collins, 2008), and Peter Armenti, "Lincoln as Poetry Reader," in *Abraham Lincoln and Poetry*, February 9, 2011: www.loc. gov/rr/program/bib/lincolnpoetry/#reader

3 See Doris Kearns Goodwin, *Team of Rivals: The Political Genius of Abraham Lincoln* (New York: Simon and Schuster, 2005), and Daniel Mark Epstein, *The Lincolns: Portrait of a Marriage* (New York: Ballantine, 2008), 95–99, 227–228.

4 See Joshua Wolf Shenk, *Lincoln's Melancholy: How Depression Changed a President and Fueled His Greatness* (Boston: Houghton Mifflin, 2005), 181–182.

5 Emerson, "Abraham Lincoln," *The Complete Works of Ralph Waldo Emerson*, vol. XI (Boston: Houghton Mifflin, 1911), 333.

6 Charles Sumner, "Eulogy," in *A Memorial of Abraham Lincoln* (Boston: Boston City Council, 1865), 134.

7 For Lincoln's relationship to Burns, see Kaplan, "The Biography," 63–70, and also Ferenc Morton Szasz, *Abraham Lincoln and Robert Burns: Connected Lives and Legends* (Carbondale: Southern Illinois University Press, 2008).

8 My account of Lincoln's early reading is indebted to Kaplan and to Armenti.

9 Johnson is particularly critical of Gray's achievement in his *Life of Gray* (1781).

10 Thomas Gray, "Elegy Written in a Country Church-Yard," 4th edition (London, 1751), February 14, 2011: http: //galenet.galegroup.com/ECCO

11 In Basler, *Collected Works*, vol. 1, p. 2, see Basler's note 2.

12 See Basler, *Collected Works*, vol. 1, p. 1, note 1, and also Kaplan, "The Biography," 38–40.

13 See Shenk, *Lincoln's Melancholy*, 39–42, Epstein, *The Lincolns*, 23–24, and "Lincoln as Poet."

14 See also Kaplan's reading of this poem ("The Biography," 158–162).

15 A final section that Lincoln mentions to Johnston was either lost or never sent. See CW vol. 1, p. 367, n. 1.

16 Kaplan says of "My Childhood Home I See Again" that the poem's "canonical influences are obvious" ("The Biography," 159).

17 See for example Kaplan, "The Biography," 159, and also Shenk, *Lincoln's Melancholy*, 78–80 and 123–125.

18 James Sloan Gibbons, "Three Hundred Thousand More," in Faith Barrett and Cristanne Miller, eds., *Words for the Hour: A New Anthology of American Civil War Poetry* (Amherst: University of Massachusetts Press, 2005), 92.

19 Ibid., 92.

20 Ibid., 93.

21 For this and other examples of poems sent to Lincoln, see Armenti, "Lincoln as Poetry Reader."

22 In a letter to Andrew Johnston, February 25, 1847, CW 1: 392.

23 From a letter to Andrew Johnston, September 6, 1846, CW 1: 385.

3

CAROL PAYNE

Seeing Lincoln: Visual Encounters

On January 18, 2009, Barack Obama delivered a brief but stirring address on the Washington Mall just two days before his historic inauguration as the forty-fourth president of the United States of America. The speech opened a widely viewed concert dubbed, "We Are One: The Obama Inaugural Celebration at the Lincoln Memorial"; Obama's already familiar eloquence established a celebratory tone for the celebrity performances that followed.

Yet, the setting of that speech was as rhetorically loaded as Obama's phrasing.[1] The then president-elect stood at a podium on the steps of the memorial, directly in front of Daniel Chester French's iconic statue of Abraham Lincoln. Meticulously choreographed for the media, the staging afforded news cameras a dramatic photo op. From their vantage point, Obama appeared as a sober but vigorous figure emerging from the stately neo-Classical surroundings (Figure 1). Behind him, appearing almost as a spectral presence was the figure of Abraham Lincoln, his extended arms at once seeming to embrace Obama and offer the president-elect up to the American nation as Lincoln's political successor. Obama referenced and associated himself with Lincoln explicitly in his speech on that day, as he often did throughout the lengthy presidential campaign. He directed the audience to look at the memorial with its statue of Lincoln "... behind me, watching over the union he saved."[2]

The orchestration of this event and the invocation of Abraham Lincoln's gaze testify to the enduring significance of the image of the sixteenth president of the United States. On pennies and five-dollar bills, television and the web, countless memorials, special exhibitions, advertising, pieces of memorabilia, and other forms of popular visual culture, Lincoln's face is ubiquitous today. Indeed, as Obama spoke on the Washington Mall in early 2009, the Smithsonian Institution was hosting a series of nearby exhibitions dedicated to the bicentennial of Lincoln's birth, including the National Portrait Gallery's "One Life: The Mask of Lincoln." Reflecting the prominence of those images, this chapter addresses the visual representation of

Figure 1. Dennis Brack, Obama at the Lincoln Memorial, January 18, 2009.
Courtesy of Getty Images.

Abraham Lincoln. Whereas most of the contributions to this volume address
Lincoln's political, historical, or literary legacy, this chapter, in contrast, takes
a visual turn. In these pages, I ponder what role the image of Lincoln has
played in the American popular imagination, arguing that these likenesses
fostered a deep bond between the public and the political figure.[3]

In formulating that argument, this chapter returns to portrayals of
Abraham Lincoln made during his lifetime, with particular attention to the
circulation of his portrait for the 1860 presidential election and during his
presidency. Lincoln was occasionally the subject of portraits in the 1840s
and 1850s before he came to national prominence;[4] but it was during and
leading up to the 1860 presidential campaign that his likeness was first

widely circulated and began its transformation from the individualized to the symbolic.⁵ Just as political campaigns today – including Obama's – use visual symbolism extensively and strategically, Lincoln, his handlers, and commercial interests also deployed images in innovative ways to speak for the candidate. I argue that the iconicity of Lincoln's likeness is rooted in the deep bond between candidate and potential voters at that time. Mid-nineteenth-century advancements in photographic technology and the mass circulation of these images were essential to that bond. But, these technologies were only effective because the public who consumed them was highly receptive to and practiced in assessing character through image. The intimacy forged in these visual technologies and through the active engagement of a viewing public established a foundation for the iconicity of Lincoln's likeness.

Few expected Abraham Lincoln to win the Republican nomination in 1860; in the end, he only received the party's nod on the third ballot. This was a critical election for the relatively new Republican Party, which had only run a presidential candidate once before, in 1856, when its nominee, John C. Frémont, lost to the Democratic ticket of James Buchanan and John C. Breckinridge. To be viable in 1860, Republicans needed to win the so-called doubtful states⁶ while satisfying a party that was divided, particularly over the Fugitive Slave Law. Republican strategists and delegates increasingly recognized that Lincoln had the potential to unify the party and to appeal to voters widely. Not only did he hail from Illinois, one of the "doubtful" states, but Lincoln, the candidate, had also carefully navigated a moderate path between Conservative Republican positions and those held by more radical, antislavery party members.⁷

Lincoln's success at the Republican convention and eventual triumph in the 1860 presidential election was also driven by a spectacular campaign, which privileged character over potentially divisive issues and featured visual symbolism extensively. Among campaign imagery, the "Railsplitter" motif was the most prominent (Figure 2).⁸ At the May 1859 Illinois State Republican convention, Lincoln's cousin John Hanks burst into the hall carrying timber rails, which the candidate was purported to have helped split for a fence many years earlier.⁹ The spectacle captured the attention of delegates and galvanized supporters. In Lincoln's subsequent presidential campaign as the Republican candidate, split rails became indispensible props at parades and rallies. Images of rails also filled scores of lithographs, placards, music sheets, broadsides, and caricatures, even supplying the name for a party journal.¹⁰ A multivalent emblem, the split rail at once signified Lincoln's much lauded industriousness and humble origins while associating

Figure 2. *The Railsplitter* (August 25, 1860): 1.

the candidate with romantic notions of the frontier, all the while remaining silent on the key issue of slavery.[11]

The popular, homespun values suggested by the Railsplitter persona were reinforced textually by familiar references to Lincoln as "Honest Old Abe" or "Uncle Abe" during the campaign.[12] The moniker was paired with Lincoln's likeness in Railsplitter images and elsewhere repeatedly throughout the campaign. "Honest Abe" or "Honest Old Abe" suggested the Republican candidate as a trustworthy alternative to the alleged corruption of Buchanan's Democratic administration. But the use of the diminutive form of Lincoln's given name was also significant. It effectively cast Lincoln in the role of a down-to-earth everyman while fabricating a semblance of familiarity or a personal bond between candidate and potential voter.

That semblance of personal familiarity was a mainstay of Lincoln campaign promotions; it was established, not only through homespun iconography, personal address, and the rhetorical device of repetition, but through portraits of the candidate. Indeed, portraiture itself became a crucial vehicle for this empathetic relationship. As Richard Brilliant has shown, the portrait is conventionally assumed to possess "some substratum of mimetic representation underlying the purported resemblance between the original and the work of art, especially because the sign function of the portrait is so strong that it seems to be some form of substitution for the original."[13]

By Election Day on November 6, 1860, Americans encountered Lincoln, through his likeness – that close substitute or surrogate for the candidate – recurrently. The country was all but saturated with portraits of Abraham Lincoln. His then clean-shaven face appeared on banners, campaign buttons, broadsides, and caricatures; Americans came to recognize that face with the familiarity of a neighbor or a friend.

The mass dissemination of Lincoln's portrait was achieved largely through new advancements in photographic technology; 1860 marked the first American presidential election to use mass-produced photographs. Reproduced in great numbers relatively quickly and at limited expense, photographs met the fast-paced demands of electioneering. Not only were photographs of Lincoln printed or reproduced by the thousands but lithographs, engravings, and other hand-rendered images were increasingly copied from photographic images then in circulation. Indeed, the popularization of Abraham Lincoln as a national figure is inextricably bound to the photographic image. Lincoln, who posed for about 120 photographs in his lifetime, is believed to be the most photographed American president of the nineteenth century and may well have been one of the most photographed Americans of his time.[14]

Agreeing to numerous sittings for photographers before and at the time of the election with even more to follow during his presidency, Lincoln was certainly aware of the role that such visuals played in public recognition and, in turn, the importance of that visual recognition to his political ascendency. At the same time, photography itself became part of the Lincoln mythos. In a widely circulated anecdote, Lincoln was purported to have said that along with his celebrated February 1860 speech at the Cooper Union in New York, it was a contemporaneous photograph by Mathew Brady (Figure 3) that "made me President of the United States."[15] As Harold Holzer has shown, this story is likely apocryphal; yet, it demonstrates the prominent role of photography in the advancement of Lincoln's political career and the candidate's efforts to use the new medium for these ends.[16]

Figure 3. Mathew Brady, Abraham Lincoln on the day of his speech at the
Cooper Union, February, 27, 1860. Carte-de-visite photograph. James Wadsworth Family
Papers, Manuscript Division, Library of Congress (046) Digital ID # al0046.

Today, photographic portraits of Lincoln appear dour and austere. Most
of the extant portraits show him alone as an unsmiling figure, stiffly posed.[17]
Technical limitations and conventions of the day account for some of these
characteristics. Sitting for a photograph, even for as practiced a model as
Abraham Lincoln, was far from a routine event in 1860 and was typically
undertaken as a formal and ritualized occasion. Cumbersome equipment
and long exposure times required that photographic portraits were almost
always taken inside in controlled settings with ample natural illumination,
usually through a north-facing skylight.[18] In order to remain motionless
during the protracted period of exposure, the sitter was typically stabilized
with an uncomfortable neck brace, given a table to lean on, or, more often,

seated in a chair. For the celebrated Cooper Union portrait, for example, Brady depicted Lincoln standing with his hand resting on a stack of books; more commonly, Lincoln is seated in photographic portrayals. Under these awkward conditions, smiling broadly for the camera was rarely feasible and would have undermined the dignity intended by the portraits.[19]

Beyond technical limitations, the routine poses demonstrate how standardized photographic practice had already become by the 1860s. According to Frederic E. Ray, in 1860 more than 3,000 photographers were working in the United States.[20] These photographic studios were competitive business enterprises, with high-profile practitioners like Brady running large and fairly opulent ventures, whereas the bulk was photographers who managed modest and often short-lived studios.[21] Large or small, photographers typically employed many of the same conventionalized and highly coded props including velvet curtains, stacks of books, tables, painted backdrops, and other furnishings for portraiture, the mainstay of photography in the nineteenth century. In the Cooper Union portrait, Brady posed Lincoln with books and beside a painted backdrop of a classical column. These props, variants of which were used in most studios of the time, suggest the learned and esteemed character of the sitter.[22] Yet, although photographers posed their clients, sitting for a portrait was a collaborative undertaking and surely a sitter as accustomed to photographic studios as Lincoln arranged himself or performed for the camera with full knowledge of the semantics of the pose.

Viewers, too, collaborated in this visual fashioning of public identity. Although to our eyes today, portraits of Lincoln often seem severe and routine, they were rich in meaning for contemporary viewers. Their reception of these images was informed in part by the cultural meanings of photography itself. As one of the most influential mechanical inventions of the day, photography embodied the authority and allure of modern science and conferred sitters, like Lincoln, with the multivalent values of the modern. Above all, however, mid-nineteenth-century viewers perceived the photograph as a direct encounter with the subject. Known at the time variously as an "exact facsimile [of nature]," a "mirror with a memory," and the "pencil of nature,"[23] photography surpassed the merely mimetic by seeming to offer the viewer a direct trace or index of the sitter.[24] In turn, this quality enhances what Richard Brilliant has termed the "indexical properties" inherent to portraiture.[25] Yet, the indexical experience of the photographic portrait was by no means unmediated; instead, it effectively invited viewers to project onto the image their own aspirations and imaginings and in this way participate in the electoral process at a highly intuitive and personal level.[26]

The perceived indexicality of photographic representations was crucial to their use during the 1860 campaign. As noted previously, mass-circulated engravings were often based on photographs; Brady's Cooper Union portrait, for example, provided the basis for the May 26, 1860, cover of *Harper's Weekly*. The use of a photographic model lent such engravings a sense of directness and authority. Contemporary understandings of photographic indexicality were also central to the effectiveness of one of the most innovative forms of Lincoln election photography: the ferrotype or melainotype campaign medal. Patented in 1860, the ferrotype, or tintype as it is commonly known, was made by coating a thin sheet of black japanned iron with a light-sensitive collodion compound and exposing it directly in a camera. A unique process photograph, the ferrotype did not use a negative and could only be reproduced by being rephotographed.[27] Perhaps largely because they were so durable and cheap, ferrotypes became phenomenally popular in the late 1850s and 1860s despite limited pictorial detail and tonal range. As campaign medals, the iron-based images were cut into circular shapes usually about 1 inch in diameter and framed by a brass border bearing the candidate's name.[28] Supporters affixed them with the aid of a wire loop threaded through a hole in the frame. Countless thousands of ferrotype medals were produced for Lincoln's 1860 campaign by rephotographing existing images.[29] Typical of them is a campaign medal from the collection of the Library of Congress (Figure 4), which features the likeness of Lincoln on one side and that of his running mate Hannibal Hamlin on the other. Lincoln's portrait was a second-generation image probably made from a photograph by Mathew Brady.[30] Ferrotype medals, like this example, performed a sense of direct connection between voter and candidate quite explicitly. Worn on the lapels of thousands of supporters, these tiny objects did not merely suggest a political allegiance; they embodied a sense of personal identification with the politician, an identification that was enhanced by the presumed indexicality of the photographic image.

Aided by photographs and photographically based images, Americans were widely cognizant of a correlation between visual codes, electoral success, and the resultant bond between voters and candidate, as testified by one of the most often recounted anecdotes about Lincoln's appearance. On October 18, 1860, less than a month before the election, eleven-year-old Grace Bedell of Westfield, New York, wrote to Lincoln personally to suggest that cosmetic improvements to his famously unkempt appearance would reap benefits in the voting booths:

> I have got 4 brother's [sic] and part of them will vote for you any way and if you will let your whiskers grow I will try and get the rest of them to vote for you you [sic] would look a great deal better for your face is so thin. All the ladies like whiskers and they would tease their husband's [sic] to vote for you and then you would be President.[31]

Figure 4. Mathew Brady, presidential campaign button with portraits of Abraham
Lincoln and Hannibal Hamlin. Ferrotype or Tintype button. Library of Congress,
Unprocessed in PR 17 CN 541.2 [item] [P&P], Reproduction number:
LC-DIG-ppmsca-19430 (digital file from original item, front);
LC-DIG-ppmsca-19431 (digital file from original item, back).

Lincoln promptly responded to the child personally, fretting in his short letter that if he grew a beard, "people would call it a piece of silly affectation."[32]
But, of course, Lincoln *did* let his "whiskers grow" during the interim
between election and inauguration. Whether this cosmetic modification
was actually prompted by little Grace Bedell is not clear; however, it does
indicate Lincoln's and the public's awareness of the power of visual self-
fashioning and the pliancy of public identity.[33] At the same time, this anecdote underscores the fact that the votership was divided by gender (as it was
by race); women – and girls like Grace Bedell – connected profoundly with
Lincoln and other public figures, but their agency was confined to swaying
the votes of husbands, sons, brothers, and fathers.

As president, Lincoln remained connected to the American public – and
the American public to him – in part through images. Indeed, Lincoln
became increasingly more visible during his presidency: He posed for photographers in ever greater numbers, sat for sculptors and painters, and

Figure 5. Alexander Gardner, President Lincoln on battlefield of Antietam, October 1862. Published in Gardner's *Photographic Sketch Book of the War* (Washington, DC: Philp & Solomons 1865–1866), vol. 1, no. 23. Library of Congress, Prints and Photographs Division, Washington, DC 20540 USA, http://hdl.loc.gov/loc.pnp/pp.print. URL: http://hdl.loc.gov/loc.pnp/ ppmsca.12544. Call Number: Illus. in E468.7.G2.

continued to use images strategically.[34] Photographers, who had much to gain financially from photographing Lincoln, regularly wrote to the president for permission to take (and market) his likeness, while individuals and charitable organizations corresponded with the White House seeking copies of Lincoln's portraits.[35] At the same time, the press issued images of Lincoln in both caricatures and more reverent depictions.[36]

If election images depicting Lincoln fostered a homely familiarity with viewers, during his presidency the character of these depictions and the public's relation to them changed. Pictorial representations of Lincoln came to reflect the gravity of contemporary events. Whimsical and nostalgic visual allusions to the frontier and homespun values would have been out of step with the harsh realities of southern secession and the ensuing Civil War. Instead, Lincoln is typically visualized during his presidency as a sober and paternalistic leader. This heightened gravitas is evident, for example, in Alexander Gardner's portrayals of Lincoln's tense meeting with General George B. McClellan on the battlefield of Antietam on October 3, 1862 (Figure 5). Issued at the time and later represented in Alexander Gardner's *Photographic Sketchbook of the Civil War*, these images present Lincoln as

Figure 6. Francis Bicknell Carpenter, *First Reading of the Emancipation Proclamation by President Lincoln* (1864). Oil on canvas (Art Collection, U.S. Senate).

commander in chief towering over the assembled members of the Army of the Potomac or addressing McClellan from across a table.[37] Visual images also commemorated Lincoln's momentous legislation as in Francis Bicknell Carpenter's 1864 canvas, *First Reading of the Emancipation Proclamation by President Lincoln* (Figure 6).[38] Although Lincoln wrote the Emancipation Proclamation alone,[39] Carpenter depicts the president surrounded by his famously factious cabinet as he presents them with a draft on September 22, 1862.[40] Nonetheless, the effect of a group portrait was, paradoxically, to enhance Lincoln's status as a statesman; seated at the center of the composition with document in one hand and pen in the other and looking out to the viewer, he is portrayed as a figure of action in contradistinction to the staid portrayals of the members of the cabinet. Lincoln's demeanor also signals his public familiarity at the time while presenting him as a figure of moral integrity. His central positioning in the composition – known widely through a mass-distributed engraving – situated him not only as a chief protagonist in the legislative drama depicted but in direct relation to the viewer.[41]

Whereas works of fine art and engravings based on them translated Lincoln's likeness into elevated forms, photography remained the central visual medium through which Americans of the time saw and related to the president.[42] One of the most widely circulated types of photographic portraits was the carte de visite, a $2\frac{1}{8} \times 3$-inch "calling card" mounted with a photographic print. Developed in France in 1854, cartes gained entry into the U.S. market in the early 1860s and soon became a fad among

Figure 7. Mathew Brady, Abraham Lincoln, U.S. President. Seated portrait, facing front, January 8, 1864. Carte de visite. Library of Congress, http://loc.gov/pictures/item/2008680391

middle-class Americans, who collected cartes by the score.[43] If the ferrotype campaign medal publicly announced an allegiance, cartes remained in the private realm of the parlor and the photo album. But they, too, performed a sense of personal bond; collectors in effect compiled autobiographical narratives in these albums with Lincoln and other celebrated figures of the day appearing as characters in their life stories.[44]

Lincoln was one of the most popular subjects of cartes de visite in the 1860s. An 1864 portrait by Mathew Brady issued as a carte shows the president at the end of his first term in office (Figure 7). His body at three-quarter view, Lincoln turns his face toward the camera, offering the viewer a direct gaze as well as an ambiguous half-smile. Unlike Brady's 1860 Cooper Union portrait, this image is almost entirely devoid of props or the sloganeering of the Railsplitter campaign. But such codes were redundant by 1864, when Lincoln's face itself was legible to Americans.

Indeed, by 1864 Americans felt able to "read" Lincoln's face like a familiar, if multivalent, text. The public interpreted faces – including Lincoln's – often through a generalized knowledge of phrenological principles, the study of cranial shape as a supposedly empirical indicator of character and aptitude. Developed in eighteenth-century Europe, phrenology was commonplace knowledge among middle-class Americans by the mid-nineteenth century. [45]

Although Lincoln's likeness was most often visually assessed with a broad understanding of the face as an index of character, he was also the direct subject of detailed phrenological readings, which render the connection between Lincoln and the American public explicit. During the 1864 election and following his death in 1865, Lincoln was, for example, the subject of analyses in the popular *American Phrenological Journal and Life Illustrated*.[46] In 1864, the journal recommended that readers

> choose their officers of trust on phrenological principles.... Then we may hope to have, not a set of noisy, drunken rowdies to fill important posts but capable honest men. Then we shall have in each department "The Right man in the Right Place."[47]

As in the 1860 campaign, character is privileged over issues but now with the aid of the pseudoscience of phrenology. Within the pages of the *American Phrenological Journal*, Lincoln, the candidate, was assessed on the basis of an engraving by R. S. Bross from a February 9, 1864, photographic portrait (Figure 8); in this, the assessment reflects the way that Americans had evaluated Lincoln since the 1860 campaign.[48] Further, this second-generation representation mediated Lincoln's appearance: The pose only renders some of his head visible, his features have been flattened out in a manner consistent with contemporary photography's optical distortions, and the engraver has slightly exaggerated the size of Lincoln's ears and positioning of his eyes. Although manipulated in this way, this representation provided evidence to the journal of Lincoln's greatness. The editors noted that his high forehead indicated advanced intellect, concluding that Lincoln's

> whole make-up denotes a matter-of-fact mind ... the forehead ample, but not ponderous ... he is open to conviction, true to his higher nature, and governed by moral principle rather than by policy. He is firm, persevering, generous, kind-hearted, affectionate, intelligent, with a high degree of strong, practical common sense. If not great, is he not good? If not the best man for the situation, where can you find a better?[49]

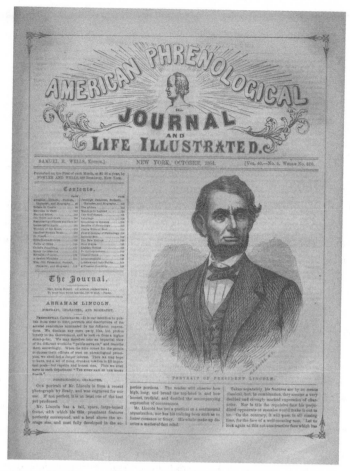

Figure 8. "Abraham Lincoln. Portrait, Character, and Biography," in *American Phrenological Journal and Life Illustrated* (October 1864): 97. Courtesy, the Collection of James M. Schmidt.

In its references to the same honorable characteristics promoted by the Republican Party four years earlier, *The American Phrenological Journal* translates the emphasis on character and a personal bond with the candidate into a pseudoscientific language.

The American Phrenological Journal's analysis of Lincoln sets into high relief the experiences of many American viewers of the time. Contemporary Americans recognized Lincoln's face with the familiarity of an old friend, and they read into that face the values of honesty, industriousness, and ethical bearing that the Republican Party had long promoted. The seeming indexicality of both photographic technology and portraiture itself enhanced the directness of that encounter, imparting a sense of personal identification and personal engagement of American voters.

Portraits of Lincoln have continued to elicit profound responses from American viewers in the generations since his assassination.[50] As Cara Finnegan has argued in her study of later nineteenth-century reception of Lincoln's image, for example, portraits of the sixteenth president functioned as "image vernaculars," focal points for the active creation of and debate over cultural values and national identity. They became, as Finnegan argues, touchstones for late nineteenth-century anxieties over new immigrants to the United States, with Lincoln signifying an exemplary "American type."[51] Barry Schwartz, too, has demonstrated that Lincoln's visage became a crucial and historically contingent symbolic element in American collective memory throughout the twentieth century.[52] And more recently on the Washington Mall on January 18, 2009, Lincoln's likeness, again, resonated with the American public. What had once been the likeness of a candidate and legislator had become an emblem in a collective narrative of American nationhood. As I have argued here, today's ubiquitous and loaded images of Lincoln had their roots in encounters between voters and Lincoln, the candidate, in the 1860s.

NOTES

1 As Obama emphasized in his speech, the Lincoln Memorial was also the rallying point for Martin Luther King's 1968 March on Washington.
2 The staging of this speech appears featured on the cover of *The New Yorker*. Bob Staake, "Reflection," *The New Yorker* (November 17, 2008): cover.
3 Any discussion of the visual representation of Abraham Lincoln is indebted to the groundbreaking work of Harold Holzer. Along with Gabor S. Boritt and Mark E. Neely, Jr., Holzer has provided a detailed catalogue of images depicting Lincoln along with instructive analyses of their iconography. See also, Carol Payne, "Photo Ops: Photography and Phrenology in the 1860 and 1864 Presidential Campaigns of Abraham Lincoln," *Retrospection: The New England Graduate Review in American History and American Studies*, vol. VI, no. 2 (1993): 23–40.
4 The earliest authenticated portrait, a daguerreotype, dates from 1846 or 1847 and is in the collection of the Library of Congress. (LOC Reproduction Number: LC-USZC4–2439). See also Philip B. Kunhardt III, Peter W. Kunhardt, and Peter W. Kunhardt, Jr., *Looking for Lincoln: The Making of an American Icon* (New York: Alfred A. Knopf, 2008), 462.
5 Portraits of Lincoln were made at the time of his celebrated 1858 debates with Stephen Douglas. However, the mass distribution of his likeness began with the 1860 presidential campaign.
6 The pivotal states of Ohio, Pennsylvania, Indiana, and Illinois were all populous, but their political allegiances were uncertain at the time.
7 Richard Carwardine, *Lincoln: A Life of Purpose and Power* (New York: Knopf, 2006), 106. See also, William E. Gienapp, "Who Voted for Lincoln?"

in John L. Thomas, ed., *Abraham Lincoln and the American Political Tradition* (Amherst: University of Massachusetts Press, 1986), 53.

8   See Harold Holzer, Gabor S. Boritt, and Mark E. Neely, Jr., *The Lincoln Image: Abraham Lincoln and the Popular Print* (New York: The Scribner Press, 1984), 1–78; Harold Holzer, Gabor S. Boritt, and Mark E. Neely, Jr., *Changing the Lincoln Image* (Fort Wayne, IN: Louis A. Warren Lincoln Library and Museum, 1985), 31–43.

9   The use of this motif has precedents in the 1840 presidential campaign of William Henry Harrison and the "Log Cabin and Hard Cider" slogan. Holzer, Boritt, and Neely, *The Lincoln Image*, 5, 16.

10 The Railsplitter persona was initiated by Lincoln supporters, but it was disseminated and popularized privately by commercial interests. See Harold Holzer, "Abraham Lincoln as Student, Subject, and Patron of the Visual Arts," in Eric Foner, ed., *Our Lincoln: New Perspectives on Lincoln and His World* (New York and London: W. W. Norton & Company, 2008), 87.

11 An 1860 Currier & Ives lithograph pictures Lincoln atop the "Republican Platform" comprised entirely of split rails with a freedman hiding beneath. Currier & Ives, "'The Nigger'" in the Woodpile, New York" (1860). Holzer, Boritt, and Neely, *The Lincoln Image*, 37.

12 Holzer, Boritt, and Neely, *The Lincoln Image*, 24.

13 Richard Brilliant, *Portraiture* (New York: Reaktion Books, 1991), 40.

14 Frederick Hill Meserve presented Lincoln photographs based on his own collection, subsequently catalogued and analyzed by his student, Lloyd Ostendorf, and Meserve's family. Along with the holdings of the Library of Congress and the National Portrait Gallery, this collection still provides the basis for the study of photographs of Lincoln. See Frederick Hill Meserve and Carl Sandburg, *The Photographs of Abraham Lincoln* (New York: Harcourt, Brace and Company, 1944); Charles Hamilton and Lloyd Ostendorf, *Lincoln in Photographs: An Album of Every Known Pose* (Norman: University of Oklahoma Press, 1963); Lloyd Ostendorf, *Lincoln's Photographs: A Complete Album* (Dayton: Rockywood Press, 1998) 3rd edition; Kunhardt, et al., *Looking for Lincoln*, 461–474; Holzer, "Abraham Lincoln as Student, Subject, and Patron of the Visual Arts," 83.

15 Roy Meredith, *Mr. Lincoln's Camera Man: Mathew Brady* (New York: Scribner, 1946); O. Henry Mace, *Collector's Guide to Early Photograph* (Radnor, PA: Wallace-Homestead Book Company, 1990), 32.

16 Harold Holzer, *Lincoln at Cooper Union* (New York: Simon & Schuster, 2004), 114.

17 See also Alan Trachtenberg, "Lincoln's Smile: The Ambiguity of the Face in Photography," *Social Research*, vol. 67, no. 1 (Spring 2000): 1–23.

18 Thanks here to John McElhone. See Mark Osterman, "Introduction to Photographic Equipment, Processes, and Definitions of the Nineteenth Century," in Michael R. Peres, ed., *Focal Encyclopedia of Photography: Digital Imaging, Theory and Applications, History and Science*, 4th edition (Amsterdam: Focal Press, 2007), 36. For Lincoln out of doors, see Kunhardt, et al., *Looking for Lincoln*, 468–470, 473–474.

19 For Lincoln's smile, see portraits by Alexander Gardner made on February 5, 1865. Trachtenberg, "Lincoln's Smile," 1–23.

20 Frederic E. Ray, "The Photographers of the War," in William C. Davis, ed., *The Shadows of the Storm: Volume One of The Image of War* (New York: Doubleday and Co., 1983), 413, quoted in Keith F. Davis, "'A Terrible Distinctness': Photography of the Civil War Era," in Martha Sandweiss, ed., *Photography in Nineteenth-Century America* (Fort Worth: Amon Carter Museum, 1991), 135.

21 For Brady's studio, see Barbara McCandless, "The Portrait Studio and the Celebrity: Promoting the Art," *Photography in Nineteenth-Century America*, 53–63.

22 For Lincoln's sitting at Brady's studio, see Holzer, *Lincoln at Cooper Union*, 102–114.

23 For an "exact facsimile," see the June 1839 announcement of Daguerre's invention; Oliver Wendell Holmes referred to photography as the mirror with a memory; and "the pencil of nature" was coined by William Henry Fox Talbot. See Vicki Goldberg, ed., *Photography in Print: Writing from 1816 to the Present* (University of New Mexico Press, 1981), 32, 36–48, 102.

24 Scholars tend to characterize photography's heightened realism following Charles S. Peirce's concept of the indexical sign. See Martin Lefebvre, "The Art of Pointing: On Peirce, Indexicality, and Photographic Images," in James Elkins, ed., *Photography Theory* (New York and London: Routledge, 2007), 220–235.

25 Brilliant, *Portraiture*, 26.

26 On how nineteenth-century American viewers viewed photography, see Franny Nudelman, *John Brown's Body: Slavery, Violence, & the Culture of War* (University of North Carolina Press, 2004), 122–126; Miles Orvell, *The Real Thing: Imitation and Authenticity in American Culture, 1880–1940* (University of North Carolina Press, 1989), 76–78.

27 Richard Benson, *The Printed Picture* (New York: The Museum of Modern Art, 2008), 120.

28 Janice G. Schimmelman, *The Tintype in America, 1856–1880* (Philadelphia: American Philosophical Society, 2007), 46–51.

29 Requests for images, including campaign medals or buttons, include William D. Kelley to Norman B. Judd, Friday, June 1, 1860. Available at *Abraham Lincoln Papers at the Library of Congress*, Manuscript Division (Washington, DC: American Memory Project, 2000–2002), http://memory.loc.gov/ammem/alhtml/ alhome.html

30 Abraham Lincoln. Albumen print, ca. 1858. On loan from the Benjamin Shapell Family Manuscript Foundation (071). Library of Congress, Digital ID # al0071.

31 Grace Bedell to Abraham Lincoln, Thursday, October 18, 1860 (typed copy). Available at *Abraham Lincoln Papers at the Library of Congress*, http://memory. loc.gov/ammem/alhtml/alhome.html

32 Abraham Lincoln to Grace Bedell, Friday, October 19, 1860. Transcribed and annotated by the Lincoln Studies Center, Knox College, Galesburg, Illinois. Available at *Abraham Lincoln Papers at the Library of Congress*, http://memory. loc.gov/ammem/alhtml/alhome.html

33 The poet Carl Sandburg quoted an unnamed source with this cutting description of Lincoln: His "anatomy is composed mostly of bones, and when walking he resembles the offspring of a happy marriage between a derrick and a windmill." Carl Sandburg, "The Face of Lincoln," in Frederick Hill Meserve, *The*

Photographs of Abraham Lincoln (New York: Harcourt, Brace and Company, 1944), 2–3.

34 Significant works include portrait busts of Lincoln by Leonard Wells Volk (1860) and Sarah Fisher Clampitt Ames (1868). For a detailed survey of Lincoln and the visual arts, see Holzer, "Abraham Lincoln as Student, Subject, and Patron of the Visual Arts."

35 See, for example, Bell & Brother to Abraham Lincoln, Saturday, January 30, 1864; James P. Root to Abraham Lincoln, Thursday, March 9, 1865; Emmeline H. Whitney to Abraham Lincoln, Saturday, October 22, 1864. Available at *Abraham Lincoln Papers at the Library of Congress*, Manuscript Division (Washington, DC: American Memory Project, 2000–2002), http://memory.loc.gov/ammem/alhtml/alhome.html

36 For caricatures from Britain, see William S. Walsh, ed., *Abraham Lincoln and the London Punch* (New York: Moffat, Yard and Company, 1909).

37 Alexander Gardner, *Alexander Gardner's Photographic Sketchbook of the Civil War* (Washington, DC: Alexander Gardner, 1866); Anthony W. Lee and Elizabeth Young, *On Alexander Gardner's Photographic Sketchbook of the Civil War* (Berkeley: University of California Press, 2008); Alan Trachtenberg, "Albums of War," *Reading American Photographs: Images as History, Mathew Brady to Walker Evans* (New York: Hill and Wang, 1989), 71–119; Davis, "'A Terrible Distinctness'," 168.

38 See Francis Bicknell Carpenter, *Six Months at the White House with Abraham Lincoln: The Story of a Picture* (New York: Hurd and Houghton, 1867).

39 Carwardine, *Lincoln*, 207.

40 William Kloss and Diane K. Skvarla, "First Reading of the Emancipation Proclamation by President Lincoln (July 22, 1862)," *United States Senate Catalogue of Fine Arts* (Washington, DC: Senate Commission on Art, 2002), 116–121.

41 Like many paintings of the day, Carpenter's 1864 canvas was known through an engraving of it that could be purchased by subscription. Kloss and Skvarla, "First Reading of the Emancipation Proclamation by President Lincoln (July 22, 1862)," 119.

42 Carpenter used photographs made in Brady's studio and at the White House as sources for the canvas. Kloss and Skvarla, "First Reading of the Emancipation Proclamation by President Lincoln (July 22, 1862)," 117–118; Holzer, "Abraham Lincoln as Student, Subject, and Patron of the Visual Arts."

43 For the carte de visite, see Elizabeth Anne McCauley, *A.A.E. Disdéri and the Carte-de-Visite Portrait Photograph* (New Haven: Yale University Press, 1985).

44 Shawn Michelle Smith, *American Archives: Gender, Race, and Class in Visual Culture* (Princeton, NJ: Princeton University Press, 1999), 51–53; Susan R. Finkel, *Victorian Photography and Carte-de-visite Albums, 1860–1880* (Ann Arbor: University Microfilms, 1984).

45 The late eighteenth-century Viennese physician Franz Josef Gall developed phrenology as closely related to physiognomy. As such, phrenology was a part of a broader biological racialist discourse. Imported to the United States by Gall's student Johann Gaspar Spurzheim, by the 1830s phrenology had become institutionalized by various American reformers. Charles Colbert, *A Measure of Perfection: Phrenology and the Fine Arts in America* (Durham: The University

of North Carolina Press, 1997), 18. Smith, *American Archives*, 31; Allan Sekula, "The Body and the Archive," *October* 39 (1986): 3–64; Trachtenberg, "Lincoln's Smile": 5–6; Finnegan, "Recognizing Lincoln": 43–45. Cara A. Finnegan, "Recognizing Lincoln: Image Vernaculars in Nineteenth-Century Visual Culture," *Rhetoric and Public Affairs*, vol. 8, No. 1 (2005), 43–45.

46 "Abraham Lincoln. Portrait, Character, and Biography," in *American Phrenological Journal and Life Illustrated* (October 1864): 97–98; "Presidents of the United States: Abraham Lincoln," *American Phrenological Journal and Life Illustrated* (July 1872): 45.

47 *American Phrenological Journal* (October 1864), 97.

48 Kunhardt, et al., *Looking for Lincoln*, 471.

49 "Abraham Lincoln," in *American Phrenological Journal*, 97–98.

50 As Holzer, Boritt, and Neely have demonstrated, following his assassination, Lincoln images flooded the market. Holzer, Boritt, and Neely, *The Lincoln Image*, 192–200.

51 Finnegan, "Recognizing Lincoln": 35–36.

52 See Barry Schwartz, *Abraham Lincoln and the Forge of American Memory*. (Chicago: University of Chicago Press, 2000); Barry Schwartz and Howard Schuman, "History, Commemoration, and Belief: Abraham Lincoln in American Memory, 1945–2001," *American Sociological Review*, vol. 70 (April 2005): 183–203.

4

STEPHEN CUSHMAN

Lincoln's Gettysburg Address and Second Inaugural Address

Among the political scriptures of the United States, Lincoln's Gettysburg Address and Second Inaugural Address, each an object of voluminous commentary and interpretation, stand preeminent. Even the Declaration of Independence, for all the stirring reverberations of its memorable opening and closing, includes an extended middle section, an inventory of specific grievances against King George III, that is rhetorically closer to legal documentation than to anything in Lincoln's two addresses. The fact that few can reproduce this section of the Declaration from memory partly reflects its generic difference from Lincoln's two famous speeches, not just its greater length. The Declaration announces and justifies the breaking of an existing contract in order to form a new one, and so, whatever the beauties and powers of its language, it belongs to the genre of the legal contract, whereas Lincoln's two speeches do not. Instead, they mix and blend various genres, among them dedication, exhortation, historical narration, political argument, psalm, and prayer. In the United States the two addresses are so often memorized, so often recited, and so often quoted in other speeches that many citizens take their generic mixings for granted.

The stature and fame of the two addresses are not confined to the United States, however. Not quite fourscore and seven years after Lincoln delivered them, for example, South African writer Alan Paton wove the two addresses and their author into his great novel of broken families and unequal races, *Cry, the Beloved Country* (1948). Reading the two addresses in the library of his son, recently murdered by a misguided Zulu boy who has moved to the city of Johannesburg and fallen into bad company there, a bereaved white father slowly begins to understand his murdered son's zealous efforts to heal the rift between races in South Africa, as Paton also uses the references to Lincoln's addresses to advance and deepen a larger vision of justice, compassion, and forgiveness, both public and private. In this novel, as in many nonliterary contexts, the Great Emancipator's two greatest speeches function as icons of an egalitarian racial vision and of an enlightened social reconciliation: the Gettysburg Address often construed as endorsing "a new birth of freedom" for an enslaved race in a true democracy and the Second Inaugural Address usually read as urging magnanimity and charity toward former enemies, once the work of correcting racial imbalance has gotten underway. But these abbreviated descriptions of the two addresses, although in wide circulation around the globe and although to some extent valid, fall seriously short of acknowledging the many complexities, both historical and rhetorical, of the two addresses.

Lincoln's Gettysburg Address has become so identified with the political aspirations and self-descriptions of the United States that in 1972 the Library of Congress published a collection of translations of the address into twenty-nine languages. Roy Basler, who gathered the translations, introduced them this way: "[S]uch a booklet might serve foreign visitors to the several Lincoln shrines with an opportunity to come to grips with Lincoln's expression of the essence of American democracy rendered beautifully into their mother tongues."[1] Although foreign tourists to Lincoln shrines no doubt benefit from the availability of Lincoln's speech in their native languages, the singling out of Lincoln's speech as the superlative encapsulation of "the essence" of democracy in the United States risks exalting it beyond our individual and collective powers to see and hear it, or the Second Inaugural Address, as a verbal arrangement by a resolutely pragmatic man working strenuously to accomplish specific goals at a particular moment of national convulsion.

In the case of the Gettysburg Address, those who intone with reverence its superbly crafted periods do not have to deny their reverence in order to bear in mind that by the time Lincoln delivered his address on the afternoon of Thursday, November 19, 1863, the victory at Gettysburg of the Army of the Potomac over the Army of Northern Virginia four months earlier had lost some of its luster, because, from Lincoln's point of view, Union General George Gordon Meade had squandered a precious opportunity to defeat the Confederate army of Robert E. Lee, allowing it to escape southward over the Potomac River. After a frustrating and inconclusive series of subsequent engagements in Virginia, Meade, under pressure from Lincoln, was about to launch the ill-fated Mine Run Campaign (November 27 to December 2, 1863). Meanwhile, in the west a decisive Confederate victory at the battle of Chickamauga, fought two months earlier in northwestern Georgia, had led to the penning up of United States forces in Chattanooga, Tennessee, and Ulysses S. Grant had not yet given Lincoln the crucial victories around that city that would convince the president to promote Grant and bring him east to face Lee in 1864, although those victories were only days away. In other words, when Lincoln delivered what many around the world now regard as the quintessential hymn to democracy in the United States, that democracy, precariously unstable, easily could have turned out a failed experiment, a quixotic delusion not worth hymning. Thirteen months after the Battle of Gettysburg, and nine months after the address there, Lincoln penned a private memorandum in which he anticipated losing the 1864 presidential election to Democratic rival George McClellan. If he had lost the election to McClellan and McClellan had concluded a peace with the Confederate States of America that recognized the independence of the latter, as he promised to do, it is questionable whether the Gettysburg Address would be read or remembered, whatever its intrinsic literary or stylistic merits.[2]

The high honor in which many hold those literary or stylistic merits is, to some extent then, an honor conferred retrospectively in light of later historical unfoldings, among them Union victory over the two major armies of the Confederacy in April 1865; the assassination of Lincoln the same month; the outpouring of Civil War memoirs and other writings in the last two decades of the nineteenth century, as many veterans' organizations began to hold local and national reunions; the development and dedication of the first national military park at Chickamauga; and the growing trend toward reconciliation, at least in public, of the white populations of North and South. If part of the rhetorical majesty of the Gettysburg Address comes from what now feels like its visionary prophetic force, that visionary prophetic force originated in November 1863, with Lee's defiant Army of Virginia dug in behind the Rapidan River in central Virginia, as a more limited exhortation in the optative mood, an exhortation on behalf of something uncertain and desired, not something inevitable and accomplished. It is important to acknowledge that in itself the Gettysburg Address made nothing happen. It did not, for example, inoculate citizens of the northern states against the extreme war-weariness of the summer of 1864, which, as Lincoln well knew, could have cost him reelection if it had not been for William Tecumseh Sherman's capture of Atlanta in September of that year, a capture that inspired northern soldiers to vote overwhelmingly for Lincoln and reflected a strategic shift to total war, subsequently prosecuted by Sherman during his famous March to the Sea, which ended at Savannah in December 1864, after his army had deliberately and systematically reduced the abilities of southern civilians to support the Confederate war effort.

To acknowledge that the Gettysburg Address does not consist of magically efficacious words, which by themselves accomplished northern war aims and preserved the Union or by themselves adequately performed public rituals of mourning and consolation – with the unparalleled casualties of 1864 still to come (in one four-week period, from May 5 to June 3, Grant lost nearly 50,000 soldiers, killed, wounded, captured, or missing), no 1863 utterance could have been adequate – in no way diminishes the distinct qualities of the address. If anything, such an acknowledgment clears the way for our realistic appraisal of the deliberate verbal means by which Lincoln achieved the distinct qualities that subsequent historical events and developments made so attractive to national retrospection and self-description.

These verbal means would not impress us so deeply in the present if a large shift in popular sensibility, taste, and expectation had not taken place since the Civil War, a shift both reflected in and furthered by changing norms in education. At Gettysburg, on November 19, 1863, Edward Everett's two-hour peroration fulfilled the expectations of educated taste and sensibility, whereas Lincoln's short speech did not attempt to. But for many reasons Everett's speech is unthinkable now, and Lincoln's, modest as it may have sounded in 1863 by comparison, now brims and resonates with sonorities that far exceed our expectations for speeches made by presidents.[3]

Consider the famous first sentence, as it appears in the Second Draft or Hay text, which recent scholarship identifies as the one Lincoln probably read: "Four score and seven years ago our fathers brought forth, upon this continent, a new nation, conceived in Liberty, and dedicated to the proposition that all men are created equal."[4] Sheer repetition of this nearly sacred sentence has made it almost impossible for us to imagine it any other way, but a comparison with translations into Romance and Germanic languages in Basler's collection, most of which open with some version of "eighty-seven years ago" (although the Italian speaks in terms of *lustri*, or five-year periods, and the German of "thirteen years" more until "it will be a century") vividly confirms Lincoln's artistry. If he had begun, "In 1776 our ancestors established a new government based on certain assumptions about individual freedom and on the principle that everyone has the same rights," he would have said much the same thing, but he would have forfeited two crucial features of the opening. The first is an echo of Psalm 90, verse 10, in the King James Version: "The days of our years are threescore years and ten; and if by reason of strength they be fourscore years, yet is their strength labour and sorrow; for it is soon cut off, and we fly away." The Hebrew original does not include a literal equivalent of "fourscore," meaning four groups of twenty; this particular locution is a flourish of the King James translators, and it is a word Lincoln's audience would connect, either consciously or unconsciously, with this well-known biblical verse, a *memento mori* acknowledging the brevity of human life in a way wholly appropriate for a speech at a new rural cemetery, although the echo carries with it some hard irony, too, because none of the soldiers interred at Gettysburg had managed to live seventy or eighty years.

The second sacrifice, which points beyond the first sentence to the entire address, as well as to the Second Inaugural, is sonority. The opening sentence bundles "Four," "score," "our," "fathers," "forth," "are" with varying degrees of rhyme, assonance, consonance, and alliteration, as it does "score," "continent," "dedicated," "created," and "equal." Since the literary modernism of the second and third decades of the twentieth century, fewer readers of English necessarily associate rhyme, or its subdivisions, with verse, let alone prose, but in fact the antecedents of Lincoln's rhyming prose include ancient Latin and Arabic precursors, although he would not have known it.[5] What he would have known, or felt, is what the writers of ancient rhyming prose knew and felt, that there are gradations and shadings on the spectrum leading from prose to verse, and certain occasions call for prose that is closer to verse. That Lincoln could also write prose wholly free of verse qualities should be immediately apparent to anyone reading through the Emancipation Proclamation. When he had to write like a lawyer and subordinate the resonating sonorities of language to more precise specifications, he certainly could do so. As the historian Richard Hofstadter commented wryly, "The Emancipation Proclamation of January 1, 1863 had all the moral grandeur of a bill of lading."[6]

Some may object at this point that to treat one of the preeminent scriptures of the United States as an aesthetic performance, without dwelling on the content of the speech, is as blasphemous as reading the Bible as literature. What about Lincoln's ignoring the Constitution, which is what legally "brought forth" the new nation and which did not dedicate the new nation to the proposition that all men are created equal, as the original version of Article 1, Section 2, which based representation and taxation on "the whole Number of free Persons" and "three-fifths of all other persons," makes perfectly clear? What about his not mentioning the South? What about his associating the war effort with bringing about "a new birth of freedom," thereby identifying emancipation as a primary war aim, although he never explicitly mentions slavery? What about the last sentence with its famous triad, "of the people, by the people, for the people" (Second Draft), which echoes, according to one dictionary of quotations, similar formulations by John Wycliffe, Daniel Webster, William Lloyd Garrison, and Theodore Parker, thereby linking Lincoln's speech with antecedents in the Protestant Reformation, antebellum Whig Unionism, abolitionism, and transcendentalism?[7]

To focus on Lincoln's verbal artistry is not to discount or dismiss any of these questions or the significance of any of the issues they raise; it is to point out that, significant as these issues were and still are, many, many people wrote and spoke about them in writings and speeches we no longer know or read. It cannot be the issues alone that keep us reading and reciting the

Gettysburg Address or the Second Inaugural, and to admit this conclusion enables us to raise another question, one that begins in verbal artistry but rapidly ramifies in several directions: What is the political or social function of eloquence? Take, for example, the famous triad in the last sentence of the Gettysburg Address. Yes, its antecedents may associate Lincoln's utterance with Protestantism, Unionism, abolitionism, and transcendentalism, with all of which he had affinities of varying complexity. But in addition to these considerations we must also recognize that Lincoln simply loved and used verbal triads throughout his writings and speeches, and the verbal triad, as a schematic rhetorical archetype, especially effective as a device for closure, descended to Lincoln with the accumulated resonances and authority of the Bible ("the power, the kingdom, and the glory"), the classical world (Caesar's *veni, vidi, vici*), Shakespeare (the Second Apparition's "Be bloody, bold, and resolute," speaking to Macbeth), and earlier statesmen (Jefferson's "we mutually pledge to each other our lives, our Fortunes, and our sacred Honor").

Many readers may want, quite understandably, to connect the verbal form of the Gettysburg Address with the content of the speech, but there is something naive about the insistence that, for example, Lincoln's careful auditory connections between and among words, phrases, clauses, and sentences – another of his favorite rhetorical devices is syntactic parallelism, which, like rhyme, is a scheme of verbal repetition – somehow reflect or represent or imitate or enact the binding together of the wounded and disintegrating Union. Lincoln's favorite verbal patterns also appear in writings composed before the Civil War, when binding together a wounded and disintegrating Union would have been neither his chief concern nor his chief responsibility. In his early Address to the Young Men's Lyceum of Springfield, Illinois, delivered January 27, 1838, a quarter of a century before the Gettysburg Address, verbal triads abound, along with anaphora (repetition of an initial word or phrase in successive clauses or sentences), as in these two consecutive sentences from the penultimate paragraph: "Reason, cold, calculating, unimpassioned reason, must furnish all the materials for our future support and defence. Let those materials be moulded into *general intelligence, sound morality* and, in particular, *a reverence for the constitution and laws;* and, that we improved to the last; that we remained free to the last; that we revered his name to the last; that, during his long sleep, we permitted no hostile foot to pass over or desecrate his resting place; shall be that which to learn the last trump shall awaken our WASHINGTON." What these two sentences demonstrate is that by the time he was approaching his twenty-ninth birthday, Lincoln had already developed his ability to organize his words into sonorous, eloquent patterns he could apply to many different subjects.

Because words are units of both sound and meaning, their sounds can never be wholly separated from their meanings, and vice versa. But the sounds of words can produce meanings beyond the sum of their dictionary definitions. Take the notorious example of Edgar Allan Poe's "The Philosophy of Composition," published in 1846, the same year Lincoln ran successfully for election to the United States House of Representatives. In that essay, which purports to explain the genesis of his poem "The Raven" and which many suspect of some degree of parody, Poe accounts for his refrain, the raven's "Nevermore," this way: "That such a close, to have force, must be sonorous and susceptible of protracted emphasis, admitted no doubt: and these considerations inevitably led me to the long *o* as the most sonorous vowel, in connection with *r* as the most producible content." With his faith in the forceful, protracted sonorities of the *o-r* pairing, Poe anticipated the first sentence of the Gettysburg Address, and subsequent theorists of expressiveness in sound patterning can illuminate why the history of childhood language acquisition might cause us to hear the *o-r* pairing as sonorous or beautiful or as integral to a feeling of aesthetic or emotional intensity.[8]

For this brief discussion, what matters more than the linguistic specifics of how or why Lincoln's combinations of particular sounds produce impressions of aesthetic or emotional intensity is *that* they produce impressions of intensity. Furthermore, especially in the case of the Gettysburg Address one could argue that whatever its other aims – to honor the soldiers killed at Gettysburg; to express sympathy for and solidarity with those bereaved by the battle and the war; to dedicate a new cemetery, with all the connotative changes Lincoln rings on the word "dedicate" (committing to a proposition, opening a new cemetery, sanctifying its ground, devoting oneself to a cause); to identify Union war aims with the Declaration of Independence rather than the Constitution – another aim was to produce feelings of emotional intensity.

Why did Lincoln want to intensify emotion in his immediate audience and his subsequent readership? In the Gettysburg Address intensity grows toward the end, as the various levels of repetition pile up, and it grows still more with the final shift in verb tenses away from the past and present to the future perfect ("shall not have died in vain") and the future ("shall not perish from the earth"). Not coincidentally, the growing intensity and the shift toward the future correspond to a loss of specificity in Lincoln's remarks. The Gettysburg Address consists of ten sentences. Each of the first nine refers to something concrete or specific: the Declaration; the Civil War; the Gettysburg battlefield; the dedication of the cemetery; the appropriateness of the dedication; the larger sense of dedication; the dead soldiers; the nature of memory (this remarkable sentence, with its fluid stream of nonspirant continuants, *w, r, l, m, n, ng*, in the phrase, "The world will little note, nor long remember," includes the only other future-tense verbs); and the need for Northerners to dedicate themselves to carrying on the war. But the tenth sentence, the longest by far and made even longer by the insertion of "under God" in some of the versions,[9] soars off into what James Joyce's Stephen Dedalus calls "vague words for a vague emotion," thrilling and intoxicating as that emotion may be. At this point, the address becomes pure exhortation, pure pep talk for the northern citizens who will be called on to pay more taxes; make do, perhaps forever, without men who have entered military service; submit to the draft instituted a few months before; submit to rigorous military training and discipline; suffer wounds, physical or mental; or lose their lives to violence or, more often, to disease.

In his final soaring sentence Lincoln mentions none of these specifics. What he does mention is that his listeners must "highly resolve" – the hazy, straining, unnecessary adverb "highly" vying for distinction as the weakest moment in the address – not to let their soldiers' deaths amount to sheer waste by preparing themselves for a new birth of freedom. In trying to stir and unify the people he governs by focusing them on a vision of newness, Lincoln is not alone. As Kenneth Burke has shown in his classic discussion of the rhetoric of Hitler's *Mein Kampf*, the promise of newness also played a significant part in the Führer's attempts to unify. Many will reject this pairing immediately as unthinkable and unacceptable, and there are vast differences between Lincoln and Hitler, neo-Confederate extremist views to the contrary notwithstanding.[10] One crucial difference is that Lincoln adamantly refused the strategy of scapegoating, whereas Hitler based his politics on it. But as Burke points out, one of the ways that Hitler appealed to Germans struggling in the crippling aftermath of World War I was by offering them a vision of "symbolic rebirth": "They can again get the feel of *moving forward*, towards a *goal*" (italics in original).[11] Different as their political methods and visions were, the sixteenth president of the United States and the first and only Führer of the German Third Reich both found themselves trying to lead at moments of acute national crisis that included severe losses in the recent past, increasing hardships in the present, and debilitating uncertainties about the future. Given their respective inabilities to restore past losses, ease present hardships, and guarantee future improvements, both leaders attempted to place the difficulties of past and present in the uplifting context of impending transformation that would compensate for those difficulties.

For Lincoln the source of language about rebirth was the Bible, specifically the Gospel according to John and the first letter of Peter (see John 1:12–13, 3:3–7; 1 Peter 1:3). In his Second Inaugural Address, Lincoln's use of the New Testament includes direct quotation, but in the Gettysburg Address New Testament sources hover implicit in the background, providing imagery and with it augmented scriptural resonance. Again, it is no coincidence that this resonance becomes more prominent at the close of the speech, as Lincoln turns to futurity, to an abstract vision of some new development still to come, in the absence of certainty in the present. With another year and a half of the war to go, and close to 100,000 casualties in major battles still ahead, Lincoln could give the people who heard and read him little more than sonorous eloquence, the function of which was to generate emotional intensity and focus them on a description of the future abstract enough to encompass the stern and mournful specificities of lost lives, wounded bodies, and expended treasure. Noted by the Associated Press reporter for the New York *Tribune*, the "[l]ong-continued applause" that followed Lincoln's speech suggests that, at least at Gettysburg in November 1863, he succeeded.[12]

Sonorous eloquence – with triads, parallelism, and various shadings of rhyme – plays an important part in the magnificent closure of the Second Inaugural Address as well, although the verb tense roots Lincoln's imperative "let us" firmly in the present, as it projects onto the impending challenge of Reconstruction a vision described in the Epistle of James, in the language of the King James Version, as pure religion: "Pure religion and undefiled before God and the Father is this, To visit the fatherless and widows in their affliction" (James 1:27). Appropriately enough, the reelected commander in chief closes this address, delivered not quite sixteen months after the one at Gettysburg, with a command. In turn, this command repeats the rhetorical form of Lincoln's version of Matthew 7:1, echoed earlier in the address but tellingly shifted from the second-person plural form of the King James original ("Judge not, that ye be not judged") to the first-person plural, in which Lincoln includes himself: "but let us judge not that we be not judged."

In the sixteen months since the Gettysburg Address, enough had changed to allow Lincoln to speak in a different mode and tone. With the capture by Union forces of Fort Fisher on January 15, 1865, a capture that meant the Confederacy could no longer use its last blockade-running port, Wilmington, North Carolina, and with Sherman's army about to cross into North Carolina and move toward connection with Grant in Virginia, Lincoln had good reason to comment at the close of his first paragraph, "The progress of our arms ... is, I trust, reasonably satisfactory and encouraging to all." Rightly judicious in venturing "no prediction" for the future – a month later the relatively quick cessation of hostilities depended in part on Lee's wise discouragement of continuing guerrilla war after Appomattox, not solely on the progress of U.S. arms – Lincoln availed himself of both the improving military picture and his own newly secured political standing to focus much of the Second Inaugural on describing the recent past in a particular way. In doing so, he was not simply exercising the victor's privilege to write the history; he was also laying the ground for his vision of Reconstruction.

Built of four paragraphs, the fourth of which is the most famous and most often quoted, the Second Inaugural, in its second and long third paragraph, does what the Gettysburg Address does not do: It names the South, it names slavery, and it narrates the past, not the distant, storied past of 1776 and the Declaration of Independence, but the immediate past of 1854, the Kansas-Nebraska Act, and what followed as a result. What is both shrewd and tricky about Lincoln's account is that he ends up having it both ways, on the one hand, calling the country to rise above sectional partisanship as it moves toward Reconstruction, on the other, assigning a little more of the blame to the South. One does not have to be a Confederate sympathizer to wonder who is included in Lincoln's "us."

To appreciate the nature of Lincoln's narration, we can compare it productively with the point of view of two outsiders deeply interested by the American Civil War. Writing in November 1861 for *Die Presse*, one of the leading newspapers in Vienna, Karl Marx and Frederick Engels summarized the war this way for their Austrian readership: "The present struggle between the South and North is, therefore, nothing but a struggle between two social systems, between the system of slavery and the system of free labor. The struggle has broken out because the two systems can no longer live peacefully side by side on the North American continent.[13] Not all students of the Civil War will find this unidealized representation of the conflict palatable. It says nothing, for example, about democracy, the Constitution, or a theory of states' rights. But it does serve as an instructive contrast with Lincoln's representation of the same war in his Second Inaugural Address.

In his short second paragraph Lincoln adopts something of the detachment of Marx and Engels, describing the moment of "impending civil war" in March 1861 also by contrasting North and South, although Lincoln contrasts them not as competing social systems but as opposites with respect to the Union, one side committed to continuing the Union – Lincoln's word is "saving" – the other to ending the Union – his not quite neutral word is "destroying." Placing the genesis of the war solely in the context of Union, Lincoln appears to refrain from assigning responsibility for the outbreak of belligerence, acknowledging a basic likeness between North and South: "Both parties deprecated war." The series of parallel constructions, in which he lays out the opposition between North and South, culminates in one of Lincoln's great sentences, a four-word marvel of concision and understatement, which contrasts with the paragraph-long sentence at the end of the address and recalls the shortest verse in the King James Bible, "Jesus wept" (John 11:35): "And the war came." Known to students of rhetoric as parataxis, this use of the conjunction "and," reminiscent of the opening verses of Genesis, leaves unspecified the logical relationship of Lincoln's short sentence to what precedes it. It withholds the causal connection, as, for example, "So the war came" would not, and in withholding that connection appears to set aside a discussion of causality altogether.

But it does so only for a moment. Leading into the long third paragraph, this short sentence functions as the hinge on which Lincoln swings his account, now moving to join Marx and Engels in explicitly identifying slavery as cause – "All knew that this interest was, somehow, the cause of the war" – while diverging from them by framing his narrative according to a pattern of apostasy and retribution straight out of the Hebrew Bible, which despite the echo of Matthew 7:1 and a quotation of Matthew 18:7, drives both vision and rhetoric, as the quotation from Psalm 19, which closes the paragraph, confirms ("the judgments of the Lord are true, and righteous altogether"): Slavery is the offence, and the war is the compensation God exacts for it.

Two stylistic features of Lincoln's biblical account of the war and its causes are particularly noteworthy and revealing. The first appears in the first clause of the sentence containing the echo of Matthew 7:1: "It may seem strange that any men should dare to ask a just God's assistance in wringing their bread from the sweat of other men's faces; but let us judge not that we be not judged." Despite his appearances earlier as detached and somewhat objective, here the lawyer in Lincoln slyly works his audience by means of the rhetorical figure known as paralipsis, a Greek word meaning "passing by omission." In paralipsis, according to the *Oxford English Dictionary*, "the speaker emphasizes something by affecting to pass it by without notice." In this case, what he affects to pass but actually emphasizes is the strangeness – an understated synonym for something like "the indefensible hypocrisy" – of slaveholders who defend slavery while thinking of themselves as entitled by their faith to divine support and favor. The irony here is that in anticipation of Reconstruction, at a moment when he hopes to prevent continued acrimony between the warring sections, Lincoln should resort to such a pointed jab at the South, whereas in the Gettysburg Address, which focuses on northern war effort and losses, and in which such a jab would be more appropriate, he does no such thing. Although he quickly follows his semicolon with an injunction against judging, he has already judged, and the "us" in "let us not judge" clearly stands for those opposed to slaveholding. If Lincoln had truly wished to leave judgment out of the Second Inaugural, or at least the judgment of one section by another, as opposed to the divine judgment to which all must answer, he could and should have left this sentence out altogether.

The second feature appears four sentences later, immediately after the long question beginning, "If we shall suppose that American Slavery is one of those offences" and climbing steadily, through various right-branching segmentations, to the high plateau of sermonic fervor. We should not be surprised that Lincoln's prose makes pronounced use of rhyme at this moment, but what many who hear the rhyme may not realize is that the prose suddenly takes the metrical shape of a four-line hymn stanza: "Fondly do we hope – / fervently do we pray – / that this mighty scourge of war / may speedily pass away." The model here is what a hymnal would identify as short meter, rhyming xaya, and Mary Stanley Bunce Dana's 1840 Presbyterian hymn "Oh, Sing to Me of Heaven" typifies any number of hymns Lincoln and his hearers might have known and sung: "Oh, sing to me of heaven / When I am called to die, / Singing songs of holy ecstasy, / To waft my soul on high."[14] This breaking into song, and not just song but hymn, marks an extraordinary moment in the Second Inaugural and distinguishes it from Lincoln's other major speeches, including the Gettysburg Address, which from start to finish may be pitched closer to the verse end of the prose spectrum than the later speech, but which as a consequence does not have to travel as far to its heights as the Second Inaugural does.

Having reached this rhetorical and auditory high ground, the Second Inaugural does not descend again. By the time he concludes, Lincoln has sounded loudly the call to northern magnanimity and forgiveness, which we can only infer and imagine would have been the hallmarks of Reconstruction if he had lived to oversee it. The final vision here is not of democracy but of peace, and, unlike the vision of the Gettysburg Address, it has no place for the words "dead" or "died." With more than six hundred thousand deaths still accumulating a month from the end of the war, Lincoln resorts to periphrastic round-aboutness in the Second Inaugural, referring to the widow and the orphan of "him who shall have borne the battle," as well as to "every drop of blood drawn with the lash ... paid by another drawn with the sword," a quaint archaism in the context of a war in which swords did a minute fraction of the killing. But nowhere bluntly does he name the dead as dead. Inaugurating a second presidency, in which war will end and rebuilding will begin, calls for different language from dedicating a cemetery while that war continues. At Gettysburg, Lincoln not only honored the dead, he also used them to strengthen northern resolve with a vision that attempted to put their deaths in a bearable perspective. On the platform in front of the Capitol, with northern resolve having nearly fulfilled its purpose, he needed to quiet the dead in order to quiet the living.

NOTES

1 Roy P. Blaser, compiled and intro., *Lincoln's Gettysburg Address in Translation* (Washington, DC: Library of Congress, 1972), n.p.

2 Lincoln's artfulness appears in John G. Nicolay, "Lincoln's Literary Experiments," *Century Magazine* 47, 6 (April 1894); Daniel Kilham Dodge, *Abraham Lincoln: Master of Words* (New York: D. Appleton and Company, 1924); Edmund Wilson, *Patriotic Gore: Studies in the Literature of the American Civil War* (New York: Oxford University Press, 1962), ch. 3; Don E. Fehrenbacher, "The Words of Lincoln," *Lincoln in Text and Context: Collected Essays* (Stanford, CA: Stanford University Press, 1987); Ronald C. White, *Lincoln's Greatest Speech: The Second Inaugural* (New York: Simon and Schuster, 2002); John Channing Briggs, *Lincoln's Speeches Reconsidered* (Baltimore: The Johns Hopkins University Press, 2005); Douglas L. Wilson, *Lincoln's Sword: The Presidency and the Power of Words* (New York: Alfred A. Knopf, 2006); and Fred Kaplan, *Lincoln: The Biography of a Writer* (New York: HarperCollins, 2008).

3 One early appreciation of the Gettysburg Address came from Ralph Waldo Emerson: "His brief speech at Gettysburg will not easily be surpassed by words on any recorded occasion." See "Abraham Lincoln," in *Miscellanies*, vol. 11 of Riverside edition of Emerson's Complete Works (Cambridge, MA: Riverside Press, 1895), 311.

4 Gabor Boritt, *The Gettysburg Gospel: The Lincoln Speech that Nobody Knows* (New York: Simon and Schuster, 2006), 272–275.

5 See O. B. Hardison, Jr., and Roger M. A. Allen, "Rhyme-Prose," in Roland Greene, Stephen Cushman, et al., eds., *Princeton Encyclopedia of Poetry and Poetics*, 4th ed. (Princeton, NJ: Princeton University Press, 2012).

6 *The American Political Tradition and the Men Who Made It* (New York: Knopf, 1948), 131.

7 John Barlett, *Familiar Quotations*, 14th edition, Emily Morrison Beck, ed. (Boston: Little, Brown and Co., 1969), 639n.

8 See, for example, Reuven Tsur, *What Makes Sound Patterns Expressive: The Poetic Mode of Speech Perception* (Durham, NC: Duke University Press, 1992), 63–66.

9 Boritt, *Gettysburg Gospel*, 264.

10 Although he does not equate Lincoln with Hitler, Thomas DiLorenzo's work has encouraged others to make the connection. See DiLorenzo, *The Real Lincoln: A New Look at Abraham Lincoln, His Agenda, and an Unnecessary War* (New York: Three Rivers Press, 2003), especially the afterword, 282–285.

11 Kenneth Burke, *The Philosophy of Literary Form: Studies in Symbolic Action*, 3rd ed. (Berkeley: University of California Press, 1973), 203.

12 Boritt, *Gettysburg Gospel*, 272.

13 Karl Marx and Frederick Engels, *The Civil War in the United States*, Richard Enmale, ed., vol. 30 of the Marxist Library, 2nd ed. (New York: International Publishers, 1940), 81.

14 Albert Christ-Janer, Charles W. Hughes, Carleton Sprague Smith, eds., *American Hymns Old and New* (New York: Columbia University Press, 1980), 557.

5

TIMOTHY SWEET

Lincoln and the Natural Nation

If, as Karl Marx said, the Confederacy was not a nation but a battle cry, what made the Union a nation? The question was not merely rhetorical when Abraham Lincoln attempted an answer in his First Inaugural Address. Introducing a territorial argument that would recur in subsequent speeches – "Physically speaking, we cannot separate" – Lincoln closed the address with a now famous emotional appeal:

> We are not enemies but friends. We must not be enemies. Though passion may have strained, it must not break our bonds of affection. The mystic chords of memory, streching [sic] from every battle-field, and patriot grave, to every living heart and hearthstone, all over this broad land, will yet swell with the chorus of Union, when again touched, as surely they will be, by the better angels of our nature.[1]

Built of an extended metaphor supported by synecdoches, the figure is more complex than is typical of Lincoln's rhetoric, perhaps because it was not originally Lincoln's but was first suggested in rough form by his Secretary of State, William Seward. Lincoln made the figure his own as he addressed the gap that the secession of seven states had opened between the discourse of sovereignty and the discourse of nationhood.[2]

Reprising the primary political claim of the speech – that "in view of the Constitution and the laws, the Union is unbroken" despite the southern states' claims of secession[3] – the "mystic chords" figure consolidated two representational problems that would recur in Lincoln's wartime speeches and would become central to the literature of the Civil War generally: (1) the production of a sovereign nation from the aggregate of individual deaths in battle and (2) the production of a national identity from a set of diverse locales, regions, and sections. Conventionally, in the production of sovereignty from deaths in battle, political meaning is ascribed to those deaths to instantiate the terms of victory and defeat.[4] Yet in the context of the First Inaugural, the post-Revolutionary production of nationhood had evidently lost its historically agreed-on tenacity and needed reinforcement in the form of "chords of memory" binding local persons and places to distant persons and places. Thus the second problem, the production of a nation from a set of locales, involves the erasure of boundaries, moving from particular places, "battle-fields," "graves," and "hearthstones," to the nation, figured as the largest natural territorial unit, "this broad land." The two means for the wartime production of national identity thus registered in Lincoln's figure specify the temporal and spatial dimensions of the general philosophical problem of the one and the many, which James Dawes argues is central to the epistemology of war.[5] The rhetorical trope for this problem is synecdoche, the trope that supports the "mystic chords" figure: individual for group or part for whole, based on some essential quality according to which the individual or part is a microcosm.[6]

In Lincoln's wartime rhetoric, these two representational problems subtend four theories of nationhood: nation as common ancestry, nation as territory, nation as social contract, and nation as embodied actor.[7] Nation as ancestry, historically enacted in colonial and U.S. dealings with Native American polities and in the writing of slave codes, forms no part of Lincoln's rhetorical strategy in the First Inaugural. Any such appeal would have evoked the Supreme Court decision in *Dred Scott v. Sanford* (1857), which arbitrated claims of citizenship on the basis of race, as defined by ancestry. Lincoln had criticized the Dred Scott decision, as much for its stipulation that Congress had no power to prohibit slavery in the territories as for its arbitration of citizenship.[8] To recall this nexus to his intended audience, which included secessionists, would have been rhetorically unproductive. After the war, the Fourteenth Amendment theoretically abolished any claim of nation as ancestry in favor of nation as territory, awarding citizenship to "All persons born or naturalized in the United States"; yet these figures remained in uneasy juxtaposition through Reconstruction and beyond. The definition of nation as territory had been bound up with the question of right of conquest from the earliest days of American colonization. However, for Lincoln and his U.S. audience, right of conquest and the material fact of empire had long since disappeared into an affective bond between citizen and land in which imagined possession was abstracted as national representativeness: "Lo, body and soul – this land," as Walt Whitman would soon write.[9] Yet questions concerning the extent of the domain bonding the citizen – that is, competing claims of local and national allegiance, the uneasy truce between federalism and antifederalism, the relation of empire to subjects – left open the potential for secession and sectionalist conflict. Any attempt to define the natural territorial extent of a nation could reanimate the original logic of right of conquest.

Whereas theories of nation as ancestry and nation as territory are expressed in figures of nature, social contract theory is expressed in figures of culture, as, for example, a language of sacrifice. Like the wartime production of national meaning from the deaths of soldiers, social contract theory posits something given for something gained, although the benefits are differently distributed. In the wartime production of nationhood, the soldier submits his civil liberties and his life to the maintenance of the state. Body counts determine the state's capacity to prosecute a war while commemorative mourning for dead and wounded soldiers transacts an affective, identity-producing bond between person and nation.[10] Analogously, in the social contract, an individual submits natural liberties to receive governmental protection of civil liberties, while joining other subjects in collective mourning for the loss of those natural liberties. Sometimes narrowly associated with the continental Enlightenment (e.g., Rousseau's 1762 treatise *Du Contrat Social*), social contract theory also had several Anglo-American manifestations, from the Mayflower Compact (1620) and John Winthrop's "A Model of Christian Charity" (1629) through the ratification of the U.S. Constitution.[11] Whereas both the citizen's and the soldier's relations to the state are structured as sacrifice, the difference between the social contract and the soldier's contract results from the soldier's body having a different representational status in accounts of war.[12]

The place of these figures of ancestry, territory, and contract in the discourse of state sovereignty remains an open question.[13] As Lincoln addressed the question of sovereignty in his wartime speeches, he first countered the claim of secession by figuring the nation as territory and later linked this to a fourth figure for nationhood, the nation as embodied actor or body politic.[14] In the First Inaugural's "mystic chords" figure, the body politic has fragmented into the myriad bodies of individual citizens, each of whose hearts was supposed to be bound to the land. However, as the war drew on and the death toll mounted, the question of the representative function of the soldier's body reanimated the Renaissance-era figure of the state as body in several cultural discourses.[15] This figure of the sovereign body politic came to coexist, sometimes uneasily, with figures of contractual, ancestral, and territorial nationhood – uneasily because, in a Civil War the representative function of the dead is especially complicated. From Lincoln's perspective, Confederate and Union dead would have to be differentiated as enemies and unified as Americans. Territorial nationhood, Lincoln's master trope, ironically made it easier to differentiate than to unify the dead. Secession and the war brought real differences in environment and cultural practices among regions into sharp political focus. Thus, where Lincoln cast territorial nationhood as a unifying trope, Southerners tapped the figure's particularizing tendency to justify secession. Early in the war, Lincoln attempted to counter the southern states' environmentally grounded arguments by linking local to national space through a figure of a "national homestead." Lincoln mapped such a claim of territorial permanence onto the provisional nature of the social contract in the Gettysburg Address (1863), a speech that anticipated the establishment of a system of national cemeteries in which Union soldiers' bodies marked Union ground. Commemorating a battle that soon became recognized as the turning point of the war, the Gettysburg Address reestablished the historical discourse of sovereignty with its supporting figure of the body politic, exemplified by Lincoln's use of the trope of authochthones (the nation born of the land). In the Second Inaugural Address (1864), when southern territory had effectively been reconquered, Lincoln proposed a calculus of "blood" that evoked both social contract and ancestral theories of nationhood. Underlying this formulation of nationhood in terms of human suffering was a territorial base that localized the source of violence in the plantation South even as it claimed to reunify North and South as a single site of violence. Thus the territorial figure for nationhood remained susceptible to particularization, as evidenced by the problematic representational status of the soldier in partisan and racially segregated postwar commemorative practices that linked or severed bodies to or from lands.

As the audience for the First Inaugural Address well knew, despite Lincoln's evasion of divisive questions such as slavery in the territories, the "chords" binding the nation had been strained through continental expansion since the Revolutionary War. "This broad land" encompassed numerous local and regional differentiations. The geographical extent of a republic, one of the first theoretical questions of classical republican theory, had been a practical question that included environmental determinants such as the apparently natural place of slavery in climates conducive to the production of staple crops.[16] According to eighteenth-century theories of environmental determinism, the territory encompassed by the United States (even before the Louisiana Purchase) might be too diverse to ground nationhood. This was the experience, for example, of Hector St. John de Crèvecoeur's Farmer James, a Pennsylvanian whose initial answer to the question "What is an American?" is successively undermined by the experience of diverse environments and their associated colonial cultures, most distressingly in the plantation culture of Charleston, South Carolina.

Recalling this question of environmental determinism from the era of the nation's founding, Seward may have taken the language of "chords of affection" harmoniously binding a nation from The Federalist Paper No. 14, in which James Madison discusses the "natural limit of a republic."[17] Madison argues that states will find it in their interest to be bound into the union despite the logistical difficulties posed by geography, which in any case would soon be remedied by numerous "improvements" facilitating communication and trade, such as canals and roads.[18] However, the problem of the natural extent of a republic persists throughout *The Federalist*, recurring for example in No. 23, which addresses the government's power to provide for a national defense. Here Alexander Hamilton answers the anti-Federalist objection that "the extent of the country will not permit us to form a government, in which such ample powers [to impose taxes, to levy troops, to build ships and fortifications, etc.] can safely be reposed." The anti-Federal alternative would be a loosely-knit set of "separate Confederacies." Hamilton asserts on the contrary that only "an energetic government" such as that provided by the Constitution could "preserve the Union of so large an empire."[19] If, in responding to an environmentally determined conflict of interests, the Constitution put the federal government in an imperial relation to the states, then a "drift to particularity" was a seemingly natural response, in which states imagined themselves as nations.

Where *The Federalist*'s repressed substructure of environmental determinism had thus ironically provided a rationale for secession, Lincoln mobilized environmental tropes to argue that territory sutured ideological difference:

> Physically speaking, we cannot separate. We cannot remove our respective sections from each other, nor build an impassable wall between them. A husband and wife may be divorced, and go out of the presence, and beyond the reach of each other; but the different parts of our country cannot do this. They cannot but remain face to face; and intercourse, either amicable or hostile, must come between them.... Suppose you go to war, you cannot fight always; and when ... you cease fighting, the identical old questions, as to terms of intercourse, are upon you again.[20]

Deriving from the figure of the body politic, the metaphor of Union as marriage allows for an easy division of territory.[21] Lincoln argues, however, that the metaphor of marriage provides a poor understanding of nationhood: Secession is not like divorce because territory is not merely a metaphor but also a material fact bearing on national sovereignty. Mary Chesnut, among others, disagreed with Lincoln's assessment. In a diary entry written in March 1861 in Montgomery (site of the first Southern Congress attended by her husband), Chesnut develops the metaphor: "We separated because of incompatibility of temper. We divorced, North and South, because we hated each other so. If we could only separate – a 'séparation à l'agréable,' as the French say it, and not a horrid fight after divorce."[22] It seemed natural to envision two bodies politic occupying contiguous territories. As Lincoln had no doubt read in *The Federalist* Paper No. 6's history of hostilities between adjoining republics, "Neighbouring Nations … are naturally enemies," motivated by "secret jealousy."[23]

The southern states' declarations of secession readily took up the territorial argument, marshaling eighteenth-century ideas of environmental determinism that had been kept alive partly through states' rights discourse in several cultural spheres.[24] South Carolina's declaration asserted that

> A geographical line has been drawn across the Union, and all the States north of that line have united in the election of a man to the high office of President of the United States, whose opinions and purposes are hostile to slavery. He is to be entrusted with the administration of the common Government, because he has declared that that "Government cannot endure permanently half slave, half free," and that the public mind must rest in the belief that slavery is in the course of ultimate extinction.[25]

South Carolina set the tone in identifying the southern states' sense of nationhood with an environmentally determined configuration of political economy, the production of agricultural staples by means of slave labor. Mississippi, the next state to secede, opened its declaration by elaborating the environmental logic of South Carolina's claim:

> Our position is thoroughly identified with the institution of slavery – the greatest material interest of the world. Its labor supplies the product which constitutes by far the largest and most important portions of commerce of the earth. These products are peculiar to the climate verging on the tropical regions, and by an imperious law of nature, none but the black race can bear exposure to the tropical sun. These products have become necessities of the world, and a blow at slavery is a blow at commerce and civilization. That blow has been long aimed at the institution, and was at the point of reaching its consummation. There was no choice left us but submission to the mandates of abolition, or a dissolution of the Union, whose principles had been subverted to work out our ruin.[26]

This environmental parsing of nationhood, said to be warranted by the "law of nature," drew on the emerging pseudoscience of race, but also on real differences between Mississippi and the northern states.[27] Mississippi's economy was indeed based on agricultural commodities "peculiar to the climate verging on the tropical regions," thus apparently naturally suggesting confederation with states of like climates. Recall that the more southerly states were the first to secede – South Carolina, Mississippi, Florida, Alabama, Georgia, Louisiana, and Texas all seceding by February of 1861. Virginia, the bellwether of the northerly tier, joined (somewhat reluctantly) in late April, after which a separate state government representing the environmentally distinct northwestern half of Virginia in turn seceded from

Virginia (or remained loyal to the Union, depending on one's Constitutional views) in 1862.

Even though the seceded states claimed to appeal to political universals such as the natural right of property (for white men), the local, environmentally specific instantiations of these universals forced the territorial sense of nationhood toward particularity. The seceded states thus had to assemble a confederation from a set of particularized claims to nationhood, each of which had used or assumed an environmental argument and a social contract argument. South Carolina, for example, announced that on secession it had "resumed [its] separate and equal place among nations." Thus Jefferson Davis, in his inaugural address of February 18, 1861, characterized the Confederacy as comprising

> an agricultural people, whose chief interest is the export of commodities required in every manufacturing country.... It is alike our interest and that of all those to whom we would sell, and from whom we would buy, that there should be the fewest practicable restrictions upon the interchange of these commodities. There can, however, be but little rivalry between ours and any manufacturing or navigating community, such as the Northeastern States of the American Union.[28]

This Jeffersonian model of political economy, as outlined in Query XIX of *Notes on the State of Virginia*, in which the nation trades agricultural staples for manufactured goods, required "so much of homogeneity that the welfare of every portion shall be the aim of the whole. When this does not exist, antagonisms are engendered which must and should result in separation."[29] The first, southernmost tier of seceded states whose representatives Davis addressed in this speech was especially homogenous, each possessing a significant cotton economy. Commemorating the occasion in his poem "Ethnogenesis," Confederate poet laureate Henry Timrod encapsulated the new nation's environmental-economic distinctiveness in a memorable paradox, a cotton field ready for harvest seen as "the snow of southern summers."[30] The plantation environmental-economic model could also accommodate Virginia's tobacco culture, as it had already done for South Carolina's rice culture and Louisiana's sugar culture (albeit with some damage to Timrod's figure). Thus tying nationhood to a distinctive human ecology, the nature-culture nexus of slave-produced, semitropical agricultural staples, Davis provided a more coherent image of nation as territory than Lincoln would be able to manage in his First Inaugural, aligning the particularity of each state's political economy with that of the Confederacy at large.

The environmental drift to particularity was not, however, unique to southern secessionist arguments. Abolitionists such as William Lloyd Garrison and Wendell Phillips had long since advocated New England's secession from the Union. Yet even Nathaniel Hawthorne's tempered Unionist meditation on nationhood in "Chiefly About War-Matters" (1862) was grounded in localism. This grounding is initially evident in Hawthorne's choice of genre, the travel essay. The opening journey from Concord to Washington provides occasion to observe regional differences of climate and manners, thus heightening our sensitivity to the question of nationalism. One of the first items on Hawthorne's itinerary in Washington is a visit to the studio of artist Emanuel Leutze, who had recently been commissioned to provide a fresco mural, *Westward the Course of Empire Takes its Way*, for the House of Representatives wing of the Capitol. Hawthorne evidently saw Leutze's study in oil and later viewed a draft of the design itself on the wall of the west stairway in the House wing.[31] He thought the work "emphatically original and American" and found it "full of energy, hope, progress, irrepressible movement onward."[32] Yet he might have seen in Leutze's depiction of a wagon train crossing the Great Divide the potential for further sectional fragmentation. In any case, Hawthorne's profession of Unionist optimism does not dispel the sense of local allegiance announced in the essay's opening. On a visit to Alexandria, Virginia, nominally Confederate territory now visibly occupied by Union troops, Hawthorne reflects on "how very disagreeable the presence of a Southern army would be in a sober town in Massachusetts." This sense of reciprocal localism leads to a larger meditation on nationhood, which broaches the problem of the representative status of death in war:

> There never existed any other Government against which treason was so easy, and could defend itself by such plausible arguments as against that of the United States. The anomaly of two allegiances (of which that of the State comes nearest home to a man's feelings, and includes the altar and the hearth, while the General Government claims his devotion only to an airy mode of law, and has no symbol but a flag) is exceedingly mischievous in this point of view.... In the vast extent of our country, – too vast by far to be taken into one small human heart, – we inevitably limit to our own State, or, at farthest, to our own section, that sentiment of physical love for the soil which renders an Englishman, for example, so intensely sensitive to the dignity and well-being of his little island, that one foot, treading anywhere upon it, would make a bruise on each individual breast. If a man loves his own State, therefore, and is content to be ruined with her, let us shoot him, if we can, but allow him an honorable burial in the soil he fights for.[33]

As Brook Thomas observes, Hawthorne's imagery of "altar and hearth" echoes, but contrasts with that of Seward's figure for Lincoln's First Inaugural.[34] Both configurations depend on synecdoche, associating

individuals with national land. Linking local "heart" and "hearth" to the landscape in a more directly embodied way than Lincoln had done, Hawthorne
points the figure toward the particularizing logic of secession by differenti-
ating between abstract sovereignty and the felt experience of nationhood.
Nation figured as contract ("airy mode of law") recedes in favor of nation
figured as territory ("physical love for the soil"). In the concluding battlefield scenario, the Confederate soldier "fights for" and dies for this sense of
nationhood. With the image of a soldier's burial in the soil he "fights for" –
recall that as of July, 1862, all the battles had taken place on Confederate
ground – Hawthorne's language shifts from the idea of contract back again
to the episode's initial register, soil-based nationalism that had been elicited
by the presence of Union troops in Virginia and the hypothetical reciprocity
of "Southern" troops occupying Massachusetts. Yet the concluding asymmetrical scenario of Union killing and Confederate dying fails to reflect on
the motivations and the representational status of the *Union* dead (who, if
buried where they fell, would not have been located in the soil *they* ostensibly fought for).

Despite such assertions of local attachment by both Southerners and
Northerners, Lincoln's initial wartime response was a more insistent deploy-
ment of the nation-as-territory topos. In the Second Annual Message to
Congress – given in December 1862, after a season of fighting that had
brought the Confederate offensive nearly to the outskirts of Washington,
to be stopped only by the bloodiest battle of the war at Antietam Creek –
Lincoln directly confronts the question of nationhood in territorial terms:

> A nation may be said to consist of *its territory, its people, and its laws*. The
> territory is the only part which is of certain durability. "One generation pas-
> seth away, and another cometh, but the earth abideth forever." It is of the first
> importance to duly consider, and estimate, this ever-enduring part. That por-
> tion of the earth's surface which is owned and inhabited by the people of the
> United States, is well adapted to be the home of one national family; and it is
> not very well adapted for two or more.[35]

As Lincoln revisits the scenario of the impossibility of national divorce
he developed in the First Inaugural, he thus names three familiar theories of nationhood: territory, ancestry, and contract. Secession and the War
had broken the social contract. The idea of ancestral nationhood easily
enough admits of divisibility into "two or more" families. Lincoln thus
hopes that an argument to territory, bolstered by biblical quotation, can
counter this divisibility. His address to what J. G. A. Pocock has called the
"Machiavellian moment," when a sovereign state confronts the prospect
of its finitude, attempts to ground time in space. Lincoln follows out the

argument for territorial nationhood by directly quoting paragraphs from the First Inaugural on the question of the expansion of slavery and the claim that separation is a physical impossibility. Yet in his recognition that generations pass away, he cuts the "chords of memory" on which he had ended the First Inaugural. Land – not people, not even law – becomes the only sure ground of nationhood. As Lincoln develops this territorial appeal, he names boundaries: rivers, mountains, valleys, "the line between free and slave country" and "the line along which the culture of corn and cotton meet".[36] Some of these boundaries are political (free and slave); some are natural (mountains and rivers); and some are both, specifying differing human ecologies (the cultures of corn and cotton). Yet Lincoln claims that the land itself demands Union, because any line drawn across "the interior region" would bar commerce and access to ports, for territorial difference demands trade, and domestic trade proceeds more smoothly than international trade. Like the secessionists, then, Lincoln aligns the sense of nation as territory with a sense of a nation as an economy – disagreeing, however, with the Jeffersonian position on internal versus external trade. The longer Lincoln goes on to develop this argument, the more the references to regional differences proliferate, thus inviting some unifying or harmonizing figure that will extend the sense of nation as economy across North and South. Lincoln concludes this section of the speech by reprising the theory of territorial nationhood, in which generations pass, but the land abides: "Our national strife springs not from our permanent part; not from the land we inhabit; not from our national homestead.... Our strife pertains to ourselves – to the passing generations of men."[37] There is a dramatic shift here from a varied terrain of slave and free, mountain and valley, cotton and corn, to this highly specific territorial synecdoche for nationhood, the "homestead."

Lincoln had in fact prepared his auditors for the "national homestead" figure by mentioning the Homestead Act earlier in the speech, thus invoking the long history of the organization of labor and capital in relation to land in North America.[38] The consolidation of this history in the American pastoral topos elided differentiation on the basis of forms of labor.[39] Jefferson's Notes, Query XIX, is most often cited as the classic formulation: "Those who labour in the earth are the chosen people of God, if ever he had a chosen people, whose breasts he has made his peculiar deposit for substantial and genuine virtue."[40] Jefferson had used the pastoral topos to support a claim about government, arguing that a republican form is preferable, as providing the greatest liberty. Agrarian independence, he claimed, was the surest ground of virtue and guard against corruption. Yet he knew that the pastoral topos had long since taken various locally specific forms such as slave labor, wage labor, tenancy, and independent owner-producer.

Such differences could be read into or out of Jefferson's canny formulation, depending on the local understanding of the key terms, "husbandman," "labor," and "industry." Slave-labor pastoral, the plantation ideal, was the dream of the southern middle class, the manifestation of material success in the leisure and security of owning land worked by a permanent underclass.[41] The plantation ideal required expansion, not only because all available land in the Old South was already owned by the planter class, but because that class's goal of perpetuating the plantation system became increasingly difficult in the face of soil exhaustion. Cotton farming was not sustainable, but rather required the taking of new land after a few years of cropping had diminished the soil's fertility. Only a few planters in the Old South owned enough acreage to sustain long fallow cycles, which would let exhausted land grow up to woods, to be cleared again for cotton after a decade or more. Sons of planters and members of the aspiring middle class thus looked to Mississippi, Alabama, Arkansas, the Missouri territory, wherever the government had removed Native Americans to permit white settlement. In the north, the wage-labor, tenant, and owner-operator configurations required westward expansion as well, as farming practices such as the culture of corn and sheep subjected the land to various ecological stresses. In antebellum New England, sons typically went west to take new land while daughters worked in the mills (which depended on environmentally unsustainable cotton and wool production). Similarly, as yields declined from soil exhaustion in Pennsylvania and New York, farmers were drawn to the fertility of the uncropped lands of the west.[42] The political conflict over expansion – that is, over configurations of land, labor, and capital in the West – from the Missouri compromise of 1820 through the Kansas-Nebraska Act of 1854, would result in secession. Recall that Lincoln's national political career was launched during the 1854 Illinois senatorial election, in which he spoke against the Kansas-Nebraska Act (which had repealed the Missouri compromise). His target was Stephen Douglas, a leading proponent of popular sovereignty, and these speeches set the stage for Lincoln's senatorial campaign against Douglas and the famous debates of 1858. Lincoln's election, the secession of the southern states, and the coming of the war finally made it possible for the Free-Soilers of the north to configure territorial expansion according to the northern version of pastoral, the "national homestead," manifested in the Homestead Act of 1862.[43]

Thus Lincoln's image of the "national homestead," although ostensibly a synecdoche undifferentiated by sectional reference, is in essence a very specific configuration of space: a structure of small farms worked by free, white owner-operators. At 160 acres, such farms were too small to ground the southern version of pastoral, the plantation ideal. Lincoln's specific intention for the "national homestead" synecdoche is clear, and his auditors at the time would have understood this specificity reference to the Homestead Act as a white, free-labor configuration of land. Like the Homestead Act, the "national homestead" synecdoche intervenes in the history of the American pastoral topos to authorize a specific configuration of labor, that of the independent owner-operator. This serial form of social organization grounds Lincoln's rhetoric of territorial nationhood early in the war.

In the opening sentence of the Gettysburg Address, Lincoln returns to the figure of territorial nationhood, which asserted the permanence of land while conceding the impermanence of people and laws: "Four score and seven years ago our fathers brought forth on this continent, a new nation, conceived in Liberty, and dedicated to the proposition that all men are created equal."[44] Lincoln counts as a mere "proposition" what Jefferson had counted as a "self-evident" truth in the Declaration of Independence, "that all men are created equal." If a vision of permanence comes from anywhere, it comes from the trope of autochthones, "brought forth on this continent," familiar to Lincoln and his auditors from the conventions of the classical funeral oration as well as the commonplace "mother earth," whereby the nation is born of the land.[45] The occasion of the speech, the establishment of the first national cemetery for Union soldiers, focuses attention on the ground itself. The only significant battle to take place in a nonslave state, Gettysburg was a highly symbolic victory, contemporarily hailed as a turning point.[46] Lincoln claims this attention to the ground through a sequence of topographical citation that draws inward from "continent" to "nation" to "battlefield," retaining this local attention through the repetition of "here" (six times) before expanding outward again in the concluding sentences, from "here" to "this nation" to "the earth."[47] At the narrow point of this hourglass-shaped rhetorical structure, reference to the "battle-field" itself, Lincoln names the occasion: "We have come to dedicate a portion of that field, as a final resting place for those who here gave their lives that that nation might live."[48]

Hawthorne had argued that Unionists ought to grant the Confederate soldier "an honorable burial in the soil he fights for."[49] At Gettysburg, unlike all other major battlefields of the war, Confederate dead rested in northern soil. As Lincoln's audience knew, only the bodies of Union soldiers had been reinterred in the Gettysburg National Cemetery.[50] These are the dead who, Lincoln resolves, "shall not have died in vain." Initial burials, necessarily hasty in the July heat, had segregated Confederate and Union bodies. Confederate bodies had been treated with less respect, often stuffed a hundred and fifty at a time into a trench. The founding of the National Cemetery had allowed for the reverential treatment of the Union dead, reinterred in October.[51]

Lincoln tropes this focus on burial places in a remarkable reversal: "We cannot dedicate – we cannot consecrate – we cannot hallow this ground. The brave men, living and dead, who struggled here, have consecrated it, far above our power to add or detract."[52] As words reach their limit ("we cannot"), Lincoln appeals to an extralinguistic arena of action and place: "The world will little note ... what we say here, but it can never forget what they *did here*" (emphasis added). The opening trope of autochthones returns to counter the moment of inexpressibility, in the prophecy that "this nation ... shall have a new birth of freedom."[53] The return of body-politic imagery here reasserts the state as sovereign actor, a dimension that had been missing from Lincoln's earlier territorial rhetoric of nationhood. At Gettysburg, dedicated ground holding the bodies of Union soldiers provided a home for the body politic, implying that freedom is born of northern soil. This was a single, unified body at home, a sovereign state actor occupying the "national homestead" of the 1862 Message to Congress.

In Lincoln's Second Inaugural Address, given on March 4, 1865, the representation of nationhood oscillates between a sectionally divided territory and a single national body. Through this oscillation, Lincoln's rhetoric inhabits the two temporalities that, conventionally, specify different representational functions for soldier's bodies, a wartime temporality in which deaths are tallied as Union or Confederate and a postwar temporality in which all deaths in the war, Confederate and Union, represent the Union victory.[54] Yet in linking wartime violence to the violence of slavery, Lincoln demonstrates how the central issue of the war strained this representational structure. He opens by mapping the cause: "One eighth of the whole population were colored slaves, not distributed generally over the Union, but localized in the Southern part of it. These slaves constituted a peculiar and powerful interest. All knew that this interest was, somehow, the cause of the war."[55] This territorial division is complicated by Lincoln's curious observation that, at the beginning of the war, neither North nor South "anticipated that the *cause* of the conflict might cease with, or even before, the conflict itself should cease."[56] Lincoln refers here to the Emancipation Proclamation, which in its final form freed all slaves in territories deemed to be in rebellion as of January 1, 1863; the document specifies a list of states or portions of states (by county) to which it applies.[57]

The Emancipation Proclamation claimed to extend federal law over territories that the federal government did not control militarily while ironically leaving slavery untouched in territories it did control.[58] Such a claim would only have weight if the said uncontrolled territories were part of the nation whose chief executive issued the Proclamation. Yet if these territories were still part of the nation, and if the war was understood to be the instrument of God's "providence" in "remov[ing]" the "offence" of slavery from the nation, then it followed that God had "give[n] to North and South, this terrible war, as the woe due to those by whom the offence came."[59] The memorable calculus of blood with which Lincoln closes this section of the speech seems to transact this logic: "Every drop of blood drawn with the lash, shall be paid by another drawn with the sword."[60] Yet within the temporality of the war – and in terms of the Old Testament frame of God's providence – the calculus balances only if the blood drawn is that of slaveholders or their representatives. What, then, was the representative status of the violence suffered by Union soldiers, some of whom were themselves former slaves: Did they too represent the slaveholders? This question shifts the calculus to the postwar temporal frame of Lincoln's final paragraph, in which each soldier, Union and Confederate, becomes a synecdoche for the figure of a single national body politic that has been punished and suffered for the offence of slavery. Here Lincoln urges his auditors to "to bind up the nation's wounds; to care for him who shall have borne the battle, and for his widow, and for his orphan – to do all which may achieve a just, and a lasting peace, among ourselves, and with all nations."[61] First subsumed into one wounded national body and then individualized into a single wounded or dead soldier who could be either northern or southern, white or black, the object of violence remains at once general and particular, national and local.

Lincoln's canny refusal, in what would be his last public address, to answer the question of "whether the seceded states, so called, are in the Union or out of it" confirms the territorial figure of nationhood but cannot dispel its particularizing tendency.[62] In a speech on Reconstruction given on April 11, 1864 – two days after Lee's surrender to Grant but two weeks before Johnston would surrender to Sherman – Lincoln states that he has "purposely forborne any public expression" on this point.[63] The immediate issue motivating this speech, the establishment of Reconstruction governments, raised the question of the states' "proper practical relation with the Union." Lincoln says that it is "easier" to establish this relation "without deciding, or even considering, whether these States have even been out of the Union."[64] Refusing thus to grant secession any legitimacy while yet refraining from any antagonistic claim, Lincoln resolves the (non)question by means of a localizing figure that links body to place: "Finding themselves safely at home, it would be utterly immaterial whether they had ever been abroad."[65] Yet the figure of "home" tends to particularity, as we have seen, here figuring each state as an embodied actor. Lincoln's uncharacteristic use of a dangling modifier locates the seceded states as subjects of a hypothetical verb that does not materialize in the passive-voice main clause. Thus shorn of any agency to wander "abroad," the state bodies repose where they had, Lincoln pretends, always been: "at home." This figure reaches back through the "national homestead" image and other tropes of territorial nationhood from Lincoln's wartime speeches to the concluding metaphor of the First Inaugural Address, where the "hearthstones" of every particular home were linked to all the battlefields and patriot graves of the Revolutionary War – that is, to a moment supposedly prior to the question of the states' relation to the federal structure.

The battlefields and patriot graves of the Civil War would soon become rallying points for Lost Cause mythologizing and white southern resentment more than they would signify the sense of natural nationhood that Lincoln had promoted. The gap between sovereignty and nationhood introduced by secession's particularizing logic would not be easy to close. During Reconstruction, Federal control of the ground itself was visibly evident in the new system of national cemeteries modeled on Gettysburg. The most expensive and elaborate government program up to that time, these cemeteries were staffed by former Union soldiers. The sense of Federal control was emphasized by the architecture of the lodges, whose Second Empire French style echoed new administrative buildings in Washington and contrasted with the local Greek Revival style of nearby plantation houses.[66] If, despite Lincoln's evasion of the territorial question in his last speech on Reconstruction, southern state bodies had ranged "abroad" after secession, in the national cemetery system individual northern soldiers (living and dead) remain displaced from their home lands. Would Hawthorne have admitted that, even so, these bodies occupied soil that they had fought for?

The new but territorially displaced Union graves soon became sites of segregated commemorative practices, which ironically served to maintain the sense of environmental differentiation initiated by secession's particularizing strain of territorial nationhood, thus cutting against any narrative of re-Union. The Memorial Day episode from Constance Fenimore Woolson's *Atlantic Monthly* short story "Rodman the Keeper" (1877) illustrates this counterforce, as marshaled through the representational function of the soldier's corpse. In the story's small southern town (possibly Andersonville, Georgia), no narrative of reconciliation has emerged to displace the war's emancipationist prospects.[67] On a May morning, the town's black community ask the keeper of the national cemetery, a former Colonel in the Union army, to "do us de hono' sah, to take de head of de processio'." At this invitation, Colonel Rodman reflects on the development of race-specific, localized commemorative customs:

> Now the keeper had not much sympathy with the strewing of flowers, North or South; he had seen the beautiful ceremony more than once turned into a political demonstration; here, however, in this small, isolate, interior town,

there was nothing of that kind; the whole population of white faces laid their roses and wept true tears on the graves of their lost ones in the church yard when the Southern Memorial Day came round, and just as naturally the whole population of black faces went out to the national cemetery with their flowers on the day when, throughout the North, spring blossoms were laid on the graves of the soldiers, from the little Maine village to the stretching ranks of Arlington, from Greenwood to the far Western burial-places of San Francisco.[68]

Associating the freedmen with specific northern grave sites – including the culminating locus of the national cemetery system, Arlington – Colonel Rodman enlists them in his own ongoing narrative of alienation from the local landscape. The northern cemeteries evoked in Rodman's vision, marking the imperial sweep of the continent suggested by Leutze's wartime mural, included the graves of Union soldiers alongside the Revolutionary-era patriot graves whose commemoration Lincoln, in his First Inaugural, had imagined binding the nation to itself. Whereas the freedmen's own local commemorative practices had originated prior to Rodman's arrival as keeper, their invitation to Rodman suggests that the prospects for emancipation depend on the strong northern presence in the South promised by the national cemetery, for "Not a white face" other than Rodman's appears at the memorial ceremony.[69] Where the secessionists' environmental argument had located black slaves in the South but denied them participation in nationhood based on a sense of nation as ancestry, Rodman's mediation offers the freedmen citizenship through participation in commemorative practices (a sense of nation as contract) but alienates them from the land where they actually live. As if to question the Fourteenth Amendment's definition of citizenship, the episode's segregation of populations, living and dead, thus reveals the imaginative dissociation of nation as ancestry from nation as territory in postbellum America.

NOTES

1 Abraham Lincoln, *Speeches and Writings, 1859–1865* (New York: Library of America, 1989), 221, 224.

2 On Lincoln's facility with figurative language, see James McPherson, *Abraham Lincoln and the Second American Revolution* (New York: Oxford University Press, 1991), 93–112. The complete textual history of the First Inaugural Address appears in Lincoln, *Collected Works*, Roy P. Basler, ed. (Rutgers University Press, 1953–1955), 4: 249–271.

3 Lincoln, *Speeches and Writings*, 218.

4 On ascription, see Elaine Scarry, *The Body in Pain: The Making and Unmaking of the World* (New York: Oxford University Press, 1985), 60–157.

5 James Dawes, *The Language of War: Literature and Culture in the U.S. from the Civil War to World War II* (Cambridge, MA: Harvard University Press, 2002).

6 Hayden White characterizes synecdoche as an integrative trope in *Metahistory: The Historical Imagination in Nineteenth-Century Europe* (Baltimore: The Johns Hopkins University Press, 1973), 31–38.

7 See Benedict Anderson, *Imagined Communities; Reflections on the Origins and Spread of Nationalism* (London: Verso, 1983) and Lauren Berlant, *The Anatomy of National Fantasy: Hawthorne, Utopia, and Everyday Life* (Chicago: University of Chicago Press, 1991).

8 Lincoln, *Speeches and Writings*, 390–403.

9 On the logic of imaginative possession, see Myra Jehlen, *American Incarnation: The Individual, the Nation, and the Continent* (Cambridge, MA: Harvard University Press, 1986).

10 See Max Cavitch, *American Elegy: The Poetry of Mourning from the Puritans to Whitman* (Minneapolis: University of Minnesota Press, 2007).

11 Eric Slauter discusses sociability in *The State as a Work of Art: The Cultural Origins of the Constitution* (Chicago: University of Chicago Press, 2009), 215–240. Michael Warner examines social contract theory in *The Letters of the Republic: Publication and the Public Sphere in Eighteenth-Century America* (Cambridge, MA: Harvard University Press, 1990), 97–117.

12 Even Sheridan's 1864 campaign in the Shenandoah Valley and Sherman's notorious "march to the sea" did not target civilian populations as would later wars.

13 Andrew Vincent argues for the logical and historical priority of the discourse of sovereignty in *Nationalism and Particularity* (Cambridge, MA: Cambridge University Press, 2002), 14–35.

14 On the historical figuration of states as persons, see Vincent, *Nationalism and Particularity*, 19–24. Slauter (*The State as a Work of Art*, 40–85) argues that during the Revolutionary era, the concept of the state became dissociated from bodily imagery.

15 Timothy Sweet, *Traces of War: Poetry, Photography, and the Crisis of the Union* (Baltimore: The Johns Hopkins University Press, 1990), 16–24.

16 On classical republican theory, see J. G. A. Pocock, *The Machiavellian Moment: Florentine Political Thought and the Atlantic Republican Tradition* (Princeton: Princeton University Press, 1975).

17 Alexander Hamilton, James Madison, and John Jay, *The Federalist* (Cambridge, MA: Harvard University Press, 1961), 154, 151.

18 Ibid., 154.

19 Ibid., 203.

20 Lincoln, *Speeches and Writings*, 221.

21 If secession was divorce, marriage would be re-Union, as in John W. DeForest's novel *Miss Ravenel's Conversion from Secession to Loyalty* (New York: Harper & Brothers: 1867). On the marriage plot as an allegory of reunion in fiction, see Nina Silber, *The Romance of Reunion: Northerners and the South, 1865–1900* (Chapel Hill: University of North Carolina Press, 1993).

22 C. Vann Woodward, ed., *Mary Chesnut's Civil War* (New Haven, CT: Yale University Press, 1981), 25. Given the date of this diary entry, sometime between March 9 and March 15, 1861, it is possible that Chesnut had read a copy of Lincoln's speech.

23 *The Federalist*, 113.

24 See the assertion of natural regional difference that governs William Gilmore Simms's 1845 cultural manifesto, "Americanism in Literature."

25 Avalon Project, "Confederate States of America: Declaration of the Immediate Causes Which Induce and Justify the Secession of South Carolina from the Federal Union," http://avalon.law.yale.edu/19th_century/csa_scarsec.asp

26 Avalon Project, "Confederate States of America: A Declaration of the Immediate Causes which Induce and Justify the Secession of the State of Mississippi from the Federal Union," http://avalon.law.yale.edu/19th_century/csa_missec.asp

27 See Bruce Dain, *A Hideous Monster of the Mind: American Race Theory in the Early Republic* (Cambridge, MA: Harvard University Press, 2002).

28 James D. Richardson, ed., *The Messages and Papers of Jefferson Davis and the Confederacy*, 2 vols. (New York: Chelsea House-Robert Hector, 1966), 1: 33–34.

29 Ibid., 1: 35.

30 Edd Winfield Parks and Aileen Wells Parks, eds., *The Collected Poems of Henry Timrod* (Athens: University of Georgia Press, 1965), 74.

31 The oil study (completed in 1861) and a cartoon detail for the mural are now held by the Smithsonian Museum of American Art.

32 Nathaniel Hawthorne, "Chiefly about War-Matters," *Atlantic Monthly* 10 (July 1862): 64.

33 Ibid., 64–65.

34 Brook Thomas, *Civic Myths: A Law-and-Literature Approach to Citizenship*. (Chapel Hill: University of North Carolina Press, 2007), 223.

35 Lincoln, *Speeches and Writings*, 403, emphasis added.

36 Ibid., 404.

37 Ibid., 406.

38 Ibid., 400.

39 See Timothy Sweet, *American Georgics: Economy and Environment in Early American Literature* (Philadelphia: University of Pennsylvania Press, 2002).

40 Thomas Jefferson, *Notes on the State of Virginia* (New York: Penguin, 1999), 171.

41 On the plantation ideal, see Louis Rubin, *The Edge of the Swamp: A Study in the Literature and Society of the Old South* (Baton Rouge: Louisiana State University Press, 1989).

42 On soil exhaustion in the middle Atlantic and the Old South, see Steven Stoll, *Larding the Lean Earth: Soil and Society in Nineteenth-Century America* (New York: Hill and Wang, 2002).

43 The Homestead Act provided for the transfer of 160 acres of public land (and no more than 160 acres) to any citizen over the age of twenty-five.

44 Lincoln, *Speeches and Writings*, 536.

45 On the classical funeral oration as a model, see Gary Wills, *Lincoln at Gettysburg: The Words that Remade America* (New York: Simon & Schuster, 1992), 41–62.

46 Newspapers likened the battle to Waterloo or Thermopylae.

47 Lincoln, *Speeches and Writings*, 536.

48 Ibid., 536.

49 Hawthorne, "Chiefly About War-Matters," 65.

50 Jim Weeks, *Gettysburg: Memory, Market, and American Shrine* (Princeton, NJ: Princeton University Press, 2003), 17.

51 Drew Gilpin Faust, *This Republic of Suffering: Death and the American Civil War* (New York: Knopf, 2008), 71–73, 99–100.

52 Lincoln, *Speeches and Writings*, 536.
53 Ibid., 536.
54 Scarry delineates the referential fluidity of the injured body in relation to these two temporalities (*The Body in Pain*, 116–117).
55 Lincoln, *Speeches and Writings*, 686.
56 Ibid., 686.
57 Ibid., 424–425.
58 Slaves were emancipated before the end of the war in some areas not named by the Emancipation Proclamation. For example, slavery was abolished in the new Maryland Constitution, effective November 1, 1864.
59 Lincoln, *Speeches and Writings*, 687. In a letter to Thurlow Weed, Lincoln speculated that the providential interpretation of the war proposed in the Second Inaugural would "wear as well as – perhaps better than – anything I have produced" (Ibid., 689).
60 Ibid., 687.
61 Ibid., 687.
62 Ibid., 699.
63 Ibid., 699.
64 In this speech, Lincoln defends the ratification of a new state constitution (including emancipation) in Louisiana by a mere twelve thousand voters.
65 Lincoln, *Speeches and Writings*, 699.
66 On the establishment of the national cemetery system, see Faust, *This Republic of Suffering*, 211–249.
67 David Blight argues that white reconciliation practices began to displace the war's emancipationist legacy in *Race and Reunion: The Civil War in American Memory* (Cambridge, MA: Harvard University Press, 2001), 64–97.
68 Constance Fenimore Woolson, "Rodman the Keeper," *Atlantic Monthly* 39 (March 1877), 273.
69 Ibid., 273.

6

BETHANY SCHNEIDER

Abraham Lincoln and the American Indians

On December 26, 1862, the Dakota Uprising ended when thirty-eight Dakota men were simultaneously executed at Mankato, Minnesota. They had been convicted of murder and rape in trials that lasted as little as five minutes, and the trials were conducted in a language – English – that most of the accused could not speak. It was and remains the largest mass execution in United States history. However, originally almost seven times as many men were scheduled to die. Military tribunals in Minnesota sentenced a total of 303 prisoners to death and sent the verdicts to Washington for the approval of the president of the United States, Abraham Lincoln. After almost a month of deliberation, Lincoln acquitted 265 of the prisoners. The new, diminished number enraged many white Minnesotans. Nevertheless, a crowd of thousands gathered around a mass gallows to watch the Dakota men – who spent the moments before the trap fell dancing in their nooses and shouting their names – plunge to their deaths. The day after the hangings, the marshal of the prison went to release Chaska, one of the many men whom Lincoln had acquitted. "I went to the prison to release a man who had been acquitted for saving a woman's life, but when I asked for him, the answer was, 'He is not here; you hung him yesterday.' I could not bring back the redskin."[1]

Without doubt the assembled crowd was bloodthirsty. But why the mass execution? One would imagine that the viewing pleasure could be prolonged, if the deaths happened consecutively, in a scene something like the extended spectacle of the guillotine during the French Revolution. One would also imagine that the grisly stagecraft of constructing a scaffold that large was both expensive and tricky. The answer to this question is indicated by the mistaken execution of Chaska: the easy disregard of whether he was acquitted or condemned; the careless loss of him into the wrong collective; the way this man and his name is engulfed by the identifier "redskin." The deaths had to happen simultaneously in order to emphasize that this was the execution of a race, not of individuals, not of Dakota, and not of men; in order, in other words, to pleasure an audience that wanted to witness genocide. "I could not bring back the redskin," the marshal said, although he knew Chaska's name. Given the ubiquitous use of the singular to refer to Indians in general – "the Red Man" most commonly – the marshal is washing his hands off responsibility for the death not only of Chaska but of all Native people. "The redskin" is a singular that erases individual, tribal, and national identification, and that means not simply a plural but a totality. When the marshal refuses Chaska his name, he is signaling that genocide has been achieved. And in several ways it had: In order to bargain down the number of executions, Lincoln promised that he would remove almost all remaining Native people from Minnesota.

The execution of the Dakota prisoners is a moment in Lincoln's presidency that receives little attention. The attention it does receive pursues the moral meaning of Lincoln's convictions and acquittals. Popular accounts are commonly anxious to show how Lincoln suffered over the decision and to remind us that he could have executed hundreds but instead only executed dozens. Scholarship on the subject acknowledges that, although Lincoln may have suffered, he also made ugly bargains to save the lives he did, and the acquitted prisoners languished and many died in custody long after the execution of their comrades. David A. Nichols, whose 1978 *Lincoln and the Indians* remains one of the most important scholarly works on the subject, asks in a later essay that we understand Lincoln's convictions of the Dakota specifically and his Indian policy in general in the following way: "If good politics is leadership toward the possible, Lincoln measures up rather well. Not much was possible, given the circumstances." He concludes: "Indian affairs show up the hard side of Lincoln's nature, a side that bordered on militarism.... This Lincoln, for all his caution and political manipulation, was obsessed with a goal and would use violence to resolve problems when Indians, or anyone else, forcibly got in the way of his highest priorities."[2] This turn in Nichols' argument is interesting. Lincoln's "hard side" "show[s] up" when we add Indians to the picture, but Nichols is careful to point out that, while Indians enable us to see it, this "hard side" was not about Indians. Lincoln could turn his "hard side" to "anyone else," as well. Indians are the filter that allow us to see something other than the soft, loving Lincoln, and they teach us how he was able to achieve a goal we are all now understood to applaud, a goal that in itself is understood to enable everyone (else's) "soft side." It is, in other words, a necessary hardness, a hardness that leads through and past Indians to the "highest priorities," priorities that are themselves founded on Indian land: the preservation of the geographical and political union of the United States.

The story that David Nichols tells is about Abraham Lincoln, not about the thirty-seven Dakota. It asks what new facet of Lincoln is revealed when we look at him, not through Native eyes or from a Native perspective, but in the light of his attitudes toward and actions regarding Native Americans. That new facet, Nichols suggests, is a violent Lincoln. This chapter is about Abraham Lincoln and what happens to him when we think about him in relation to Native people, and it will therefore also be about the "hard side of Lincoln's nature." This chapter will also travel far from Native realities in its exploration of the Lincoln phenomenon. In order to do so, I am going to turn away from historical facts, which in the case of Native Americans and their relationship to Abraham Lincoln seem to slide from collective memory, and from thirty-eight Dakota deaths that were recorded and witnessed but almost successfully forgotten in the Lincolnalia, although certainly not by Dakota people. I am going to turn away from both the enigma of Lincoln's feelings and the pragmatics of his "politics of the possible." Instead, I am going to turn to literary legend in order to construct a genealogy of an almost entirely fictional Native American man, probably Shawnee, who makes his brief and fatal appearance in the hagiographies of the assassinated president, and who continues to appear here and there to this very day.

Like Chaska, whose mistaken death and violently reinscribed anonymity underlines the equally mistaken and anonymous deaths of the other thirty-seven Dakota with whom he died, this legendary Shawnee points the way to many more dead Indians buried in the mythical story of Abe Lincoln. And finally, I turn to this dead Shawnee man and the long history of his myth because it is through him, literally through his bullet-pierced body, that we may be able to construct a Native view on Lincoln, as opposed to Lincoln's view on Native people. If dead Indians "show up the hard side of Lincoln," as they most assuredly do, I will argue that the only way *not* to show the hard side of Lincoln, the only way to produce the benevolent, all-loving, antiracist Lincoln who persists in fantasy if not in scholarly histories, is to hide the Indian bodies.

In the early 1780s, a man named Abraham Lincoln moved with his wife and four children to northwest Kentucky, an area hotly contested between white settler colonists and the Shawnee; the family lived near Hughes' Fort for protection. The Northwest Indian Wars, in which the Shawnee, Cherokee, and their allies fought the expanding United States, were waged over land that the Native alliance of nations considered their shared hunting ground and that the United States considered the Kentucky Territory. Across the decade, thousands of people on all sides were killed in raids and pitched battles. Sometime in the mid 1780s – most accounts say 1784, but some say earlier and some later – Abraham Lincoln was shot and killed by Native gunfire. His death was one of many and would be of no more historical importance than the deaths of countless others were it not for the fact that some four-score years later his grandson, also named Abraham Lincoln, would become the sixteenth president of the United States. This Abraham Lincoln would be shot by a very different kind of assassin, and he would become a figure of almost absurdly towering myth. Grandfather Abraham's obscure frontier death became a building block of that myth.

Grandfather Abraham's death was a family story before it was a national story. In 1854, the future president was an Illinois lawyer gearing up to run for the U.S. Senate. He received a letter from a man named Jesse Lincoln, who wanted to know if the two might be related. Lincoln replied, "As you have supposed, I am the grandson of your uncle Abraham; and the story of his death by the Indians, and of Uncle Mordecai, then fourteen years old, killing one of the Indians, is the legend more strongly than all others imprinted upon my mind and memory."[3] Jesse Lincoln's letter is lost, as is the original of the reply. It is clear, however, that the two men established and agreed on their blood relation by trading in a narrative about the violent deaths of a white man and a Native American. When he begins the sentence, Lincoln uses "story" to describe his grandfather's death, but after referencing the teenaged Uncle Mordecai's killing of an Indian, Lincoln upgrades "story" to "legend." It seems that it is Uncle Mordecai's murderous retaliation, rather than the killing of Grandfather Abraham, that appears most mythic to Lincoln.

Lincoln – the autodidact and voracious reader – imagines his memory to be a page and the legend of his uncle's youthful act a text "imprinted" on his being more forcefully than any subsequent narrative. To what extent that early impression shaped Lincoln's actions as president, most particularly his administration's Indian policies, his attitude toward the western expansion of the United States, and his own decisions regarding the conviction of hundreds of Dakota prisoners, is impossible to say. The letter to Jesse Lincoln is the only time Lincoln references his Uncle Mordecai's actions in writing.

The letter from Abraham Lincoln to Jesse Lincoln was unknown until it was printed in the *Chattanooga Times* in 1883, and it wasn't until one year later that the story of Mordecai jumped from family to national legend. Earlier biographies of Lincoln treat his grandfather's death very briefly. John Locke Scripps, who wrote a biography for the campaign trail in 1860, says simply, "Abraham Lincoln removed to Kentucky about the year 1780, and four years thereafter, while engaged in opening a farm, he was surprised and killed by Indians."[4] Four biographies published closely after the president's death make little more of the event. Three have him working far from the cabin, alone. Two assert that his body – scalped – was not found until the next morning. None have anything to say about Mordecai in relation to the killing. The most interesting of these biographies is Isaac Newton Arnold's 1866 *The History of Abraham Lincoln and the Overthrow of Slavery*. Arnold was a very close friend of Lincoln's, a Democrat turned Republican who served in the Senate across Lincoln's presidency and drafted important anti-slavery legislation. He describes Grandfather Abraham's death succinctly, again with no reference to Mordecai's presence: "He was shot by an Indian, while at work in his field, near his log cabin. Thomas Lincoln, the father of Abraham, was only six years of age when he was left an orphan."[5]

After 1883 an entirely new story emerges, one that proffers extra details about Mordecai's murderous action. Remarkably, the first writer who puts forward this expanded version of the story is the self-same friend of Lincoln who printed such a bland account almost two decades earlier: Isaac Newton Arnold. In *The Life of Abraham Lincoln*, published in 1884, Arnold retells the story this way:

> Shortly after this, he was one day, while at work in the field, waylaid, shot, and instantly killed, by a party of Indians. Thomas Lincoln, born in 1778, and the father of the President, was in the field with his father when he fell. Mordecai and Josiah, his elder brothers, were near by in the forest. Mordecai, startled by the shot, saw his father fall, and, running to the cabin, seized the loaded rifle, rushed to one of the loop-holes cut through the logs of the cabin, and saw the Indian who had fired; he had just caught the boy, Thomas, and was running towards the forest. Pointing the rifle through the logs, and aiming at a silver medal on the breast of the Indian, Mordecai fired. The Indian fell, and the boy, springing to his feet, ran to the open arms of his mother, at the cabin door. Meanwhile, Josiah, who had run to the fort for aid, returned with a party of settlers, who brought in the body of Abraham Lincoln, and the Indian who had been shot. From this time throughout his life, Mordecai was the mortal enemy of the Indians, and, it is said, sacrificed many in revenge for the murder of his father.[6]

From whence do these new details come? Perhaps Isaac Newton Arnold got hold of that original letter from Jesse Lincoln, which must have told some of the story in order to elicit acknowledgment from Abraham Lincoln. If so, he doesn't cite it. Perhaps the president told Arnold the story, but Arnold simply didn't think it was that important when he was writing about Lincoln in 1866. Or perhaps Arnold made the details up as he considered that tantalizing fragment of information in Lincoln's letter and tried to imagine what exactly about the killing and Mordecai's response might have been so strongly imprinted on the president's mind and memory. We cannot know. But we can know that this different historical moment produces a different version of events and a different understanding of the role of Indians in the life of Abraham Lincoln.

It is historically plausible that the adult Mordecai Lincoln made a regular habit of killing Native people. In 1881, a 100-year-old Kentucky doctor by the name of Christopher Columbus Graham dictated what he knew of the Lincoln family to an interlocutor. His testimony was of interest because he could prove that Lincoln's parents had been married, thus putting to rest the rumor that the president was illegitimate: "I was hunting roots for my medicines, and just went to the wedding to get a good supper, and got it," he said. But in the midst of his rambling discourse he has something very interesting to report about Mordecai. "Mordecai Lincoln … was a good Indian fighter," he says, as if affirming something everyone already knows. But "the story of his killing the Indian who killed old Abraham Linkhorn is all 'my eye and Betty Martin.'"[7] The old man is perfectly comfortable saying that Mordecai *did* kill Indians, regularly and efficiently. However, Christopher Columbus Graham counters Isaac Newton Arnold at the level of narrative causation, asserting that Lincoln's uncle killed Indians simply because he wanted to; he didn't need any primal trauma to goad him on. Perhaps Lincoln knew that his uncle hunted and killed Indians for pleasure. Maybe stories about Mordecai were in circulation in the family, and the legend of his first killing was concocted, with a wink, to explain his murderous pleasures.

It does not matter if Mordecai's transformation through primal trauma into a lifelong "mortal enemy" of Indians is the legendary aspect of the story to which Lincoln refers, or if it is Arnold's embellishment. Either way, it is entirely generic, tapping into the literary tradition of the "Indian hater," who, driven mad by the sight of his slain family, becomes an enraged serial killer. Robert Montgomery Bird's 1837 novel, *Nick of the Woods*, is set across the exact same years and in the exact same region of Kentucky where Grandfather Lincoln met his fate. Bird creates an Indian hater in Nathan Slaughter, an otherwise pacifist Quaker who fails to save his family from death. Slaughter's psychotic drive to kill Indians teaches others how to become nation-building, Indian-killing American males.[8] These scenes of foundational violence seem to pivot on the body or bodies of dead white family members: The sight of their bodies turns the father or brother or son into a serial Indian killer. But I would argue that it is the body of the dead Indian, which the Indian killer is driven to make again and again, which turns the "story," in Lincoln's own formulation, into "legend." Everyone agrees that Grandfather Abraham was really and truly, historically and bodily, killed by Native gunfire. No one can say, and not many people care, if Mordecai killed an Indian in return. The killing of Indians is historically and literarily ubiquitous. Generic and specific Native deaths cannot be allowed to matter, or be said, in any given moment, to have been true. The violence that may or may not have been perpetrated by Uncle Mordecai, and that may or may not have been repeated across the course of his life, can only ever be understood under the heading "legend."

This is why it is important to pay attention to the legendary Indians that appear here and there in stories of Abraham Lincoln's early life. These legends deserve more attention than a simple cluck-clucking over the recycled silliness of Lincoln hagiographies. The inability to tell the story of Indian hating, to read that which is most deeply imprinted, to know the life history of anti-Indian violence, is all part of Indian hating – and therefore of America making – itself. Herman Melville, writing in 1857 of the phenomenon of the Indian hater, frames his distinction between the intermittent Indian hater, who goes on killing sprees, and the "Indian hater par excellence," who dedicates his life to the extermination of Indians and disappears forever into the forest to pursue them, as a difference between that which can be told and that which cannot:

> How evident that in strict speech there can be no biography of an Indian-hater par excellence.... The career of the Indian-hater par excellence has the impenetrability of the fate of a lost steamer. Doubtless, events, terrible ones, have happened, must have happened; but the powers that be in nature have taken order that they shall never become news.[9]

In his 1831 decision deciding that the Cherokee Nation could not bring suit against the state of Georgia, Chief Justice John Marshall explains that "if the Cherokee nation have rights, this is not the tribunal in which those rights are to be asserted. If it be true that wrongs have been inflicted, and that still greater are to be apprehended, this is not the tribunal which can redress the past or prevent the future."[10] Genocidal violence against Indians, in other words, is a given, but it cannot be spoken in official documents like biographies and laws. It lies forever outside the realm of news and can only be hinted at in the realm of fiction. If its legend is imprinted most deeply on the minds and memories of our leaders, the text is so overwritten by other texts that it can never be deciphered – but that very illegibility ties a forgotten past of Indian killing to a certain future of the same.

Arnold's biography was published in a window of time between the Battle of Little Big Horn in 1876 and the massacre of Wounded Knee in 1890. It was a period of massive western expansion coupled with the violent killing, suppression, and containment of Native people. It is in this national mood that Arnold's biography made what quickly became and still seems, when the sober face of a benevolent Lincoln glints from our very pennies, a scandalous claim: Arnold's Abraham Lincoln was of and for Indian hating as a founding characteristic, and it is that hate that made him, and America itself, great. It was that hate, indeed, that furnished America with the strength to end slavery, for it is this heroic feat that Arnold most admires in Lincoln. Grandfather Abraham's death and Mordecai's primal scene is immediately followed by this pedagogical exegesis:

> It was in the midst of such scenes that the ancestors of the President were nurtured. They were contemporaries of Daniel Boone ... and other border heroes and Indian fighters on the frontiers, and were often engaged in those desperate conflicts between the Indians and the settlers, which gave to Kentucky the suggestive name of "the dark and bloody ground."

> Those Kentucky hunters, of which the grandfather and the father of the President are types, were a very remarkable class of men ... of greater endurance and of far superior intellect, the Kentucky hunter could outrun his Indian enemy, or whip him in a man to man fight. This man, who has driven away or killed the Indian, who has cleared the forests, broken up and reclaimed the wilderness, and whose type still survives in the pioneer, is one of the most picturesque figures in American history. From this sort of ancestry have sprung Andrew Jackson and David Crockett, Benton and Clay, Grant and Lincoln.[11]

Here, Arnold teaches his readers to understand Abraham Lincoln's (and other great Americans') ancestry as steeped in racially driven violence and his legacy as an endorsement to continue that violence. Arnold would have us understand that the text most deeply imprinted on Abraham Lincoln's mind, the text that made him end slavery and save the union, is a primer for genocide.

Arnold's story of Grandfather Lincoln's death was taken up and expanded on in dozens of biographies that followed. But almost every one of Arnold's followers dropped the point about Mordecai's drive to revenge and left out discussions of inherited Indian-hating tendencies. Certainly such claims became troubling when Indian killing went out of fashion as a topic if not a practice after Wounded Knee. Sympathy for the "poor Indian" began to restructure the feelings of white Americans. After the founding of Carlisle Indian School in 1879, Indian schools cropped up everywhere, their stated goal the assimilation of Native children into white society. It was a project that hid its genocidal intentions in plain sight; the infamous tag line of the founder of Carlisle was "kill the Indian and save the man." Indian killing was now disguised as Salvationist benevolence, and this so-called sympathy for the Indian was easily recognizable as akin to the calls for sympathy for slaves that characterized the Abolitionist movement. The "hard side" of Lincoln receded from view again. How could Abraham Lincoln, who freed the slaves out of his great love for all mankind, be, in his very sinews, a racist serial killer?

It is a perverse fact that in Arnold's version, the Native man who is both the killer of Grandfather Abraham and the victim of Mordecai's retaliation marks the place of Native resistance. Valorizing the labor of genocide that went into the making of Kentucky and Illinois at least acknowledges that the bucolic western setting of Abraham Lincoln's infamous rail splitting was violently wrested from Native people. The reader understands that something was at stake for Native people, even as the reader is taught to celebrate the destruction of Native lives and cultures by white nation-building killers. Indians fade along with Lincoln's "hard side" when the biographies shift attention from the story of nation building to the story of national division and reunification. Grandfather Abraham's frontier death took place before the ratification of the Constitution, but the story of the three brothers as it develops in and after Arnold's original version is deeply invested in the "new birth of freedom" that Lincoln proposed at Gettysburg, and that has come to be seen as a moment of refounding. Lincoln carefully avoids speaking of race or slavery in the Gettysburg Address, and in these later versions of the story of Grandfather Abraham's death, the Shawnee man's brief appearance spurs a similarly whitewashed vision of a unified America.

In *The Ancestry of Abraham Lincoln*, written in 1909, James Henry Lea explains that President Lincoln should have been a Kentucky aristocrat because of the size of his grandfather's stake in the territory. It comprised

in all some 3200 acres, a goodly domain of the finest farming land in the world, which, had all prospered, would have placed his descendants among the first in wealth and position in their community as the wilderness crystallized into an infant state. But, at least for the hapless younger son, the bullet of the savage marauder changed everything.

One morning in the early summer of 1785, going out to his daily task in the fields with his two elder sons and the child Thomas, Abraham Lincoln was shot dead by an Indian from an ambush in the forest. The two young men, aged twenty-one and nineteen respectively, fled – the elder to the cabin and the younger to the nearest stockade, Fort Hughes, leaving the helpless infant of five years to his fate beside his father's body. As the savage stooped to lift the terrified child from the ground, Mordecai, who had secured his rifle, shot the Indian through the heart, and little Thomas, thus released, escaped to the cabin, where his brother held the enemy at bay until Josiah returned from the fort with assistance, and the assailants fled.[12]

In this version, the "hapless" Thomas is made insignificant by his status as youngest, his loss of wealth, and by his infancy. And indeed, the adult Thomas Lincoln, whose relationship with his son was not happy, is largely depicted as ineffectual in biographies of the president. But in Lea's account, Thomas plays an important if entirely passive role in restructuring the shattered world of the Lincoln sons in the aftermath of their father's death. Thomas is at first abandoned – but he is structurally important, for without the need to protect him, the elder brothers, whose first impulse is to flee, would have no reason to turn back to the scene of violence and reconstitute the family along new lines. Because of Thomas and the ethical magnetism of his innocent passivity, the flawed older brothers are folded back into the story as political agents. Mordecai chooses individual action and kills the Indian who killed the father, thus revenging his death and protecting the child. Josiah turns to the social infrastructure for help, thereby saving the now barricaded Mordecai (notice that the mother, to whom Thomas runs in Arnold's version, is now written entirely out of this newly founded family of brothers), and by extension the community itself against Indians in general.

Here the Shawnee killer of Grandfather Abraham recedes from centrality, becoming a mere prompt to actions that are now of more national importance than a dead Indian. The Indian serves as a metaphor for the divisive issue of slavery, the "red man" standing in for the "black man" as the problem over which two white brothers will first struggle, then find united maturity. Christopher Columbus Graham made it clear that racism itself could be the catalyst for many people's antislavery sentiments: "Many great men of the South and North were then opposed to slavery, mainly because the new negroes were as wild as the Indians and might prove as dangerous."[13] In Lea's version, the Lincoln family is shattered and reconstituted through Indian-white violence, but it is the reconstitution rather than the cause of the shattering that is important, prefiguring the shattering and reconstituting of the American nation in Lincoln's Civil War. The implicitly white blood brotherhood between the sons, rather than the blood shed by the father and the Indian, is the point. Thomas may be a weak child in the story, and may grow to be a less-than-ideal father, but in saving him his brothers discover in themselves qualities that bypass Thomas to be carried on and greatly amplified in his famous son, their nephew. The lost paternal inheritance of land and wealth becomes a fraternal inheritance of character: Mordecai's valor (which readers would understand as a southern characteristic) and Josiah's civic duty (which readers would understand as northern). The direct line of inheritance – idle wealth from a grandfather and weakness of character from a father – are interrupted and rechanneled, and President Lincoln is shown to be the heir of brave and ultimately united brothers rather than rich or indolent fathers. This version of the "legend" piercingly prefigures as family drama the dramatic intensity of the scene at Gettysburg, where, among the dead "on a great battle-field," Lincoln rededicated the nation in the name of brothers and futures rather than fathers and pasts.

This chapter has worked to show how a process of Indian removal in the legend itself produces a benevolent, antiracist Lincoln. Indians, in other words, reveal a Lincoln and an America motivated by race hatred, and the further the hagiographies take us from Indians, the easier it is for them to argue that Lincoln was an antiracist father figure motivated by love. But I believe we can nevertheless find a "real" Indian in this story, and we find him if we follow the bullet.

Isaac Newton Arnold's savoring of the legend in his second biography of Lincoln has the young Indian killer "pointing the rifle through the logs, and aiming at a silver medal on the breast of the Indian. Mordecai fired." The lethal gaze fixes on the glint of a medal: What is that medal? Native leaders commonly wore "peace medals" given to them by European colonizing powers and then the United States. These medals, like coins, had the heads of state leaders depicted on them. U.S. medals bore likenesses of U.S. presidents. So when Mordecai aims at and presumably shoots the Indian through the medal, he is both saving Thomas Lincoln and prefiguring the assassination of Thomas's president son; Abraham Lincoln was shot through the head. Thus Arnold's Mordecai compresses the entirety of Lincoln's life into that moment, ensuring both his birth and death.

The Indian through which Mordecai's bullet passes is left for dead – generic, unnamed, and inconsequential. But I would like to suggest a name and suggest some consequences. The medal can be used to refract another history of an American (although not U.S.) leader besides Lincoln, another war chief who led his divided people into battle to try to save the political and geographic integrity of a homeland: a Sauk named Makataimeshekiakiak, or Black Hawk. Black Hawk is remembered largely because of the catastrophic 1832 war that bears his name, which ended with the massacre of hundreds of starving Sauk and Mesquakie-Fox, and because, in 1833, he told his life story to an amanuensis. It was published as *Life of Ma-Ka-Tai-Me-She-Kia-KIak or Black Hawk – Dictated by Himself*, and it was a best seller. Black Hawk's autobiography is peppered with French, British, and U.S. peace medals. Indeed the action of the autobiography and the long history of Sauk dispossession are inaugurated several generations in the past when a Frenchman gives a peace medal to Black Hawk's ancestor, and for the rest of the book Black Hawk uses the medals to distinguish between more and less trustworthy colonizing powers. Kendall Johnson notes "as U.S. peace medals recur throughout the narrative, they not only signal dishonesty but outline the rhetorical pattern of marking peace with Indians in the act of dispossessing them."[14] Black Hawk refuses, in the biography, ever to wear U.S. peace medals. But, Johnson points out, in Charles Bird King's 1837 portrait, Black Hawk is shown wearing an enormous one, with the profile of President Martin van Buren clearly depicted. Johnson shows that many aspects of this portrait, but especially the medal that readers of the autobiography would

know Black Hawk despised, scorn the Sauk leader and cast him as finally
subject to U.S. control. Building from Johnson's attention to the importance
of peace medals in *Life of Ma-Ka-Tai-Me-She-Kia-Kiak or Black Hawk*,
I propose that the peace medal in Arnold's biography of Lincoln would
signal Black Hawk to readers familiar with the autobiography. And there
is plenty of reason to think readers of Arnold's 1884 Lincoln biography
would be familiar with Black Hawk, as a highly dramatized new revision
of it had been published under the title *The Autobiography of Ma-Ka-Tai-
Me-She-Kia-Kiak* in 1882. For Arnold, this connection was simply another
dramatization of the prefiguring of Lincoln's life that he was spinning in his
autobiography. Lincoln served in the Black Hawk War; here Black Hawk's
defeat is foretold along with everything else.

Beyond unpacking Arnold's literary flourishes, it is important to find Black
Hawk in the permanently two-dimensional figure of the Shawnee warrior
who killed Lincoln's grandfather. Abraham Lincoln, as a young man, joined
up to fight in the Black Hawk War, was elected captain of his company,
and although he never saw action, he was twice present in the aftermath of
battles. He helped bury the white dead on the battlefields where they fell.
Serious historians of Black Hawk and the Black Hawk War have nothing
to say about Lincoln's service; he played a less-than-minor part, and his
future presidency has no bearing on the historical events of 1832. Serious
biographers of Lincoln note only that he made important political connections across those months. Hagiographers of Lincoln make much of a story
in which he was said to have saved a wandering Potawatomie man from
bloodthirsty white soldiers, and they are titillated by the portentous-in-
hindsight fact that the future president of the Confederacy and Lincoln's
archenemy, Jefferson Davis, also served. In other words, historians are not
interested in understanding what relationship Abraham Lincoln had to the
politics of Indian fighting, or what passions led him to join a war that was
essentially a manhunt and that even the contemporary press condemned,
after its horrifying conclusion, as "the most disastrous Indian campaign of
modern times."[15] Instead they pursue Lincoln's service in the Black Hawk
War for what it can tell them about the future greatness of the man, either
as an historical or a mythical figure, and the future destiny of the nation.
Why, when rail splitting is understood to have formed the very backbone
of Abraham Lincoln's persona, is the actual political situation of the Black
Hawk War, or the persona of Black Hawk himself, not allowed to stick to
Lincoln in any way?

Let us compare 214 words of Black Hawk in which he makes an argument for national belonging and justifies war, and 278 words of Lincoln that
argue the same points. First, Black Hawk's description of the considerations

that led him to convince several thousand of his people to follow him back across the Mississippi River to reclaim their land:

> We were a divided people, forming two parties. Ke-o-kuk being at the head of one, willing to barter our rights merely for the good opinion of the whites; and cowardly enough to desert our village to them. I was at the head of the other party, and was determined to hold on to my village, although I had been *ordered* to leave it. But, I considered, as myself and band had no agency in selling our country – and that as provision had been made in the treaty, for us all to remain on it as long as it belonged to the United States, that we could not be *forced* away. I refused, therefore, to quit my village. It was here, that I was born – and here lie the bones of many friends and relations. For this spot I felt a sacred reverence, and never could consent to leave it, without being forced therefrom.
>
> When I called to mind the scenes of my youth, and those of later days – and reflected that the theatre on which these were acted, had been so long the home of my fathers, who now slept on the hills around it, I could not bring my mind to consent to leave this country to the whites, for any earthly consideration.[16]

Now, Lincoln's famous speech that he made at the dedication of the National Cemetery at Gettysburg:

> Four score and seven years ago our fathers brought forth on this continent, a new nation, conceived in Liberty, and dedicated to the proposition that all men are created equal.
>
> Now we are engaged in a great civil war, testing whether that nation, or any nation so conceived and so dedicated, can long endure. We are met on a great battle-field of that war. We have come to dedicate a portion of that field, as a final resting place for those who here gave their lives that that nation might live. It is altogether fitting and proper that we should do this.
>
> But, in a larger sense, we can not dedicate – we can not consecrate – we can not hallow – this ground. The brave men, living and dead, who struggled here, have consecrated it, far above our poor power to add or detract. The world will little note, nor long remember what we say here, but it can never forget what they did here. It is for us the living, rather, to be dedicated here to the unfinished work which they who fought here have thus far so nobly advanced. It is rather for us to be here dedicated to the great task remaining before us – that from these honored dead we take increased devotion to that cause for which they gave the last full measure of devotion – that we here highly resolve that these dead shall not have died in vain – that this nation, under God, shall have a new birth of freedom – and that government of the people, by the people, for the people, shall not perish from the earth.[17]

Perhaps this comparison is a cheap trick. Perhaps the many parallels between these two texts – and I won't pursue them all – are accidental. But if Gary

Wills can contemplate the European and Anglo-American texts that influenced the Gettysburg Address, I will suggest here, only briefly, the possibility that a Native American text – and the memory of a Native American War – might be "more strongly than all others imprinted upon my mind and memory." Lincoln served in the Black Hawk War. His labor in that war was to bury the white dead in the battlefields where they fell. Black Hawk's autobiography does not appear on the list of books that we know Lincoln read. But surely the famously voracious young reader got his hands on the book that describes the very war in which he had served a year earlier.

The Sauk had not lived for very long in the land they fought to regain. They did not argue that this was the land that a Creator made for them many generations ago. Black Hawk carefully explains that the Sauk only arrived in that land one hundred years earlier, and he painstakingly traces their right to the land through histories of both European and Native warfare and treaty making. His autobiography is an argument for belonging that is as fragile, in some ways, as the United States' arguments. Again and again – not only in the section quoted previously – Black Hawk explains that the foundation of Sauk national belonging to the land he fights to regain is the presence of Sauk dead in that land. More than that, he describes how rituals of mourning enacted at graves between generations of warriors create a feedback between dead and living men that "rededicate" both to the continuing sanctity of the land, defined by fighting on and for it, being buried in it, and doing what one does in its name for the honor of those who have already died in its service: "The brave, with pleasure, visits the grave of his father, after he has been successful in war, and repaints the post that shows where he lies!"[18]

Telling the life of Abraham Lincoln, whether you do it backward or forward, is to follow the bullet. I am proposing that we follow the bullet much further than we are wont to do, and that we follow it back through myth and metaphor and peace medal until it leads us to a different leader, whose passionate war making was in the service of another people and whose catastrophe was the fracture and loss of a different nation (although of course the problem was that its acreage was coextensive with the United States' claims to belonging). This is not to say that Black Hawk is the Native American Lincoln. Black Hawk was not martyred for his cause. The war that carries his name was disastrous for the Sauk, and it isn't clear if he was self-deluded or deluded by others into pursuing it. He didn't die with his people in the massacre that ended it, but he stayed safely away from the melee. It is difficult to understand why he chose to "dictate" his autobiography to a white interlocutor, and it is impossible to pin down, in that translated, edited, and rewritten "autobiography," what one might want to call his "voice." Black Hawk, in other words, slips away from the promises of biographical inquiry to the same degree that studies of Lincoln seem inexorably drawn to those same promises. But finding Black Hawk – a different leader, another war, another injustice, a different shattered sovereignty and devastated nation – shows us something other than the hard side of Lincoln, which is all Indians seem to be able to reveal about Lincoln in the histories and hagiographies (a vision of hard Lincoln that leads us right past Indians themselves and back to the "highest priorities" of national union). Rather, finding Black Hawk finally allows us to see something other than Lincoln. It should teach us that national union is founded on Indian land, and that the dead at Gettysburg repose in Indian land. When Lincoln rededicated the nation at Gettysburg, speaking "the words that remade America," as Wills puts it, he remade America on Indian land.[19] And he remade it not for the second time and not for the last time. It is a remaking – and a removal – that the United States ceaselessly reenacts on Indian bodies and Indian land and through Indian words.

At the site of the battle of Stillman's Run in Illinois, where twelve United States militiamen were killed in an encounter with Sauk warriors, there is a monument that was erected in 1901. The monument reads, "The presence of soldier, statesman, martyr, Abraham Lincoln assisting in the burial of these honored dead has made this spot more sacred."[20] More sacred than what? The monument surely intends to convey that Lincoln's presidency and martyrdom proleptically made the land more sacred than the interred soldiers could possibly make it on their own. This is not the lesson Lincoln teaches at Gettysburg, when he says that his words and our actions are not what sanctify the soil, but only the dead themselves. The writer of the inscription knows better. Only Lincoln can erase the stain of genocide – we need him to be benevolent for this reason, and it is for this reason that Indians disappear in his presence. The burial of common soldiers in the land cannot undo the scandal of genocide, but Lincoln buried these dead as he buried the dead at Gettysburg, and then he died for our sins. Abraham Lincoln makes "this spot" – and by extension perhaps all Sauk land, or even all Indian land, which is to say the whole United States, sacred soil.

The inscription makes it clear that we think back through Lincoln's assassinated body all the time, and that we read pre-Lincoln America through his wounds. But it is possible to think back through Lincoln to another body altogether, another country, another polity. It is possible to let go of Lincoln's singularity and his genius and his martyrdom that stopped time and started it up again in an eternal *anno domini* of national self-congratulation. It is possible to un-imagine the singularity, the mystical union, and the immortality of the United States. The land was *already* sacred. It *already* had governments by the people and for the people. It was *already* peopled with the sacred and sanctifying dead: "There is no place like that where the bones of our forefathers lie, to go to when in grief. Here the Great Spirit will take pity on us!"[21]

NOTES

1 John D. Bessler, *Legacy of Violence: Lynch Mobs and Executions in Minnesota* (Minneapolis: University of Minnesota Press, 2003), 62.
2 David A. Nichols, "Lincoln and the Indians," in Richard W. Etulain, ed., *Lincoln Looks West: From the Mississippi to the Pacific* (Carbondale: Southern Illinois University Press, 2010), 226.
3 Abraham Lincoln, "April 1, 1854 – Letter to Jesse Lincoln," in John George Nicolay and John Hay, eds., *Abraham Lincoln: Complete Works Volume 1* (New York: The Century Company, 1907), 177.
4 John Locke Scripps, *Life of Abraham Lincoln* (Bloomington: Indiana University Press, 1961), 24.
5 Isaac Newton Arnold, *The History of Abraham Lincoln and the Overthrow of Slavery* (Chicago: Clark and Company, 1866), 69.
6 Isaac Newton Arnold, *The Life of Abraham Lincoln* (Chicago: Jansen, McClurg and Company, 1884), 16.
7 Christopher Columbus Graham, "Dr. Graham's Statement," in Ida Minerva Tarbell and John McCan Davis, *The Early Life of Abraham Lincoln: Containing Many Unpublished Documents and Unpublished Reminiscences of Lincoln's Early Friends* (New York: S. S. McClure, 1896), 233–234.
8 See Robert Montgomery Bird, *Nick of the Woods* (Chicago: College and University Press, 1967).
9 Herman Melville, *The Confidence Man* (New York: Oxford University Press, 1999) 200–201.
10 John Marshall, "Cherokee Nation v. Georgia," in Francis Paul Prucha, ed., *Documents of United States Indian Policy* (Lincoln: University of Nebraska Press, 2000), 60.
11 Arnold, *The Life of Abraham Lincoln*, 17.
12 James Henry Lea, *The Ancestry of Abraham Lincoln* (New York: Houghton Mifflin Company, 1909), 82.
13 Graham, "Dr. Graham's Statement," 233.
14 Kendall Johnson, "Peace, Friendship, and Financial Panic: Reading the Mark of Black Hawk in Life of Ma-Ka-Tai-Me-She-Kia-Kiak," in *American Literary History* 19 (4) (Winter 2007), 781.
15 Cited in Johnson, "Peace, Friendship, and Financial Panic," 772–773.
16 Black Hawk, *Life of Black Hawk, or Ma-ka-tai-me-she-kia-kiak: Dictated by Himself* (New York: Penguin Classics, 2008), 61–62.
17 Abraham Lincoln, *The Life and Writings of Abraham Lincoln* (New York: Modern Library Classics), 787–788.
18 Black Hawk, *Life of Black Hawk*, 46.

19 Gary Wills, *Lincoln at Gettysburg: The Words that Remade America* (New York: Simon and Schuster Lincoln Library, 2006).

20 Cited in Ralph Geary, *Following in Lincoln's Footsteps: A Complete Annotated Reference to Hundreds of Historical Sites Visited by Abraham Lincoln* (New York: Basic Books, 2002), 173.

21 Black Hawk, *Life of Black Hawk*, 46.

7

DEAK NABERS

Abraham Lincoln and the Self-Governing Constitution

Abraham Lincoln unfolded his political career as a series of responses to threats to the very idea of democratic legitimacy in the United States. Crisis is the central narrative mode of his political discourse; American self-government itself inevitably lies in the balance. Even as early as 1838, in the first major address of his political career, Lincoln sensed "something of ill-omen amongst us," suggesting a serious threat to "the preservation of our political institutions" (1:28–29). This something would only grow more ominous in the years to come, through the tumultuous 1850s when the "divided" nation had reached a point where it could no longer "stand" to a Civil War that put into question whether "a constitutional republic, or a democracy" – "government of the people, for the people" – could survive. The terms feel more or less inevitable. Even when they have disputed Lincoln's accounts of its origins and its proper resolution, historians have long considered the antebellum sectional conflict a constitutional crisis, and they have addressed Lincoln's legal thinking accordingly, explicating it largely in terms of the environment of local political controversy that served as its most obvious immediate occasion.[1] Approaching Lincoln's legal thinking from the vantage of this environment can be slightly misleading, however, for the crises at the heart of his constitutional thought tend to be more fundamental and abstract than the terms of the specific debates in which he developed them. His legal imagination persistently honed on to difficulties he identified with the very idea of legal authority in democratic states, difficulties engaged by the sectional conflict over the status of slavery but nonetheless largely incidental to it. We might say that Lincoln was as troubled by the simple idea of democratic law as he was by any of the myriad of concrete constitutional questions slavery ignited throughout the 1850s and 1860s.

In his Special Message to Congress on July 4, 1861, for instance, Lincoln suggested that the secession crisis "presents" a fundamental "question" to the "whole family of man": "Must a government," especially a "constitutional republic, or a democracy," "of necessity, be too *strong* for the liberties of its own people, or too *weak* to maintain its own existence?" (2:250; emphasis added).[2] This tension obviously loomed large throughout the Civil War, when the exigencies of a full-scale military conflict seemed to reveal the nation's constitutional institutions as too weak and too strong by turns. "Many wondered during the conflict whether the Constitution would ... be a casualty of war," the legal historian Daniel Farber has explained. "Others must have questioned whether the Constitution would survive Lincoln's own efforts to save it."[3] But Lincoln's exposition of the question proceeded more or less without reference to the specific dilemmas he faced in confronting the secession crisis itself. "Of necessity," "whole family of man": At issue for him was not simply the survival of a particular nation so much as the very possibility of democratic government. He went on to ask what authorizes "government of the people, by the same people" (2:250) in a world in which "unanimity is impossible" (2:220)? What remains of democratic ideals once we acknowledge that the set of people administering the government and choosing its policies (by the people) will never be exactly the "same" as the set of people comprising the nation (of the people)? Lincoln insisted that self-government necessarily depends on the ability of majorities to "control" the "administration" of the government. Allowing the disapproval of "discontented individuals" or "domestic foes" to obstruct the functioning of the state would "practically put an end to free government upon the earth" (2:250). But as "government of the people, by the same people" becomes "government of the people, by *some* of those people" the moral force of democratic self-government loses a little of its luster. Lurking in any scheme of majoritarian democracy is the danger that nothing more than what Lincoln called "the mere force of numbers" would entitle a majority to administer the state (2:229, emphasis added; 2:119). The democratic state might become strong enough to govern only at the cost of its strongest claim to legitimacy.

In American constitutional discourse, the Constitution itself has generally been offered as a solution to this problem. Numbers do not empower a majority; the Constitution does, and it does so, at least in theory, in such a way so as to ensure that the majority's will cannot "deprive a minority," as Lincoln put the point, of any "vital" "right" (2:219). Farber offers a clear formulation of the basic idea: "If ... sovereignty resides in a society's 'supreme, irresistible, absolute, uncontrolled authority,' no government in America since 1789 has ever fit this description. All units of government are subject to the Constitution."[4] As the very phrase "subject to the Constitution" might imply, however, the turn from numerical majorities to constitutional frameworks can itself seem somewhat awkward if the ultimate goal is "government of the people, by the people." Although Lincoln would not go so far as the novelist Lydia Maria Child in worrying that "wholesale lauding of the Constitution has made it an object of idol worship" rather than the vehicle of democratic expression,[5] he was carefully attentive to the prospect that an excessive veneration of the Constitution could involve our substituting ancestor-government for self-government. "Now, and here, let me guard a little against being misunderstood" (2:119), he paused to explain at the Cooper Union in February 1860, in the midst of his most detailed effort to reconcile the Republican free-soil antislavery agenda with "the frame of Government under which we live," "the Constitution of the United States" (2:111). "I do not mean to say that we are bound to follow implicitly in whatever our fathers did" (2:119).

The point was especially pressing with respect to the particular set of political controversies that gave rise to most of Lincoln's constitutional thinking. "Between the black race and its freedom," observed Frederick Douglass, "the constitution is always interposed. It always is."[6] Interposed: The authority of the Constitution summons the looming specter of the mediating interpretive powers of the courts as well as the persistent claims of previous generations. Given that "whatever our fathers did" with respect to slavery had hardly undermined the peculiar institution, the "frame" they had left behind was readily adaptable to mid-nineteenth-century proslavery judicial initiative. Even if many antislavery activists and thinkers, including Douglass himself, ultimately would have concluded that emancipation was wholly compatible with the "idol worshipped" Constitution, the likely decisions of the Supreme Court under its conservative Chief Justice Roger Taney ensured that there would always remain a palpable tension between the most vigorous forms of constitutional fealty in antebellum America and democratic projects devoted to the cause of African-American freedom.[7] But the problem could not be confined to Taney's personal intransigence on the issue of slavery. The "candid citizen must confess," Lincoln explained in his First Inaugural Address, "that if the policy of the government ... is to be irrevocably fixed by decisions of the Supreme Court ... the people will have ceased, to be their own rulers." (2:221).

Lincoln's account of "the only true sovereign of a free people" could thus give "constitutional checks and limitations" only a decidedly subordinate role: So far as democratic sovereign legitimacy is concerned, constitutions are hardly better than mere numbers. "A majority," Lincoln claimed in his First Inaugural Address, "held in restraint by constitutional checks and limitations, and always changing easily, with deliberate changes of popular opinions and sentiments, is the only sovereign of a free people. Whoever rejects it, does, of necessity, fly to anarchy or to despotism" (2:220). The phrases go by so quickly that it is easy to overlook how much they leave unanswered. How is the majority held in restraint? Who determines the nature and scope of the constitutional checks and limitations? Who enforces them? What is a deliberate change "of popular opinions and sentiments," and how does it differ from a nondeliberate one? What does it mean for a majority to change easily? The pressure of these questions and others like them determines the contours of Lincoln's constitutional thinking. At the core of all of his major constitutional claims is a relentless effort to reconcile American self-government with American constitutionalism, to present a framework within which constitutional checks and limitations could result from democratic practice as well as restrain it. The task is daunting, and we will see that the vagueness on offer here is not entirely accidental: In Lincoln's hands concrete institutional frameworks almost inevitably came to threaten the integrity of the majorities they empowered and organized.[8] The result was a scheme in which both the Constitution and the institutions authorized within its domain took on such dynamic roles as to stretch the idea of constitutionalism itself almost to its breaking point.

"Let us re-adopt the Declaration of Independence," Lincoln suggested in 1854, "and with it, the practices, and policy, which harmonize with it.... If we do this, we shall not only have saved the Union; but we shall have so saved it, as to make, and to keep it, forever worthy of the saving" (1:340). When one "readopts the Declaration of Independence" is he reaffirming the old nation or starting a new one? And when one "so saves" a nation "as to make it worth saving" has he preserved that nation or transformed it? Lincoln's great project, as a legal theorist and as a political agent, was to reconcile these two possibilities – to produce a framework within which the Constitution could be saved and reformulated in a single gesture, a framework within which the Constitution could stem from popular will even as it governed its expression. We will be able to understand the structure and design of this framework only after we first register how seriously Lincoln took the opposition, between legal institutional authority and popular sentiment, it would be asked to reconcile.

The "House Divided" (1858) speech famously began by announcing that American slavery stood at a crossroads: "Either the *opponents* of slavery, will arrest the further spread of it, and place it where the public mind shall rest in the belief that it is in the course of ultimate extinction; or its *advocates* will push it forward, till it shall become alike lawful in *all* the States, *old* as well as *new* – *North* as well as *South*" (1:426). The formal symmetry implied by scenario on offer here sits awkwardly with the conspicuously asymmetrical terms in which Lincoln conjures these two possible futures. Our choice is not between slavery's becoming "alike lawful in *all* States" and its becoming alike unlawful in all of them; it is rather between complete institutional and legal acquiescence to slavery on the one hand and some vague public confidence that slavery's course tends toward "ultimate extinction" on the other. Insofar as it allowed Lincoln to claim that "the chief and real purpose of the Republican party is eminently conservative" (2:35) and to disown any inclination to "interfere" with slavery in any state where it already existed (1:603), this emphasis was no doubt good politics in late 1850s Illinois. However, we should nonetheless note how little Lincoln's agenda demands. The cause of liberty does not require that we eliminate slavery. It only asks that slavery be "placed" on course to that result – a result of our choosing, perhaps, but not exactly of our enterprise; we are dealing with extinction, not murder, as Lincoln would sometimes make clear by emphasizing that the extinction he had in mind would be thoroughly "peaceable" and that it would come only "in God's good time" (1:582).[9] The process is not entirely removed from a specific political project, but if Lincoln claimed the result would follow from "restricting" slavery to "the limits it has already covered" (1:603), he certainly was not eager to specify exactly how it would so follow. His oft-repeated phrases about public minds and ultimate extinction seem designed to obscure the workings of what Stephen Douglas called "the policy by which this would be done" (1:752) rather than clarify them. By the end of their famous series of debates, Douglas was moved to exasperation. Lincoln "says that he is not now and never was in favor of interfering with slavery where it exists in the States," Douglas acknowledged. "Well, if he is not in favor of that, how does he expect to bring slavery in a course of ultimate extinction?" (1:752). Douglas's half-mocking suggestion that Lincoln's strategy must revolve around the eventual starvation of African Americans only reinforced his contention that his opponent's real policy amounted to nothing more than agitation. "Why he will agitate, and he will induce the North to agitate until the South shall be worried out, and forced to abolish slavery" (1:753).

The problem here was not simply that Lincoln was generally unwilling to explain how the policy of restricting the spread of slavery would lead to the goal of abolishing the institution; it was also that the restriction of slavery's territorial expansion was not really a policy in the first instance for Lincoln. Other Republicans could make this policy look quite aggressive. But Lincoln would take none of Charles Sumner's palpable delight in the prospect of a confined slavery's dying "as a poisoned rat dies of rage in its hole."[10] The hole in which he sought to place slavery was, after all, a good bit more virtual than Sumner's vivid metaphor would suggest. To Douglas's amazement, Lincoln would not rule out supporting the admission of future slave states into the Union. At least so far as he understood it, "the admission of a single

Slave State" would not necessarily be a problem, as it would not "permanently fix the character and establish this as a universal slave nation" (1:576). Lincoln's antislavery project thus involved a national "character" only partially indexed to the nation's actual legal institutions. We can hardly fail to note in this context that Lincoln's oft-repeated credo looked to the status of "the public mind" as much as the "place" of slavery, and that, indeed, its interest in the public mind superseded its interest in slavery's actual posture: "Place it where the public mind shall rest in the belief that it is in the course of ultimate extinction." Slavery's place achieved its significance here only in its relation to the public mind, whose status was in turn given a value independent of the conditions it might seem to assess. The public would not rest in the certainty, or even in the confidence, that slavery was headed toward extinction; it would rather rest only in such a "belief." Nor was it by any means certain, even on Lincoln's terms themselves, that this belief would be well founded. Lincoln routinely announced that his only goal was to restore the institution of slavery to "the original basis – the basis on which our fathers placed it" (1:515). But how well exactly did that original setup restrict the growth of slavery? If slavery was in the course of its ultimate extinction until the passage of the Kansas-Nebraska Act in 1854, when a "new era" was "introduced in the history of the Republic, which tended to the spread and perpetuation of slavery" (1:574), it was dying a very peculiar death. Lincoln was adamant that "the public mind *did* rest in the belief that it was in the course of ultimate extinction" (1:514). But who in 1859 would see slavery's course over the first eighty years of the nation's life as tending toward an ultimate extinction? Evidently the public could rest in the belief that slavery was on the course of its disappearance without its actually following such a path – which gives new meaning to the famous quip in the "House Divided" speech that "we shall *lie down* pleasantly dreaming that the people of *Missouri* are on the verge of making their State *free*; and we shall *awake* to the *reality*, instead, that the *Supreme* Court has made *Illinois* a *slave* State" (1:432).

If that meaning was not lost on Douglas, who often observed that the peculiar institution had hardly suffered on its original constitutional basis, it was entirely lost on Lincoln himself. Remarkably, for all of his paranoia about the potential advances of slavery, Lincoln evinced little anxiety on this particular front. Throughout the 1850s he remained steadfast in the belief that in "the way our fathers originally left the slavery question, the institution was in the course of ultimate extinction" and in the belief that slavery "no doubt ... *would* become extinct, for all times to come, if we but re-adopted the policy of the fathers by restricting it to the limits it has already covered – restricting it from the new Territories" (1:603). Lincoln's confidence hinged on a somewhat unexpected understanding of slavery's "position" in 1789, of the "basis" on which it stood when subject to a "policy ... restricting it to the limits it [had] already covered."

> I was glad to express my gratitude at Quincy, and I re-express it here to Judge Douglas – *that he looks to no end of the institution of slavery*. That will help the people to see where the struggle really is. It will hereafter place us with all men who really do wish that the wrong may have an end. And whenever we can get rid of the fog which obscures the real question – when we can get Judge Douglas and his friends to avow a policy looking to its perpetuation – we can get out from among them that class of men and bring them to the side of those who treat it as a wrong. Then there will soon be an end of it, and that end will be its "ultimate extinction." Whenever the issue can be distinctly made, and all extraneous matter thrown out so that men can fairly see the real difference between the parties, this controversy will soon be settled, and it will be done peaceably too. There will be no war, no violence. (1:811)

When slavery's "end" finally emerged on the horizon, it was strangely detached from the territorial policy that was supposed to occasion it, detached indeed from any policy whatsoever. It stemmed from aspiration rather than application, from the simple amassing of a political coalition around a moral judgment rather than the implementation of any political program: A great deal hinged on the mere "wish" that slavery would end. Treating slavery as wrong has virtually emerged as its own policy; the "basis that our fathers originally placed it upon" is a basis of stigma as much as limitation. By Lincoln's autumn 1859 address at Columbus, this transformation would become explicit, the fathers' "basis" and "policy" simply a "tone": "[The Republican Party] proposes nothing save and except to restore this government to its original tone in regard to this element of slavery, and there to maintain it" (2:35).[11] "*As those fathers marked it, so let it be again marked,*" he claimed at the Cooper Union the next February, "*as an evil not to be extended, but to be tolerated and protected only because of and so far as its actual presence among us makes that toleration and protection a necessity*" (2:120). The policy so closely follows the judgment here that it is hard not to conclude that the policy simply *is* the judgment. Legislation preventing the spread of slavery morphed into a symbolic condemnation of slavery: "seal of legislation *against its spread*" (1:514). Rather than sealing slavery from new territories, legislation now simply marked it for disapproval. If the "framers of the Constitution ... found the institution existing among us, and they left it as they found it," Lincoln noted, they also "left this institution with many clear marks of disapprobation upon it" (1:802). The new era inaugurated in 1854 hinged less on a new territorial policy than an observable changing of the original tone, a definitive indication that these seals and marks had faded over time.[12] The antislavery cause emerging in response to that era "must be intrusted to, and conducted by" its own "undoubted friends" "who *do care* for the result" (1:434) precisely because caring for the result is more or less all that comprised its agenda.

Douglas was not altogether wrong, then, in maintaining that Lincoln expected to "worry" slavery "out" of the South, although the interest of Lincoln's position has much less to do with the persistence of protest in his schema than in the absence of government from it. For all of his emphasis on the importance of public judgment, the end goal here, at least as Lincoln tells it, was "rest" rather than agitation. And even if this quasi-magical thinking that distilled emancipation from nothing more than public sentiment reeks of political opportunism, especially in light of the real "war" and "violence" emancipation would ultimately require, this line of argument had theoretical benefits to match its practical ones. For in occasionally obscuring the logistical difficulties of effecting emancipation, Lincoln was also exempting slavery's extinction from the problems of democratic legitimacy. In transforming the majority's will into the nation's destiny, public sentiment allowed Lincoln to retain a vision of democracy so pure that even the institutions of the state – electoral, constitutional, legislative, administrative – might count as obstacles to self-government.

Actual governmental action was hardly any more central to Lincoln's sense of the proslavery cause than it was to his visions of slavery's ultimate extinction. Although he was happy to marshal a case in the "House Divided" speech for a grand conspiracy designed to nationalize slavery, Lincoln's emphasis more routinely fell on liberty's vulnerability than its enemies' cunning. Nothing was more common in his writing from the late 1850s than a persistent concern about the state of public moral judgment. His critiques of popular sovereignty and its leading spokesperson mirror his celebration of free-soil emancipation. Douglas claimed that his career was based on the "grand principle" that the people of every sovereign entity should be left, in Douglas's own terms, "to decide for themselves" (1:601) whether to exclude or allow slavery "without interference, direct or indirect" (1:603). Yet Lincoln considered the Little Giant "the best" imaginable "instrument" for "making the institution of Slavery national" (1:717). Douglas's work assumed such a sinister hue because Lincoln assessed it in a frame of reference in which tone and policy were virtually indistinguishable from one another. Insofar as the senator had done "all in his power to reduce to the whole question of slavery to one of a mere *right of property*" (1:433), he had systematically undermined what Lincoln considered the only possible basis for liberty. "What constitutes the bulwark of our own liberty and independence?" Lincoln asked at the close of his reply to Douglas in the first debate at Ottawa. "It is not our frowning battlements, our bristling sea coasts, the guns of our war steamers, or the strength of our gallant and disciplined army." All of these "may be turned against our liberties, without making us stronger or weaker for the struggle," as might even those legal institutions generally associated with liberty. Instead, "our reliance is in the *love of liberty* which God has planted in our bosoms" (1:585). Douglas's championing of a policy of states' rights was of little use when he also advanced an ideology within which that love would not thrive. "If ... he shall succeed in moulding public sentiment to a perfect accordance with his own, what barrier will be left against slavery being made lawful everywhere?" (1:493–494).

Removing barriers to slavery's becoming universal, of course, is not quite the same as universalizing slavery; Lincoln acknowledged in the same breath that he identified Douglas as slavery's "best" and "most ingenious" "instrument" that "I do not charge that he means it so" (1:717). But Lincoln's investment in public sentiment was so great that he considered the remaining work nothing more than a "formality" (1:527) – both in the sense that it seemed to involve little initiative and in the sense that it merely made visible the results of a project already carried out on other terms. "Then what is necessary for the nationalization of slavery?" he asked at Ottawa. "It is simply the next Dred Scott decision.... When that is decided and acquiesced in, the whole thing is done" (1:524). The point here is not simply that Lincoln clearly thought this "next Dred Scott" decision less important than the work Douglas might do in "moulding public sentiment." It is rather that public sentiment did even the work of the decision. "The whole thing [was] done" when the case was decided "and acquiesced in," not simply when the Court announced its opinion. Legal policy is quite literally now a function of the status of the nation's moral lights. The technical policy questions that lead Douglas to his joking speculations about slave starvation did not emerge for Lincoln precisely because their resolution was simply assumed within the sentimental and moral framework in which he meant to cast his argument. "The whole thing is done": The politics of public sentiment effectively dissolve any interest in the process of political change.

"In this and like communities," Lincoln had noted earlier at Ottawa, "public sentiment is everything.... [It] makes statutes and decisions possible or impossible to be executed" (1:524–525). This emphasis on the execution of statutes and decisions, as opposed to their validity, might suggest that Lincoln understood the legal significance of public sentiment in largely practical terms: Whatever its technical legal standing, any given legal initiative, be it a law or a judicial decision, will have force only to the extent of its broader public acceptance. Public sentiment would matter chiefly as a prerequisite of political efficacy. Lincoln advanced versions of this point throughout his career, sometimes even going so far as to underscore the essentially logistical significance of public sentiment by pointedly refusing to assess the ethical standing of various "universal feelings" (1:316).[13] But the interaction between public sentiment and legal authority in Lincoln's thinking was more complicated than such sequences might imply. He often insisted that the categories are mutually constitutive as well as functionally codependent. Lincoln's claims about the importance of public sentiment were almost always pegged to the particular problems of governance in "this and like communities": "We know that in a Government like this, ... a Government of the people, where the voice of all men in the country, substantially enter into the execution, – or administration rather – of the Government – in such a Government, what lies in at the bottom of all of it, is public opinion" (2:63). Needless to say, public opinion will assert considerable practical influence if the public itself ("all the men in the country") must "substantially enter into the execution" and "administration" of the government. But public opinion will also bear substantial *normative* weight in any "government of the people" in the democratic, as opposed to administrative, sense in which Lincoln tended to use the phrase. When the government depends on "the voice of all men in the country" as well as their labor and talents, public opinion secures the state's authority as well as its functionality; it legitimates legal regimes as well as enables them.

Lincoln took this point seriously enough to follow it to extreme ends. Discussing his commitment to "maintaining the government" even for a succeeding administration bent on terminating the Civil War without reuniting the nation, Lincoln told a group of serenaders on October 19, 1864,

> This is due to the people both on principle, and under the constitution. Their will, constitutionally expressed, is the ultimate law for all. If they should deliberately resolve to have immediate peace even at the loss of their country, and their liberty, I know not the power or the right to resist them. It is their own business, and they must do as they please with their own. (2:635–636)

The interest here surrounds the phrase "constitutionally expressed," by which Lincoln no doubt meant to refer to the role specifically granted to elections under the Constitution: Elections formalize the people's sentiments into a constitutionally valid will.[14] The rest of the sequence, however, raises a number of questions about how the 1864 election would actually perform this function. Regular readers of Lincoln's public pronouncements might well have wondered whether the drive for "immediate peace even at the loss of their country" could have any valid "constitutional expression," and they would certainly have wondered whether an ordinary election would be the proper vehicle for such a project. Given that Lincoln had long been committed to the idea that "in contemplation of universal law, and of the Constitution, the Union of these States is perpetual" (2:217), the expression of the people's will along these lines would seem to be constitutionally questionable, whether or not it arose from a constitutionally valid election. Although Lincoln acknowledged that "this country, with its institutions, belongs to the people who inhabit it," he was quick to add that any changes so radical as the prospect on offer in this account of the stakes of the presidential election of 1864 would require extraordinary public ratification: "Whenever they shall grow weary of the existing government, they can exercise their *constitutional* right of amending it, or their *revolutionary* right to dismember, or overthrow it" (2:222). As a practical matter, to be sure, Lincoln would have had little recourse against a popular impulse "to dismember, or overthrow" the government by way of a regular election in 1864. But his comments gave the people not only the power to lose their country in this way but also right to do so: "It is their own business, and they must do as they please with their own." If the people's will threatens to supersede the Constitution here, it does so largely by becoming the Constitution; constitutionally expressed in this manner, the public's resolve determines both the Constitution's fate and its form.

Such a nebulous boundary between public sentiment and constitutional authority attended almost all Lincoln's constitutional pronouncements. Even when he most directly referred to the text Constitution and the circumstances of its composition and ratification, he carefully blurred the boundaries between the legal instrument and popular will. "What is the frame of Government under which we live?" Lincoln asked at Cooper Union.

> The answer must be: "The Constitution of the United States." ... Who were our fathers that framed the Constitution? I suppose the "thirty-nine" who signed the original instrument may be fairly called our fathers who framed that part of the present Government. It is almost exactly true to say they framed it, and it is altogether true to say they fairly represented the opinion and sentiment of the whole nation at that time. (2:111)

For such an uncontroversial identification of the nation's founding fathers, the sequence is amazingly hesitant. Lincoln began by evincing at least a modest reluctance to assent to the Constitution as the frame of our government – his begrudging "must be" hinted that isolating any particular framing instrument might move the frame further from "the people" than he would like. He then carefully, and pointedly, unwound his ambivalence through three discrete stages. Those who signed may only "be fairly called our fathers who framed that part of the Government"; but "it is almost exactly true" that they framed the document; and it is "altogether true" to say that they "represented the opinion and sentiment of the whole nation at that time." If these equivocations feel slightly arbitrary, they nonetheless drive home a clear rhetorical effect: The further we move from the personal paternal authority of these historical personages to the broader public sentiment they may or may not have represented, the closer we approach "true" legitimacy.[15] Lincoln continued to push along this course throughout the first half of the speech until he assimilated this group of thirty-nine not only into "the whole nation at that time" but also the set of "all other living men within century in which it [the Constitution] was framed" (2:119).[16] The invocation of the founders' frame merely steers us back to the population as whole.

This interarticulation of legal frame and popular also laid at the heart Lincoln's extremely complicated wrangling with the Dred Scott decision. Insofar as Taney's opinion concluded that Congress lacked the authority to regulate slavery in the territories, it obviously stood as a major obstacle to the realization of Republican free-soil aspirations. But if Lincoln led his party in making "war" (1:597) on the decision, as Douglas would put it, his campaign involved a good deal more than a simple refutation of Taney's opinion. In his June 1857 speech on the case in Springfield, Lincoln contended that the political authority of judicial decisions derived from their uses: Judges settle disputes (they "absolutely determine the case decided"), and they provide expectations as to how future disputes might be settled ("indicate to the public how other similar cases will be decided when they arise"). In a striking anticipation of the claim later advanced in Oliver Wendell Holmes's classic essay, "The Path of Law" (1897), Lincoln traced legal authority not to the statements of judges but rather to the course of development those statements imply. The upshot is to immerse the Court within a complicated extralegal process of lawmaking, in which the relevant question is not how the courts have decided a given issue but rather how much deference their treatment of the issue has received in a broader political environment. Lincoln said that "judicial decisions are of greater or less authority as precedents, according to circumstances." Lincoln claimed to believe "as much as Judge Douglas" "in obedience to, and respect for, the judicial department of government," but his ultimate loyalty was less to that department than the broader process in which its decisions received ultimate ratification. "We think its decisions on Constitutional questions, when fully settled, should control, not only the cases decided, but the general policy of the country" (1:392).

Given that Lincoln thought that the Dred Scott decision was "erroneous," that it reflected "partisan bias," and that it was "based on assumed historical facts which are not really true" (1:393), one can easily see why Douglas would conclude that Lincoln considered the constitutional issues at stake "unsettled" simply because he disagreed with Taney's resolution of them. However, Lincoln's criteria for judicial settlement were not limited to the terms of legal argumentation: He also cared about "legal public expectation," the "steady practice of the departments throughout our history," and regular affirmation and reaffirmation "through a course of years" (1:393). He wanted to invoke something like a legal culture, not to castigate the court simply for reaching the wrong conclusion about a particular constitutional topic.[17] In maintaining that Taney's decision became "binding" on "every good citizen" simply by virtue of its having been delivered by the "highest judicial tribunal in the world" (1:597), Douglas countered this kind of thinking by insisting that the Court should not been seen as participating in the legal culture so much as determining it. Even he tended to approach the Dred Scott decision in terms of its prospects as a rule of political action rather than its status as a binding authority: "Judge Taney expressly lays down the doctrine. I receive it as law" (1:600). The route from Taney's opinion to "the law of the land" involved something more than his simply delivering that opinion as the Chief Justice of the Supreme Court. Taney's "doctrine" became "law" in Douglas' acceptance ("I receive it").[18] This is why it made sense for Lincoln to emphasize the "extraordinary tenacity" with which Douglas "espouses the decision, and denounces all opposition to it" (1:492). At issue in his debate with Douglas was less how much authority any given legal opinion should receive as a matter of general judicial deference than how much authority Douglas and others could attach to Taney's doctrine in the realm of public opinion. "The sacredness that Judge Douglas throws around this decision," Lincoln remarked in Chicago shortly before the run of debates, "is a degree of sacredness that has never before been thrown around any other decision" (1:451).[19] If Douglas was in some sense right that Lincoln meant to "appeal from the Supreme Court to every town meeting" (1:728), Lincoln would respond that Taney's opinion could not assume decisive political authority by any other process: The Little Giant's very expressions of judicial fealty constituted the same basic appeal.

The removal of constitutional arguments from the courthouse to the town meeting substantially changed the terms in which they would be conducted. It mattered intensely to Lincoln that Taney's opinion was mistaken as a matter of textual interpretation and historical understanding, but he did not let the fact that it was mistaken count, in and of itself, as a reason for rejecting it. Controversies over "questions" unanswered by "express provisions" in the Constitution do not produce answers; they produce "majorities and minorities" (2:220). They are consequently resolved less at the level of constitutional argument than that of public sentiment, which comes to inform, and indeed determine, the resolution of even those constitutional questions on which Lincoln had well-formed and deeply held views. In a remarkable sequence in his July 4, 1861, Special Message to Congress, for instance, Lincoln maintained that the outcome of the war would settle the question of secession's constitutionality: "What is now combated, is the position that secession is *consistent* with the Constitution – is *lawful*, and *peaceful*" (2:257). The suggestion that combat would somehow reveal whether secession was "peaceful" comes right out of *Catch-22*, of course, but it is in some respects the least surprising feature of this sentence. Only moments before, Lincoln had pilloried the idea "that any state of the Union may, *consistently* with the national Constitution, and therefore *lawfully*, and *peacefully*, withdraw from the Union, without the consent of the Union, or of any other state" as nothing more than "an ingenious sophism" spread by traitors in an "insidious debauching of the public mind" (2:254–255). Now that position is somehow merely under review, and under a review that would seem to have nothing whatsoever to do with the legal merits of the claim. If elections at least constitute a recognized mode for constitutional self-determination, battle would seem another matter entirely. War cannot provide a meaningful *legal* resolution to any dispute, and in this case Lincoln seems to have thought that there was not even a reasonable legal controversy to begin with. Such considerations inevitably lose their force, however, as we move from the realm of constitutional interpretation to the arena of constitutional resolution. Legal niceties aside, the outcome of the combat certainly set the constitutional norms under which the nation proceeded in the wake of battle; it thereby settled the issue of secession. The jarring contrast between the two moments in the speech merely marks the potential tension between the Constitution as a legal text and the Constitution as a frame of sentimental culture.

Lincoln organized his presidency around the project of keeping these two constitutions in alignment, of making the case for his account of the Union while winning the war that would authorize that case. In this sense his duty would always derive from two sources simultaneously – from the Constitution's specific legal framework and from the broader cultural setting in which that framework would be established in actual practice. Lincoln allowed that the "Constitution expressly enjoin[ed] upon" him a "duty" to combat secession (2:218), but his most emphatic accounts of his wartime obligations trace them to the slightly more capacious duty of preventing "free government" (2:250) from "perishing from the earth." (2:536). Lincoln's immense rhetorical skill frequently allowed him somehow to make the enterprise of his preserving "free government" for "the whole family of man" (2:250) look identical with that of his carrying out "what the Constitution expressly enjoins me." But given the range of influences filtered into Lincoln's sense of duty, we might well wonder whether there was anything more than mystification at work here. What endows the view on offer in the Gettysburg Address with a specifically constitutional purchase? Lincoln's Constitution can often seem so elastic that it appears as nothing more than the name he gave to any given moment's prevailing agenda. In what sense do we have a Constitution at all if its meaning can be determined by combat or by a regular election?

I am not sure that Lincoln had a theoretically sound answer to these questions, but I think he did have an explanation of how even so tenuous a construction as his Constitution can survive the various forms of combat that surround and inform it. The key can be found in the striking significance of oaths in his constitutional thinking. He opened his First Inaugural Address by attributing his appearance before Congress to "compliance with a custom as old as the government itself," namely that the president "take, in your presence," "the oath prescribed by the Constitution" (2:215). It was altogether fitting that he foreground the role of the oath as he assumed his office. His political career had begun with a speech in which he had effectively recommended that the nation as a whole participate in a similar custom. The call in his 1838 Lyceum Address for "*political religion*" comprised of "reverence for the laws" (1:32) amounted to a demand that "every American" "swear by the blood of the Revolution, never to violate in the least particular, the laws of the country; and never to tolerate their violation by others" (1:32). If the point here was to ensure what Farber plainly calls "the rule of law," Lincoln was not pursuing it simply by requesting "obedience" (1:177). His focus was not on the citizen's compliance with given regulations so much as her disposition toward legality. The force of the distinction, of course, is to replace a sense of the law as a set of commands with the set of the law as a set of practices, to replace legal deference with legal participation.[20]

What governs in a world of oaths is a legal regime, not a legal code – note, for instance, that Lincoln did not, and could not exactly, propose a law commanding his political religion; and also note that although Lincoln took the oath prescribed in the Constitution at the beginning of the First Inaugural Address, he placed the occasion under the banner of custom, not a provision of positive law. Within the oath's regime, differences of the kind that produce majorities and minorities get subsumed within a shared commitment to the enterprise in which those differences surface and become salient. Consider, for instance, the closing lines of Lincoln's First Inaugural

Address, which explicitly peg their appeal to national solidarity to Lincoln's constitutional oath:

> In *your* hands, my dissatisfied fellow countrymen, and not in *mine*, is the momentous issue of civil war. The government will not assail *you*. You can have no conflict, without being yourselves the aggressors. *You* have no oath registered in Heaven to destroy the government, while *I* shall have the most solemn one to "preserve, protect and defend" it.
>
> I am loath to close. We are not enemies, but friends. We must not be enemies. Though passion may have strained, it must not break the bonds of affection. The mystic chords of memory, stretching from every battle-field, and patriot grave, to every living heart and hearthstone, all over this broad land, will yet swell the chorus of the Union, when again touched, as they surely will be, by the better angels of our nature. (2:223–224)

At first glance it might be hard to see, at least in practical terms, how Lincoln's oath would offer Southerners much comfort. Preserving, protecting, and defending the government, at least as he understood that government, are not alternatives to the "conflict" in question in 1861; they would in fact almost inevitably entail it. But for Lincoln the oath effaces this difference rather than focusing it. It invokes a form of solidarity so powerful as to render any conflict simply a momentary disagreement. The appeal here is pointedly not to legal requirement or duty: Lincoln did not remind the Southerners that they were bound by the Constitution. Instead, he deployed the Constitution as way of activating a set of cultural forms that actually supersede it in his hierarchy of values – "friends," "bonds of affections," "affection," "mystic chords of memory."

If this gesture depends on the notion that the Constitution might command a greater loyalty than any of the particular governments assembled under it, it does not exactly depend on loyalty to the Constitution as a legal text. It depends rather on loyalty to the very idea of constitutional loyalty. The appeal to the constitutional values summoned at the end of Lincoln's First Inaugural Address quite literally could have come at the expense of recognized constitutional provisions. In his Special Message of July 4, 1861, for instance, Lincoln would go so far as to insist that his oath, properly interpreted, could oblige him *not* to comply with the Constitution's habeas corpus provisions: "To state the question more directly, are all the laws, *but one*, to go unexecuted, and the government itself go to pieces, lest that one be violated? Even in such a case, would not the official oath be broken, if the government should be overthrown, when it was believed that this question was presented" (2:253)? Within this schema the Constitution would be governed by public sentiment and local contingency as it in turn governed them. The convenient upshot is that the oath defused the conflict between Lincoln and his adversaries even as it rewrote his side of the disagreement as Constitutional necessity. It allowed Lincoln's readoption of the Declaration of Independence to count both as a transformation of the nation and a saving of it. It made his military suppression of secession the gesture of the nation rather than a partisan one, and it made his military emancipation of slaves an expression of constitutional necessity rather than executive authority. We are by no means obliged to enter into this logic with Lincoln. We can always hold his actions up against a text rather than against a context, as of course many people did throughout his political career and as even more have done since. But we will not understand Lincoln's Constitution unless we recognize that it worked as an enterprise, not a set of regulations, and that it thrived on engagement, not obedience. Moreover, it is a tribute to the power of his vision that, whatever problems it may have posed for traditional accounts of the Constitution, the constitutional crisis of the mid-nineteenth century seems ultimately to have reaffirmed the centrality of the Constitution to American civic life rather than undermined it.[21]

NOTES

1 See, for instance, Mark A. Graber, *"Dred Scott" and the Problem of Constitutional Evil* (Cambridge: Cambridge University Press, 2008), and Don E. Fehrenbacher, *The "Dred Scott" Case: Its Significance in American Law and Politics* (New York: Oxford University Press, 1978).

2 All quotations from Abraham Lincoln and from the Lincoln-Douglas debates come from Abraham Lincoln, *Speeches and Writings, 1832–1865*, 2 vols., Don E. Fehrenbacher, ed. (New York: Library of America, 1989). In-text citations denote volume and page number from *Speeches and Writings*.

3 Daniel Farber, *Lincoln's Constitution* (Chicago: University of Chicago Press, 2003), 7–8. See also J. G. Randall, *Constitutional Problems Under Lincoln* (1926; rev. ed., Champaign: University of Illinois, 1964), Farber, *Lincoln's Constitution*; Mark E. Neely, Jr., *The Fate of Liberty: Abraham Lincoln and Civil Liberties* (New York: Oxford University Press, 1992); and Graber, *"Dred Scott" and the Problem of Constitutional Evil*.

4 Farber, *Lincoln's Constitution*, 29.

5 Quoted in Michael Vorenberg, *Final Freedom: The Civil War, the Abolition of Slavery, and the Thirteenth Amendment* (Cambridge: Cambridge University Press, 2001), 30.

6 Quoted in Vorenberg, *Final Freedom*, 35.

7 Several Democrats suggested that antislavery and pro-civil rights amendments would "invest the amending power," as Senator Garrett Davis put the point, "with a faculty of destroying and revolutionizing the whole government" (Vorenberg, *Final Freedom*, 107).

8 The foundational texts in this field are Edward S. Corwin, *The Doctrine of Judicial Review: Its Legal and Historical Basis* (Princeton: Princeton University Press,

1914), and Charles Grove Haines, *The American Doctrine of Judicial Supremacy* (New York: Macmillan, 1914).

9   Lincoln stated, "I think Slavery is wrong, morally, and politically. I desire that it should be no further spread in these United States, and I should not object if it should gradually terminate in the whole Union" (*Speeches and Writings*, 2:62).

10 Quoted in Vorenberg, *Final Freedom*, 73.

11 Lincoln regularly transforms fixing slavery within its current limits into fixing the idea in "the public mind" (2:57) that slavery should and will end.

12 Lincoln noted that Taney's reasoning in the Dred Scott case hinged on his inability to see this "very important change" "in the public mind" (2:57).

13 With respect to the possibility that African Americans might be made "political and socially, our equals," Lincoln explained in his condemnation of the Kansas-Nebraska Act in 1854, "My own feelings will not admit of this; and if mine would, we well know that those of the great mass of white people will not."

14 Throughout the Civil War Lincoln would maintain that regular elections were a constitutional "necessity" (2:641; cf. 2:431–433).

15 Lincoln sought to relocate "the frame" of our government from a specific text to a broader set of beliefs.

16 Lincoln disclaims the idea "that we are bound to follow implicitly in whatever our fathers did" (2:119).

17 Lincoln resisted the decision's taking on the status of what he called a "rule of political action."

18 Even when Douglas looks most deferential, his remarks emphasize *his* deference as much as the *Court's* authority.

19 Lincoln's argument effectively counts as an early version of Whittington's more recent claim that "Judicial supremacy itself rests on political foundations" (Keith Whittington, *Political Foundations of Judicial Supremacy: The Presidency, The Supreme Court, and Constitutional Leadership in U.S. History* (Princeton: Princeton University Press, 2007: 9).

20 Douglas had sought to reconcile Dred Scott's prohibition of congressional interference with slavery in the territories with his popular sovereignty.

21 On the issue of constitutional failure, see Mark E. Brandon, *Free in the World: American Slavery and Constitutional Failure* (Princeton: Princeton University Press, 1998).

8

HAROLD K. BUSH, JR.

Abraham Lincoln and Spiritual Crisis

On December 13, 1862, thousands of Union troops were ordered to cross a temporary bridge over the Rappahannock River and into the town of Fredericksburg, Virginia. Almost 13,000 soldiers died in that slaughter, which many observers considered a suicide mission. George Whitman was injured at Fredericksburg and stated that the battle "was lost in my opinion solely through incompetent generalship"; his brother Walt called it "the most complete piece of mismanagement perhaps ever yet known in the earth's wars."[1] Oliver Wendell Holmes, later to become Justice of the United States Supreme Court, was a soldier in a regiment that lost forty-eight men at Fredericksburg: "I firmly believe ... that the men who ordered the crossing of the river are responsible to God for murder."[2] Those orders, believed Holmes, came from a deranged form of certainty on which the entire war was premised. As one historian has argued, "The lesson Holmes took from the war can be put in a sentence. It is that certitude leads to violence." Late in his life, Holmes wrote to a friend, "I detest a man who knows that he knows." The "highly cultivated, homogeneous" world in which he had been raised had been efficiently destroyed by the events of the war. Certainty breeds violence – and so certainty must be abandoned.[3]

Disasters like the Battle of Fredericksburg, undertaken in the name of God and country, caused participants and observers alike to question their deeply held convictions about the nature of the conflict. These growing metaphysical doubts appear here as symptomatic of and contributing to a larger spiritual crisis that rocked the American evangelical world of the period. This crisis simultaneously marked the life of Abraham Lincoln and informed the rapid mythologizing of his memory in the aftermath of the assassination. Much of Lincoln's greatness as a leader and visionary was linked to his uncanny ability, not only to navigate the treacherous waters dividing the Union and the Confederacy, but also to navigate those dividing the warring factions of the spiritual realm. In these contexts, it is a bit surprising that Lincoln's contributions as a prescient theological thinker and writer have been underappreciated even though his status as a spiritual leader and ultimately as a martyr became iconic within weeks of his death, culminating in the construction of the greatest "spiritual" shrine in our nation's history, the Lincoln Memorial.

Much has been documented about the reasons soldiers gave for fighting the war.[4] Both Union and Confederate leaders went into the war quite certain about the Christian righteousness of their causes. Union chaplains, for instance, often preached an American civil religion. According to Gardner Shattuck, "Equating the cause of their nation with the cause of God, they entered the army with clear consciences.... At a moment when all citizens were united in a common struggle, the duties of a minister and a patriot seemed to be thoroughly compatible, perhaps almost identical."[5] Such beliefs informed the work of Confederate chaplains as well, and the extent to which the Confederacy operated according to its own peculiar version of a civil religious ideology is easily overlooked.[6] Both sides were motivated by the certainties of a deeply felt civil religion informing their causes; both sought the blessing of a benevolent God in their sacred effort. Or, as Lincoln stated simply and directly in his Second Inaugural Address: "Both [sides] read the same Bible and pray to the same God, and each invokes His aid against the other."[7] In so few words, Lincoln captured a crucial irony of the religious petitions of millions of Americans: In effect, these believers sought to have God's wrath poured out on their adversaries.

By the war's weary end, and in the context of horrific eyewitness accounts of the butchery at Antietam, Fredericksburg, Gettysburg, or the Wilderness, Christian prayers in support of either side had begun to resemble pagan acts of moral degeneracy, a resemblance that would be famously captured decades later by Mark Twain in the feud chapters of *Adventures of Huckleberry Finn* (1884) and, even later, in his wickedly accurate satire "The War Prayer" (unpublished in his lifetime). As Edward Blum notes, Twain understood the "ghastliness" of such prayer: that "in their supplications for protection of their sons, [the congregants] were asking God for the deaths of others. The silent prayers approached God as a murderer and a nationalist."[8] The Civil War's spiritual foundations, including a clear-eyed moral certainty with both sides praying for the destruction of other Americans, became threadbare after four grueling years, and thus contributed to the emerging national crisis of belief.

The war's ramifications for religion and belief have been staggeringly overlooked ever since. Many contemporary Americans are embarrassed to admit their nation's sad record of violence in the name of religious fanaticism, an admission that seems decidedly antimodern, even anti-American. But the Civil War was very much a clash of religious worldviews; it was, as Mark

Noll has argued, effectively a religious war deriving from a theological crisis.[9] Much recent historical work counters this omission by analyzing how, "in fundamental respects, religion stood at the center of the American Civil War experience."[10] If we accept these views, then we can begin to recognize also the extent to which religious conflict characterized American culture during and after Abraham Lincoln's lifetime: what historian Paul Carter has called "the spiritual crisis of the Gilded Age."[11] A crucial ingredient of this crisis was the lingering grief and trauma from the Civil War, which spawned widespread epistemological doubt about God, Providence, and the American mission. As Menand argues so powerfully, a good deal of that crisis emanated from the growing assault on certainty.

The initial period of mourning both the Civil War dead and the mythic, slain president, saw Christian beliefs forced to weather additional philosophical attacks. Three primary intellectual challenges reigned supreme – the sheer metaphysical horror of the war's carnage; the German higher criticism of the Bible; and the rise of Darwinian evolution. In effect, the uncanny emergence of these two additional philosophical phenomena at almost exactly the same time (and, more to the point, during the despair-ridden aftermath of the Civil War) produced a devastating attack on the traditional dogmas of the Christian church. In particular, evangelical certainty about human origins, biblical inerrancy and historicity, and American civil righteousness about being a "chosen nation" were all being radically assaulted and demythologized at precisely the same moment.[12] The result was a spiritual crisis that shook the faith of American evangelicals – a crisis from which American Christianity is still trying to recover.

The "reconstruction" of Lincoln in cultural memory took place in the midst of these attacks. Clashing accounts of Lincoln's Christianity reflected theological crises. The chief figure in these debates was William Herndon, whose obsessive designs to sketch an agnostic Lincoln set the terms. Herndon was Lincoln's law partner beginning in 1844, and he later became one of the key biographers for the remainder of his life. He is best known today for the materials he gathered from friends, family members, and co-workers after the president's death. Herndon's collaboration with Jesse Weik, known as *Herndon's Lincoln*, was published in 1889.[13] Controversial during his lifetime, Herndon remains so today, largely for his highly idiosyncratic readings of Lincoln materials, including his insistence that the dead president was committed to neither Christian orthodoxy nor evangelical religion. Versions of Lincoln as a pious, Christian gentleman, as typified by Josiah G. Holland's characterization in the first major biography, *The Life of Abraham Lincoln* (1866), enraged Herndon, and he spent much of the remainder of his life angrily disputing them.

In a plethora of essays regarding Lincoln's religious beliefs, Herndon seemed convinced that it was his duty and vocation to set the record straight: Holland's account, he sniffed, was *"romantic ... all mere bosh, a lie."*[14] Herndon's version focused on Lincoln's Jeffersonian liberalism and fatalism. Herndon presents traces of both biblical critique and vulgar Darwinism, as in these remarks from a letter Herndon wrote in 1886, according to which Lincoln "believed that what was to be would be, and no prayers of ours could arrest or reverse the decree; he was a thorough fatalist, and thought the fates ruled the world; he believed that the conditions made the man.... Men were mere tools in the hands of fate – were made as they are made, by conditions; and to praise or blame men was pure folly." Herndon proceeds to contrast Lincoln with the Transcendentalist moralist Ralph Waldo Emerson: "Emerson had the genius of the Spiritual and ideal. Lincoln had the genius of the real and the practical. Emerson lived high among the stars – Lincoln lived low among men. Emerson dreamed, Lincoln acted. Emerson was intuitional, Lincoln reflective. Both were Liberals in religion and were great men."[15]

Much of this account rings true. However, Herndon's views of Lincoln's beliefs were often questionable, deeply prejudiced by his own misgivings about evangelical religion. For instance, Herndon's dismissal of Lincoln's belief in prayer ignores the plentiful evidence of Lincoln praying, especially in the latter half of his stay in the White House. Herndon also avoids use of specific terms like Providence, with which Lincoln became quite comfortable. Thus Herndon's remarks illustrate his inability to speak authoritatively about Lincoln's changing attitudes during the White House years, when he had no firsthand knowledge.

Herndon's depiction of Lincoln is symptomatic of a broader movement in American religion after the war. His liberalized, free-thinking version of Lincoln was copied by Robert G. Ingersoll (1833–1899), one of America's flashiest and most brilliant orators, and himself a great champion of the late president. Ingersoll, the man known as "America's infidel,"[16] was far riskier than the controversial Herndon could ever imagine, as in this comparison between Lincoln and the quintessential scientist of the century:

> On the 12th of February, 1809, two babes were born – one in the woods of Kentucky, amid the hardships and poverty of pioneers; one in England, surrounded by wealth and culture. One was educated in the University of Nature, the other at Cambridge. One associated his name with the enfranchisement of labor, with the emancipation of millions, with the salvation of the Republic. He is known to us as Abraham Lincoln. The other broke the chains of superstition and filled the world with intellectual light, and he is known as Charles Darwin.

> Nothing is grander than to break chains from the bodies of men – nothing nobler than to destroy the phantoms of the soul.[17]

According to Ingersoll's vision, Lincoln becomes, like Darwin, a great liberator of men insofar as he works to destroy the myths and ideologies imprisoning them. Lincoln is best understood as a slayer of myths, says Ingersoll, a liberator of men from their prisons of thought – the chief prison for Ingersoll always being, of course, institutional religion and its hardshell interpretations of the Bible. In Ingersoll's brilliant hands, Lincoln becomes a tool for the destruction of all hypocrisy, mystical cant, and superstition: what Ingersoll famously dubbed the "ghosts" of our archaic, religious past.[18]

The remarks by Herndon, Ingersoll, and others like them were widely scorned for claiming that Lincoln was not an orthodox Christian. The scorn multiplied as the Lincoln myth of the profound, Job-like Christian prophet was simultaneously being etched deeper into stone. The heterodox accounts received extensive criticism, often from Lincoln's intimate friends from the White House years, such as the following remarks of Noah Brooks in 1872: "Mr. Lincoln was at heart a Christian man, believed in the Savior, and was seriously considering the step which would formally connect him with the visible church on earth. Certainly, any suggestion as to Mr. Lincoln's skepticism or Infidelity, to me who knew him intimately from 1862 till the time of his death, is a monstrous fiction – a shocking perversion."[19] Brooks's comments were printed in a remarkable article in *Scribner's Monthly* by James A. Reed, which contained more than a dozen detailed reports culled from Lincoln intimates. Among them were comments by John T. Stuart ("Mr. Lincoln had changed his opinion, and become a believer in the truth of the Christian religion"), by the Rev. Phineas Gurley ("after the death of his son Willie and his visit to the battlefield of Gettysburg, he said, with tears in his eyes, that he had lost confidence in everything but God, and that he now believed his heart was changed, and that he loved the Saviour"), and by many others.[20]

Interestingly enough, Herndon was such a committed and thorough researcher that much of the best and most damning evidence against his position was gathered through his own tireless efforts to interview witnesses and to correspond with those who knew Lincoln best. Thus, much of the treasure trove of Herndon's collection of information about Lincoln is not only unavailable from any other source, ironically, much of what he uncovered is directly opposed to many of Herndon's own conclusions. Many readers responded with anger and emotion to Herndon's attacks against their beloved president. For example, perhaps the strongest rebuttal of Herndon's dismissal of Lincoln's faith came from the Rev. James Smith, a Presbyterian pastor in Springfield who knew the Lincolns well. Smith's famous account is among the most direct:

> I was Pastor of the 1st Presbyterian Church of Springfield, Mr. Lincoln did avow his belief in the Divine Authority and Inspiration of the Scriptures.... This then for the present is the Vindication of the Character of the Martyred president, from the foul aspersions, You Sir have Cast upon it.... To the arguments on both sides Mr. Lincoln gave a most patient, impartial and Searching investigation. To use his own language "he examined the Arguments as a lawyer who is anxious to reach the truth investigates testimony." The result was the announcement by himself that the argument in favor of the Divine Authority and inspiration of the Scripture was unanswerable.[21]

Taking this pro-religious position to its most extreme, there are even more radical accounts of Lincoln's faith and orthodoxy. With their focus on Lincoln's Christian fidelity and frequently on his return to faith and prayer, these versions have been generally eliminated from consideration. But these accounts are symptomatic of larger crises. Moreover, Herndon's and Ingersoll's depictions were similarly prejudiced by their own symptomatic positions against faith in the supernatural. In particular we might consider such examples as the famous narrative of Colonel James Rusling, in which he recalled meeting Lincoln not long after Gettysburg. Rusling was surprised to hear Lincoln say he was not at all worried about the recent great battle at Gettysburg. The president explained his assurance: "I went into my room one morning and locked the door, and got down on my knees, and prayed Almighty God for victory at Gettysburg.... I made a solemn vow with my Maker, that if He would stand by you boys at Gettysburg, I would stand by Him! I prayed, 'Oh God, have mercy upon me and my afflicted people! ... Come now and help us, or we must all likewise perish! And Thou canst not afford to have us perish! We are Thy chosen people, the last best hope of the human race!' And so I wrestled with Him, as Abraham or Moses in ancient days."

According to Rusling, Lincoln explained that "after so 'wrestling' with God, sincerely and devoutly, in solemn prayer, for a considerable time, ... somehow or other a sweet comfort crept into my soul, that God Almighty had taken the whole business up there into His own hands, and things would come out all right at Gettysburg. And He did stand by you boys there, and now I will stand by Him!" Although this tale has been questioned by historians, it was corroborated on many occasions. Rusling famously claimed, "I wrote home about it the same day, and now give it here as the very truth of history."[22]

Among the voluminous accounts of Lincoln's religion, many were like Rusling's: Evangelical and even boastful, they present a view of the president ready to "witness" in a manner that seems, like Herndon's similarly flawed accounts, strongly tinged by a particular pole of the religious controversies at hand. Still, it is worth noting that the vast majority of first generation memoirs depict a deeply religious president, and many were based on eye-witness testimony. For instance, Elizabeth Keckley recalled,

> I discovered that Mr. Lincoln was reading that divine comforter, Job. He read with Christian eagerness, and the courage and hope that he derived from the inspired pages made him a new man.... What a sublime picture was this! A ruler of a mighty nation going to the pages of the Bible with simple Christian earnestness for comfort and courage, and finding both in the darkest hours of a nation's calamity. Ponder it, O ye scoffers at God's Holy Word, and then hang your heads for very shame![23]

Keckley's view places Lincoln totally at odds with "scoffers" such as Herndon and Ingersoll.[24] Although the terms are often disparate, the sense of Lincoln's belief is the central point of agreement.

Overall, while Herndon might correctly note Lincoln's skepticism early in life and his general unwillingness to talk about Jesus Christ or specific doctrinal matters, Rusling in contrast notes the sincerity of Lincoln's faith in an unseen God superintending the war and the nation. These two poles of a paradox reflected American religious rhetoric after the war: A largely evangelical consensus still held sway in the North, even though its powers were waning as its doctrinal beliefs were being questioned and often dismissed by freethinkers and agnostics alike. In such a rancorous milieu, the memory of Lincoln became a highly contested object of desire for both sides.

If we conceive the religious debate as being characterized by an intensive rationalism pitted against a sentimentalized moralism, it thus conforms to what was often understood to be a masculine head pitted against a feminine heart.[25] And yet the most ingenious accounts of Lincoln's religion found creative ways to combine the feminine elements of his faith with those considered more masculine. This compromise was to be found in any number of proclamations of Lincoln's Christian faith as a vague civil nationalism combining the best of the head and the heart, constructions that now seem rather muted and poetic, but which also stress the ongoing crisis of the age. Harriet Beecher Stowe wrote of Lincoln, "We do not mean to give the impression that Lincoln is a religious man in the sense in which that term is popularly applied. We believe he has never made any such profession, but we see evidence that in passing through this dreadful national crisis he has been forced by the very anguish of the struggle to look upward, where any rational creature must look for support." Stowe signifies her sense that Lincoln's faith may not quite measure up to the rigorous demands of prewar evangelicalism. Nevertheless, she states, the "evidences" of Lincoln's faith were clear, and the "anguish" of the president forced him, despite his free-thinking tendencies, to "look upward." All particular doctrines aside, Stowe celebrated "[Lincoln's] simple faith in God, the ruler of nations, and [his] humble willingness to learn the awful lessons of his providence."[26]

Like Stowe, Lincoln's belief tended toward the romantic, or as Mary Lincoln put it, "Mr Linc(oln) had a Kind of Poetry in his Nature."[27] Mary's sentiments are elaborated in James Russell Lowell's stunning essay, in which he found it difficult to state the precise nature of this aspect of the president's genius: "That penetrating fire ran in and roused those primary instincts that make their lair in the dens and caverns of the mind. What is called the great popular heart was awakened, that indefinable something which may be, according to circumstances, the highest reason or the most brutish unreason."[28] Whatever it was ("that indefinable something"), it tapped into the "great popular heart" – or, as Lincoln memorably described it, those "mystic chords of memory." Similarly, Phillips Brooks stated:

> Not one of all the multitudes ... can tell you today whether the wise judgments that he gave came most from a strong head or a sound heart.... This union of the mental and moral into a life of admirable simplicity is what we most admire in children; but in them it is unsettled and unpractical. But when it is preserved into manhood, deepened into reliability and maturity, it is that glorified childlikeness, that high and reverend simplicity, which shames and baffles the most accomplished astuteness and is chosen by God to fill his purposes when he needs a ruler for his people, of faithful and true heart, such as he had who was our President.[29]

Brooks's analysis is useful insofar as he surmises Lincoln's ingenious balancing act in the face of the ongoing spiritual crisis of the period. The solution, according to Brooks, was another sort of union: Lincoln, says Brooks, succeeded by wedding head and heart, male and female, rationality and sympathy; "This union of the mental and moral" sprang from Lincoln's frontier youth. For Brooks, this "union" constituted Lincoln's genius; indeed, it was the unique character of the Union as well – and suggested a way of solving other crises.[30] It was a "reaching out to both sides" that Lincoln mastered in the political realm, as is evident in his most powerful statements.

Religious thinkers would have done well, as it turned out, to heed Lincoln's centrist approach in the theological battles. Both sides of the cultural battle over the nature of Lincoln's religious belief were right about certain aspects but wrong about others. It would be for later commentators to see more fruitfully the extent of Lincoln's theological contributions and especially how Lincoln's theistic belief informed his major writings.[31] Considering the sheer mountain of material available, one might forget that Lincoln's account of his own spiritual crisis, as deduced from various writings, is fascinating. His spare meditations, including his uncannily modern solution to the crisis, provide much useful wisdom. In the Second Inaugural Address, Lincoln composed one of the most theologically astute interpretations propounded at the end of the Civil War, as numerous historians have recently claimed. Much of that genius derived from Lincoln's uncanny ability to navigate the raging river between the two competing sides, which included not only the North and South of the war, but also the head and the heart of the religious. Lincoln was, as Mark Twain noticed, necessarily a "man of the border": He sympathized with both of the feuding sides, and his genius wedded the scientific and pragmatic with the romantic and the sympathetic.[32]

Historians suggest that Lincoln's religious views did in fact change drastically in the period surrounding the death in the White House of his son Willie (February 1862) as well as the great battles of the Civil War throughout 1862–1863. The consensus is that Lincoln underwent his own "crisis of doubt" that led him back to the earlier convictions of frontier religion.[33] Profound grief and trauma plagued the president, and Lincoln was almost certainly afflicted with what we might characterize as clinical depression. The deaths of two of his sons – Eddie in 1850 and Willie in 1862 – affected him strongly. He had also had two episodes that were characterized as breakdowns (in 1835 and 1840–1841).[34]

Several trends can be identified as central to Lincoln's religious philosophy in the months and years after Willie's death. In particular, he relied more heavily on fundamental biblical concepts and allusions in his later speeches, and he embraced the concept of continued bonds with the dead. Most significantly, he relied more explicitly on a mysterious Providence. Earlier in his career, Lincoln exhibited a more freethinking theism. As Nicholas Parrillo notes, "Lincoln's deep commitment to republicanism never lost its motive power, but by the end of the war, his new Calvinist tendencies acquired strength equal to that of his never-changing democratic beliefs."[35]

In *The Varieties of Religious Experience* (1899), William James defines religion as "the feelings, acts, and experiences of individual men in their solitude, so far as they apprehend themselves to stand in relation to whatever they may consider the divine."[36] According to such a Jamesian focus on Lincoln's experiences of the divine in solitude, one of the most remarkably "modern" extant texts is surely Lincoln's "Meditation on the Divine Will." Its direct relation to the stunning Second Inaugural has become a commonplace of Lincoln studies:

> The will of God prevails. In great contests each party claims to act in accordance with the will of God. Both may be, and one must be wrong. God can not be for, and against the same thing at the same time. In the present civil war it

is quite possible that God's purpose is something different from the purpose of either party – and yet the human instrumentalities, working just as they do, are of the best adaptation to effect His purpose. I am almost ready to say this is probably true – that God wills this contest, and wills that it shall not end yet. By his mere quiet power, on the minds of the now contestants, He could have either saved or destroyed the Union without a human contest. Yet the contest began. And having begun He could give the final victory to either side any day. Yet the contest proceeds.[37]

According to the most authoritative accounts, the fragment was written "in September, 1862, while his mind was burdened with the weightiest question of his life.... It was not written to be seen of men."[38] The precise dating remains a mystery, but those closest to the president associate it with the "weightiest question of his life," which certainly must be the question of emancipation. This scrawled meditation probably came after the Second Battle of Bull Run, which plunged the president into one of the deepest depressions of the war, only six months after the death of Willie.[39]

John Hay, one of Lincoln's closest confidantes who called the Second Inaugural "a new chapter of Hebrew prophecy," provided a telling account of the fragmentary meditation's composition and meaning: "Mr. Lincoln admits us into the most secret recesses of his soul.... It shows ... the awful sincerity of a perfectly honest soul, trying to bring itself into closer communion with its Maker."[40] The "Meditation" certainly predated Antietam, which was invaded by Lee's forces in early September and which was obviously looming as one of the major battles on the horizon, if not the crucial scene of success or failure for the war up until that moment. McLellan fought Lee at Antietam on September 17, and the victory there (with unprecedented casualties) led directly to Lincoln's call for emancipation, a decision that needed to be made at a time of evident military superiority.[41]

It appears that Lincoln pursued a Gideon-like search for providential direction at almost precisely the moment he inscribed his fragmentary vision in September 1862. As John Stauffer puts it, for Lincoln, God was "inscrutable rather than indwelling. The most one could hope for on earth was to discover signs of God's presence and to establish a covenant (or sacred agreement) with Him.... God would reciprocate this trust by guiding the faithful toward righteousness."[42] The most interesting evidence that Lincoln viewed Antietam in the mystical terms of God giving a sign comes from the diary of Gideon Welles, then Secretary of the Navy. Welles convincingly recalls that Lincoln defined the great battle of Antietam in religious terminology:

[Lincoln] remarked that he had made a vow, a covenant, that if God gave us the victory in the approaching battle, he would consider it an indication of

Divine will, and that it was his duty to move forward in the cause of emancipation. It might be thought strange, he said, that he had in this way submitted the disposal of matters when the way was not clear to his mind what
he should do. God had decided this question in favor of the slaves. He was
satisfied it was right, was confirmed and strengthened in his action by the vow
and the results.[43]

Welles describes a covenantal agreement made through a vow, the strangeness of such a method, the submission of a weighty matter to God's answer
through a specific sign, and most crucially a deep yearning for the clear
indication of God's will. There is even the added irony that the incident
was recorded by a man named Gideon – reminiscent of the Hebrew judge
and military leader. Finally, the seemingly providential elements of the battle itself (before which Union soldiers discovered General Lee's battle plans,
which had been wrapped tidily around some cigars and then carelessly
dropped in a field) punctuated the seemingly miraculous nature of the events
at Antietam.[44] As Allen Guelzo has argued, it is rather astonishing to consider the possibility that the president committed America to full emancipation "on the strength of a sign he had asked from God."[45]

While most commentators in the North spoke confidently about the
ways of God in the aftermath of the war, Lincoln injected a strong note
of modern uncertainty before a great and awesome God who is very difficult for mankind to size up.[46] As such, Lincoln's analysis anticipated
major shifts in postbellum thinking by articulating a progressively modern view of the providence of God as mysterious and obscure. Lincoln
emphasized to his listeners his firm belief that the will of God is not easily
discerned, and it is often affected by contingencies and human stupidity.
Certainly, the episodes surrounding Antietam indicate a profound, heartfelt desire to know for certain God's providential plan. And yet, his head
told him that God was inscrutable to human understanding. As Noll has
well stated, "This combination of convictions – confidence in Providence
along with humble agnosticism about its purposes – transformed the central section of the second inaugural into a theological statement of rare
insight," an insight that pushed Lincoln "into post-Protestant, even post-
Christian theism."[47]

When James Russell Lowell noted in 1864, "In our opinion, there is
no more unsafe politician than a conscientiously rigid *doctrinaire*....
Mr. Lincoln's perilous task has been a rather shaky raft through the rapids,
making fast the unrulier logs as he could snatch opportunity," he reminded
readers of Lincoln's frontier experience on a flatboat.[48] In retrospect,
Lowell's figure might remind readers of the abused fourteen-year-old Huck

Finn with the runaway slave Jim, caught up in a monstrous river set directly between North and South, freedom and slavery; perhaps even of the borders separating head and heart. Lincoln evinced a sort of protomodern religion that navigated expertly the fashionable intellectual ways of the freethinkers as well as the conservative old-school theologians, taking the best from both heritages. He seemed to understand intuitively the sea change Noll has recently identified: "The Civil War proved to be the climax, but also the exhaustion, of the synthesis of common sense, republicanism, and evangelical Christianity" in America.

Similarly, our grand memorial to Lincoln on the Mall in Washington signals both the climax and the exhaustion of the nation's embrace of a providential past. Lincoln sits beneath the inscription: "In this temple, as in the hearts of the people for whom he saved the Union, the memory of Abraham Lincoln is enshrined forever." Given this concrete expression of America's understanding of his metaphysical legacy in this unsurpassed "temple," it is ironic that Lincoln was also a key prophetic observer signaling the inevitable demise of the homogeneous religion that the Memorial ostensibly represents. Lincoln was one of the very few clarion voices who recognized how the war had called into question America's brazen confidence in a "clear-eyed moral certainty about God and His will."[49]

NOTES

1 Roy Morris, *The Better Angel* (New York: Oxford University Press, 2001), 57.
2 Louis Menand, *The Metaphysical Club* (New York: Farrar, Strauss and Giroux, 2001), 61.
3 Menand, *The Metaphysical Club*, 62, 68–69.
4 See James McPherson, *What They Fought For, 1861–1865* (Baton Rouge: Louisiana State University Press, 1994); James Moorhead, *American Apocalypse: Yankee Protestants and the Civil War, 1860–1869* (New Haven, CT: Yale University Press, 1978); Gardner Shattuck, *A Shield and Hiding Place: The Religious Life of the Civil War Armies* (Macon, GA: Mercer University Press, 1987); and Stephen E. Woodworth, *While God Is Marching On: The Religious World of Civil War Soldiers* (Lawrence: University Press of Kansas, 2001).
5 Shattuck, *Shield*, 58.
6 On the Confederacy's civil religion and Lost Cause ideology, see Randall M. Miller, et al., *Religion and the American Civil War* (New York: Oxford University Press, 1998); Charles Reagan Wilson, *Baptized in Blood: The Religion of the Lost Cause, 1865–1920* (Athens: University of Georgia Press, 1980); Gary W. Gallagher and Alan T. Nolan, eds., *The Myth of the Lost Cause and Civil War History* (Bloomington: Indiana University Press, 2000); David W. Blight, *Race and Reunion: The Civil War in American Memory* (Cambridge, MA: Harvard University Press, 2001); and Thomas L. Connelly and Barbara L. Bellows, *God and General Longstreet: The Lost Cause and the Southern Mind* (Baton Rouge: Louisiana State University Press, 1982).

7   Abraham Lincoln, "Second Inaugural," in Roy P. Basler, ed., *The Collected Works of Abraham Lincoln*, vol. 8 (New Brunswick, NJ: Rutgers University Press, 1953), 332–333.

8   Edward Blum, "God's Imperialism: Mark Twain and the Religious War Between Imperialists and Anti-Imperialists," *Journal of Transnational American Studies* 1.1 (2009): 35.

9   Mark Noll, *The Civil War as a Theological Crisis* (Chapel Hill: University of North Carolina Press, 2006).

10 Randall M. Miller, Harry S. Stout, and Charles Reagan Wilson, "Introduction," in *Religion and the American Civil War* (New York: Oxford University Press, 1998), 3–4.

11 Paul Carter, *The Spiritual Crisis of the Gilded Age* (DeKalb: Northern Illinois University Press, 1971).

12 Besides Carter, *The Spiritual Crisis of the Gilded Age*, see Ferenc Morton Szasz, *The Divided Mind of Protestant America, 1880–1930* (Tuscaloosa: University of Alabama Press, 1982).

13 The definitive edition is Douglas L. Wilson and Rodney O. Davis, eds., *Herndon's Lincoln: Letters, Interviews, and Statements about Abraham Lincoln* (Urbana: University of Illinois Press, 2006).

14 Herndon to Jesse W. Weik, Feb. 26, 1891, in Emanuel Hertz, ed., *The Hidden Lincoln, from the Letters and Papers of William H. Herndon* (New York: Viking Press, 1938), 266–267.

15 From a letter of 1886, reprinted in Harold K. Bush, ed., *Lincoln in His Own Time* (Iowa City: University of Iowa Press, 2011); 191–192; hereafter *LIHOT*.

16 Susan Jacoby, *Freethinkers: A History of American Secularism* (New York: Metropolitan, 2004), 149.

17 "On Abraham Lincoln," in no ed., *The Works of Robert G. Ingersoll*, vol. 3, (New York: Farrell, 1900). Reprinted in *LIHOT*: 193–194.

18 On this topic, see Robert Ingersoll, *The Ghosts, and Other Lectures* (Washington, DC: Farrell, 1878).

19 James A. Reed, "The Later Life and Religious Sentiments of Abraham Lincoln," *Scribner's Monthly* (July 1873): 340.

20 Reed, "The Later Life and Religious Sentiments of Abraham Lincoln," 336, 342.

21 Douglas L. Wilson and Rodney O. Davis, eds., *Herndon's Informants: Letters, Interviews, and Statements about Abraham Lincoln* (Urbana: University of Illinois Press, 1997), 547, 549.

22 From Col. James Rusling, "Lincoln and Sickles," undated pamphlet of a speech given by Col. Rusling on May 5, 1910. Parish Memorabilia of the Asylum Hill Congregational Church, in the Connecticut State Library.

23 Elizabeth Keckley, *Behind the Scenes; Or, Thirty Years a Slave, and Four Years in the White House* (New York: Carleton, 1868); reprinted in *LIHOT*: 67–68.

24 Ervin Chapman, ed., *Latest Light on Abraham Lincoln and War-Time Memories* (New York: Fleming H. Revell, 1917), 507.

25 For background on the gendering of religion in the church during the Gilded Age period, see Donald Hall, ed., *Muscular Christianity* (New York: Cambridge University Press, 1994); Clifford Putney, *Muscular Christianity* (Cambridge, MA: Harvard University Press, 2001); and Ann Douglas, *The Feminization of American Culture* (New York: Farrar, Strauss, and Giroux, 1998).

26 Harriet Beecher Stowe, "Abraham Lincoln," *The Living Age*, February 6, 1864; reprinted in *LIHOT*: 111.

27 Wilson and Davis, *Herndon's Informants*, 360. On Lincoln's romantic imagination, see Stewart Winger, *Lincoln, Religion, and Romantic Cultural Politics* (DeKalb: Illinois University Press, 2003).

28 James Russell Lowell, "Abraham Lincoln" (1865), in *The Writings of James Russell Lowell, Vol. 5: Political Essays* (Cambridge: The Riverside Press, 1890); reprinted in *LIHOT*: 114–115.

29 Phillips Brooks, *Addresses* (Boston: C. E. Brown, 1893), 166–96. Reprinted in *LIHOT*: 157.

30 On this opposition in the nineteenth century, see Garry Wills, *Head and Heart: American Christianities* (New York: Penguin, 2007).

31 For works about Lincoln's religion, see Allen C. Guelzo, *Abraham Lincoln: Redeemer President* (Grand Rapids: Eerdman's, 1999), and Richard Carwardine, *Lincoln: A Life of Purpose and Power* (New York: Knopf, 2008). See also, John Patrick Diggins, *On Hallowed Ground: Abraham Lincoln and the Foundations of American History* (New Haven, CT: Yale University Press, 2000); Joseph R. Fornieri, *Abraham Lincoln's Political Faith* (DeKalb: Northern Illinois University Press, 2003); Lucas E. Morel, *Lincoln's Sacred Effort: Defining Religion's Role in American Self-Government* (Lanham, MD: Lexington Books, 2000); John Stauffer, *Giants: The Parallel Lives of Frederick Douglass and Abraham Lincoln* (New York: Twelve, 2008); James Tackach, *Lincoln's Moral Vision: the Second Inaugural Address* (Jackson: University Press of Mississippi, 2002); and Stewart Winger, *Lincoln, Religion, and Romantic Cultural Politics* (DeKalb: Northern Illinois University Press, 2003).

32 See Mark Twain, "A Lincoln Memorial," *The New York Times*, January 13, 1907; reprinted in *LIHOT*: 210.

33 See Timothy Larsen, *Crisis of Doubt: Honest Faith in Nineteenth-Century England* (New York: Oxford University Press, 2007), passim.

34 See Joshua Wolf Shenk, *Lincoln's Melancholy: How Depression Challenged a President and Fuelled His Greatness* (Boston: Houghton Mifflin, 2005).

35 Nicholas Parrillo, "Lincoln's Calvinist Transformation: Emancipation and War," *Civil War History* 46.3 (September 2000): 227–253.

36 William James, *The Varieties of Religious Experience* (New York: Touchstone, 1997), 42.

37 Lincoln, *Collected Works*, vol. 5, 403–404.

38 John Hay and John Nicolay, *Abraham Lincoln: A History*, vol. VI (New York: Century, 1914), 341–342.

39 Basler's note is in Lincoln, *Collected Works*, vol. 5, 404.

40 John Hay, "Lincoln's Faith," in no ed., *Addresses of John Hay* (New York: Century, 1906), 239.

41 See Mark E. Neely, *The Last, Best Hope of Earth: Abraham Lincoln and the Promise of America* (Cambridge, MA: Harvard University Press, 1995), 106–110.

42 Stauffer, *Giants: the Parallel Lives of Frederick Douglass and Abraham Lincoln*, 251.

43 Gideon Welles, *Diary of Gideon Welles* (Boston: Houghton Mifflin, 1911), 1:143.

44 See James McPherson, *Crossroads of Freedom: Antietam* (New York: Oxford University Press, 2002).

45 Guelzo, *Abraham Lincoln: Redeemer President*, 153.

46 On these three themes in Lincoln's work, see Mark Noll, *America's God: From Jonathan Edwards to Abraham Lincoln* (New York: Oxford University Press, 2002): 426–432.

47 Mark Noll, "'Both ... Pray to the Same God': The Singularity of Lincoln's Faith in the Era of the Civil War," *Journal of the Abraham Lincoln Association* 18.1 (1997): 13, 26.

48 Lowell, "Abraham Lincoln," in *LIHOT*, 116.

49 Noll, *America's God*, 426, 425.

9

PAUL GILES

America and Britain during the Civil War

Of all eminent American public figures over the past 230 years, perhaps none has been as hostile in principle to the idea of transnationalism as Abraham Lincoln. Lincoln's professed goal was to consolidate the United States as "one national family," a nation predicated on "territorial integrity," whose Constitution, so he argued in 1864, represented the country's "organic law."[1] Lincoln began his own career as a policer of national boundaries during the Black Hawk War, Indian skirmishes "in what was then the West." His life-long attempt to define and circumscribe the parameters of the nation always impelled him toward a deep suspicion of anything that might undermine the idea of such "organic" unity.[2] Characteristically, Lincoln opposed the Mexican War of the 1840s and expressed no enthusiasm for the annexation of Texas, on the grounds that such expansionist moves might unsettle the U.S. national framework. He himself never set foot outside the country, even when serving as president, and he also resisted moves to reopen the Atlantic slave trade – partly on moral grounds, but also to protect the United States from disruptive foreign influences. In his "Address to the Young Men's Lyceum" in Springfield, Illinois, delivered in 1838 at an early point in his public career, Lincoln suggested that fears for "some transatlantic military giant to step the ocean, and crush us at a blow" were much less plausible than the likelihood that "danger ... if it ever reach us ... must spring up amongst us," and he stuck to this basic design throughout the rest of his political life.[3]

Lincoln's recognition of such homegrown "danger" being potentially more destructive than anything from "abroad" led him consistently to incorporate the United States within a range of familial metaphors. We see this in his famous "House Divided" speech of 1858, as well as through the comparison in his 1861 Inaugural Address of an impending Civil War to the prospect of divorce between husband and wife. This rhetoric of sentimental domesticity was, as George B. Forgie has noted, quite common in public life during the antebellum period, when the nation was frequently represented by politicians as a "growing youth," with emerging states depicted as women about to be "married" to the Union.[4] In Lincoln's case, however, this conception extended beyond the merely metaphorical and became the source of his foundational investment in the integrity of the nation. Lincoln's professed belief, as expounded in his First Inaugural Address, in a nation whose "perpetual" Constitution was guaranteed by "universal law" was regarded with some incredulity among the political classes in London, where the political framework of the new U.S. republic was regarded as a much more contingent and mutable phenomenon.[5] In this sense, Lincoln's frequent elevation of the Constitution and other aspects of U.S. life to transcendent status – linked by the "mystic chords of memory" to purportedly metaphysical dimensions of the nation's past and future – was widely understood in Britain as part of the president's dim-witted folksiness and religiosity: British lawyer and historian George Wingrove Cooke wrote scathingly in the London *Times* of October 7, 1862, of how Lincoln by his Emancipation Proclamation "constitutes himself a sort of moral American POPE," and even Richard Cobden, the proselytizer for free trade who was generally well disposed toward the Union, described Lincoln as "intellectually inferior."[6] Conversely, it is in large part for this metamorphosis of national identity into a transcendent idea that Lincoln has so often been celebrated in the United States itself. Walt Whitman's famous elegy, "When Lilacs Last in the Dooryard Bloomed," deliberately associates the "corpse" of the slain president, "the sweetest, wisest soul of all my days," with the "varied and ample land, the South and the North in the light" that Whitman regards Lincoln's brilliantly integrative spirit as having encompassed politically.[7] This, of course, is the same cherished land that Whitman represents Lincoln's martyred body as traversing on its final journey.

Yet Lincoln's mystification of the idea of federal union was a high-risk strategy, the ultimate success of which was facilitated by various roundabout pieces of good fortune. One came from the formal protests made by Honduras, Costa Rica, and Nicaragua against Lincoln's elaborate scheme in 1862 to establish an African-American colony in the Chiriqui province of Colombia (now part of Panama). This well-developed plan had already attracted funding from Congress, but, had it been carried into effect, it would certainly have undermined aspirations for racial integration on a national basis during the Reconstruction era and afterward. Another piece of good luck was the absence during the war years of a transatlantic telegraph: Even though the first cable across the Atlantic had been laid in the summer of 1858, with Queen Victoria sending the first transoceanic cable message to President James Buchanan in August of that year, the cable broke down a few weeks later, and it was not repaired until after the Civil War had ended.

Such national isolation proved a particular boon to Lincoln in the wake of the *Trent* affair in November 1861, described by Craig L. Symonds as "Lincoln's Cuban missile crisis," when Britain's wrath toward the North was roused by the U.S. Navy's seizure, on the initiative of Captain Charles Wilkes, of two Confederate diplomats, James Mason and John Slidell, from a British mail ship.[8] Although Britain had officially declared neutrality at the outbreak of the Civil War – much to the irritation of Lincoln, who thought Britain was thereby acknowledging the Confederacy as an independent entity rather than merely a rebellious faction – there was nevertheless the prospect for a time of Union forces being forced also to engage in warfare on a transatlantic front. Prime Minister Lord Palmerston expressed outrage in Parliament at the way Captain Wilkes "had the courage to insult the British flag," while one British newspaper editor insisted there were "only two ways of settling the difficulty, an ample apology or an appeal to arms."[9] In this tense political situation, the absence of an international telegraph system proved advantageous to Lincoln, because, to his great relief, the long delays incumbent on the transmission of diplomatic notes by sea allowed this controversy eventually to subside.

All of this suggests ways in which Lincoln's understanding of the Civil War as above all a domestic dispute, analogous to a quarrel between husband and wife, served at times to obscure in his eyes the ways in which this conflict also carried a global resonance. As Symonds has observed, Lincoln was not comfortable even with the idea of war expanding into the "continental" west, and the whole world of naval affairs was "utterly foreign" to him when he first took office.[10] Karl Marx in his writings of the 1850s described the U.S. Civil War as merely one aspect of a larger global economic crisis, with the loss of cotton trade between Lancashire and the American South being linked systematically for Marx to the glutted markets that had similarly led to economic catastrophe for cotton workers in Asia. Lincoln's perspective, however, was much more doggedly nationalistic, and he even alarmed natural British supporters of the North such as Cobden, John Bright, and Harriet Martineau by his imposition of protectionist tariffs and his reluctance to endorse the principles of free trade across an international axis. Martineau was particularly incensed by the Morrill Tariff, initiated in 1861 by President Buchanan but supported in two subsequent bills introduced by the Lincoln administration, which increased import duties to raise revenue for the war and thereby effectively discouraged foreign trade. Martineau in 1862 accused Americans of replacing their motto, "Our country is the world, our countrymen are all mankind" with a new slogan, "Our country, right or wrong," and, as R. J. M. Blackett has observed, Lincoln's support of the Morrill Tariff "brought her to the brink of severing ties with American abolitionists with whom she had worked for thirty years."[11]

It was generally acknowledged in Britain at this time that no other overseas event had ever impacted the country's national life so much as the American Civil War. "The Civil War in the United States," declared the London *Times* on August 21, 1862, "affects our people more generally even than the Indian Mutiny."[12] One obvious effect stemmed from the North's naval blockade of cotton exports from the South, something that led in Britain to a lack of raw materials and consequent economic distress, particularly in the mill towns of Lancashire. Mary Ellison has suggested this induced the workers of Oldham, Accrington, and other hard-hit towns to express support for the Confederacy, although the pattern here seems to have been mixed, with other workers (particularly in Scotland) who were affected almost as badly nevertheless continuing to support the Union cause.[13] The British MP and antislavery activist George Thompson toured the country with some success urging his followers not to "allow any temporary suffering to lead you to give your sympathies to the enemies of human freedom on the other side of the Atlantic."[14] But the other major strand of British interest at this time involved more profound anxieties about how the long-term political and economic well-being of the British Empire might play itself out in a world where it had to compete with a fully integrated and modernized United States. As Howard Temperley has written, during the second half of the nineteenth century Britain was entering directly into "imperial" competition with the United States, and in 1862 the *Times* saw clearly that it would be in London's interests to be dealing henceforth with "two friendly Unions of moderate power and temper" rather than one burgeoning colossus.[15] Indeed, toward the end of his life Lord Salisbury, who had three spells as Conservative prime minister between 1885 and 1902, wrote to his son that it was "very sad" Britain had not "interfered in the Confederate War" when it had the opportunity, so as "to reduce the power of the United States to manageable proportions." As it is, concluded Salisbury, "I am afraid America is bound to forge ahead and nothing can restore the equality between us."[16]

It is clear, then, that British views of Lincoln were governed by many factors other than the probity or wisdom of his own domestic policies. Goldwin Smith, at that time the Regius Professor of History at Oxford, wrote in 1862 to Charles Eliot Norton in Boston of how the Confederacy drew its support in Britain from the aristocracy, the "great capitalists" influenced by the London press and the Church of England, while on the other hand "a good deal of the intellectual, the religious heart of the middle classes, the ministers of most of the Free Churches, and the great mass of the intelligent lower classes" were with the Union. As a rough template this was probably true enough, although, as Blackett has noted, there was a great deal of general confusion in British public opinion, with many clubs and associations springing up that were more or less informed about events on the other side of the Atlantic. Lincoln always did his best to control information networks overseas as well as at home, and he himself crafted personally a series of resolutions to be transmitted in advance to public meetings in Britain, passing them on to Charles Sumner, chair of the Senate Committee on Foreign Relations, for transmission to the staunch Union supporter in England, John Bright. However, the rowdy nature of British working-class life was not so easily susceptible to this kind of presidential executive power, with the organizers of a meeting in Bristol to congratulate Lincoln on his reelection in 1864 being surprised by what one observer described as a "half-drunk" mob calling for three cheers for Confederate heroes such as Jefferson Davis, Stonewall Jackson, and Robert E. Lee.[17] There had been a widespread hardening of racial attitudes in Britain since the 1834 emancipation of all slaves in the British Empire, with Thomas Carlyle, in his "Occasional Discourse on the Nigger Question" (1849), influentially suggesting that this policy had been an abject failure. Carlyle's principal focus here was on the West Indies, although his essay cross-references this region with the "American epitaph on the Nigger child," while attacking the "froth-oceans" of "Emancipation-principle" and "Christian Philanthropy" as "baleful and all-bewildering jargon."[18] For Carlyle, the practices of slavery were validated in part by their empirical particularity, the beneficent situations of caring and comfort they apparently provided, whereas the theorems of emancipation were associated in his mind with the language of abstraction and rationalization that was, as David Simpson has shown, fiercely resisted by the English "social-theological hierarchy," particularly in the nineteenth century.[19]

Such hostility to what were considered the more abstruse forms of emancipation doctrine heightened in Britain around the time of the American Civil War. Although Frederick Douglass garnered much public support for abolition during the period he spent in Britain between 1845 and 1847, when he returned to Britain for a second visit in 1859 and 1860, just before the outbreak of the Civil War, he found the atmosphere considerably less hospitable. Indeed, it is remarkable that in the House of Lords at this time there were only five bishops (out of twenty-six) who were favorable to the cause of emancipation. Goldwin Smith explained to his incredulous American friends that Bishop Wilberforce, son of the famous abolitionist William Wilberforce, was hostile to the Union because, unlike his father, the younger Wilberforce was "a bishop of the State Church" and thus saw it as his duty to represent the interests of the British Establishment.[20] In 1866 Smith joined the Jamaica Committee, a pressure group that, after Governor Eyre's brutal suppression of the Morant Bay rebellion the previous year when nearly five hundred black Jamaicans were killed by the British army, called for Eyre to be tried for his actions. Also on the Jamaica Committee were such liberal luminaries as John Stuart Mill, Thomas Huxley, John Bright, and Charles Darwin, but they were opposed by an Eyre Defence Committee that included, among others, John Ruskin, Charles Dickens, Alfred Lord Tennyson, and, of course, Carlyle. The former group had strong personal links with the Union cause in the United States, whereas those in the latter party were more instinctive supporters of the Confederacy; indeed, the *Times* after the Civil War used the example of events in Jamaica as a cautionary tale against the desirability of extending "political rights" to African Americans in the United States.[21] Smith himself came under attack at Oxford at this time for his political views, with Conservative leader Benjamin Disraeli calling him "an itinerant spouter of stale sedition ... a wild man of the cloister, who goes about the country maligning men and things." Indeed, Smith eventually found his position so uncomfortable that he chose in July 1866 to resign his professorship at Oxford to move to Cornell University in New York, from where he went on a few years later to the University of Toronto. The Regius professorship of History at Oxford was subsequently occupied by the much more traditional figure of William Stubbs, whose version of medieval antiquarianism constructed a reverential version of the English past that emerged, as Kathleen Biddick notes, "within well-articulated racisms, imperialisms, and nationalisms."[22]

Indirectly, then, the U.S. Civil War and associated disputes about customs of slavery created fissures in British as well as American life. Defense of Governor Eyre was one of the primary motives for Carlyle's essay "Shooting Niagara: And After?," published in August 1867, which also linked the prospect of "Swarmery" in Britain with malevolent pressures toward "democracy" that Carlyle linked to the outcome of the Civil War:

> By far the notablest case of *Swarmery*, in these times, is that of the late American War, with Settlement of the Nigger Question for result. Essentially the Nigger Question was one of the smallest; and in itself did not much concern mankind in the present time of struggles and hurries. One always rather likes the Nigger; evidently a poor blockhead with good dispositions, with affections, attachments, – with a turn for Nigger Melodies, and the like: – he is the only Savage of all the coloured races that doesn't die out on sight of the White Man; but can actually live beside him, and work and increase and be merry. The Almighty Maker has appointed him to be a Servant.[23]

Carlyle goes on to blame "frantic 'Abolitionists,' fire-breathing, like the old Chimaera" for generating an empty rhetoric of "Liberty" and "Constitutional Government." In his eyes, such pressures helped to bring about not only the senseless destruction of the American war itself but also the Second Reform Act in Britain, passed in 1867, which doubled the number of parliamentary voters, but which Carlyle saw as a fatal blow to the country's "Aristocracy of Nature." The well-nigh pathological contempt here for both "nigger" and abolitionism – Carlyle talks of "rabid Nigger-Philanthropists, barking furiously in the gutter" – makes this a deeply troubling piece of work, perhaps one of the most offensive essays ever written in the English language.[24] It is clear, however, that Carlyle attributes political reform in Britain as well as imperial controversies in the Caribbean to the fallout from the American Civil War, and also that he was only expressing more in a more naked fashion what were, in fact, common racist and anti-American sentiments among British conservatives at this time. Carlyle was not hostile to Lincoln personally, calling him a "brave, sincere kind of man" who summoned his country to follow him with no idea of where he was leading it, but the Scottish polemicist's response to the issue of slavery in general suggests the long transatlantic shadows thrown by the American Civil War over British life.[25]

A more measured and thus in some ways more interesting example of British skepticism toward Lincoln during the early part of the Civil War can be found in Anthony Trollope's travel narrative *North America*, based on a visit the British novelist undertook to the United States between August 1861 and May 1862. As Trollope explained in his introductory chapter, he had long planned "to write a book about the United States" and had scheduled his trip before the nation's "intestine troubles" manifested themselves: "I have not allowed the division among the States and the breaking out of civil war to interfere with my intention," commented Trollope, "but I should not purposely have chosen this period either for my book or for my visit."[26] What ensues, in fact, is a very detailed critical account of the political situation of the United States, one that even goes so far as to include three appendices that reprint in their entirety the Declaration of Independence, the Articles of Confederation, and the U.S. Constitution, because the author said he is concerned that readers "who desire to look into this matter may be anxious to examine them without reference to other volumes."[27] Most of this political commentary is normally excised in modern editions of *North America*, which tend in the more conventional manner of travel writing to focus on Trollope's fleeting impressions of particular towns and cities, but the weighty nature of these political observations bears ample testimony to how pressing a concern the American Civil War appeared for Englishmen at this time. Although Trollope was generally supportive of the North and its right to wage war on the South, he was also adamant that the differences between these regions of the United States were so extensive – "different instincts, different appetites, different morals, and a different culture" – that the real issue was simply where the line of secession should ultimately be drawn.[28] According to Trollope, the war was worth fighting on the North's part only because it would make it more likely that border states such as Maryland, Virginia, and Kentucky would be saved for the Union. Trollope's implicit sympathy for Southern regionalism was echoed in other parts of the British Establishment at this time: Although Lord Palmerston in May 1861 declared it would be a happy day when "we could succeed in putting an end to this unnatural war between the two sections of our North American cousins," his Chancellor of the Exchequer, William Gladstone, remarked in a speech of 1862 that, regardless of one's feelings about slavery, Jefferson Davis should be commended for having "made a nation."[29]

In relation to the broader culture of the Union states, Trollope saw the erosion of personal liberties by the Lincoln administration as deeply disturbing. "Newspapers have been stopped for advocating views opposed to the feelings of the North," he complained, "as freely as newspapers were ever stopped in France for opposing the Emperor."[30] He also described the "executive power" of the president as "almost unbounded," saying that Lincoln "is much more powerful than any minister can be with us" and accusing him of breaching the U.S. Constitution by suspending habeas corpus without the authority of Congress.[31] Trollope also reserved particular venom for Secretary of State Seward, who he said "has instituted passports and surveillance" and "locked men up with reason and without."[32] The English author was also particularly incensed by the circumstances of the *Trent* affair: "Up until this period my sympathies had been with the North," he explains: "But this stopping of an English mail-steamer was too much for me."[33] Trollope's own professional commitment to mail services would doubtless have increased his outrage at this incident, and indeed in 1859 he himself had traveled on the *Trent* between San Juan del Norte and Colon, when visiting the West Indies on behalf of the British Post Office.[34]

Trollope's indictment of Lincoln's overbearing power foreshadows various critiques of the institution of the American presidency that have become a standard feature of political analysis in modern times. The political historian James Bryce, who served between 1907 and 1913 as British ambassador to the United States, described Lincoln in his famous book *The American Commonwealth* (1890) as akin to "a Roman dictator," someone who "wielded more authority than any Englishman has done since Oliver Cromwell," and more recently American historian Don E. Fehrenbacher depicted Lincoln as having invented a "modern imperial presidency ... built to a considerable extent upon the concept of emergency power."[35] Such critiques of presidential authoritarianism were particularly marked in the early years of the twenty-first century, in the wake of George W. Bush's invocation of "homeland security" as a rationale for the exercise of state surveillance. Whereas Bush was generally abhorred in Europe for bringing the good name of American liberty into disrepute, it is remarkable how quickly Lincoln became sanctified as a folk hero, both at home and abroad, for the way he manipulated the power of his presidency to bring about the end of slavery. It was, of course, Lincoln's assassination on Good Friday, 1865, that changed everything, with the chairman of a memorial meeting in Huddersfield shortly after the news reached England declaring that "all sects, all parties, and all classes" in Britain were united in their revulsion at this dastardly act.[36] The *Times*, which on November 22, 1864, had declared Lincoln's reelection as "an avowed step towards the foundation of a military despotism," was by April 29, 1865, proclaiming antithetically: "Abraham Lincoln was as little of a tyrant as any man who ever lived." In terms of his own subsequent political reputation, Lincoln can thus be said to have timed his departure perfectly.[37] In a general election held in Britain in July 1865, not a single sitting member who had supported the Union failed to be returned to the new parliament.

After 1865, Lincoln went on to be fêted as the embodiment of a democratic legend by various radical and liberal groups in Britain. He was particularly popular in Wales, where his abolitionist triumph was widely associated with his abiding Nonconformist Christian principles. *Uncle Tom's Cabin* had been the first novel ever translated into the Welsh language, and the Welsh-speaking Liberal Prime Minister David Lloyd George, who unveiled a statue of Lincoln at Westminster in 1920, was particularly effusive in his praise for the American president, describing him as "one of those giant figures, of whom there are very few in history, who lose their nationality in death," because they "are no longer Greek or Hebrew, English or American" but "belong to mankind."[38] At the same time, however, Lincoln found himself also appropriated by political conservatives, who hailed him as the quintessential Anglo-Saxon hero, someone who had managed to uphold the dignity and integrity of his country against forces of internal subversion. Some of the chameleonic capacity that Lincoln displayed during his lifetime, his skill in presenting many different faces to different factions, was consequently preserved in the multifarious ways in which his presidential aura was exploited after his death. Characteristically, his legacy was invoked by both sides on the Irish Home Rule question in the early twentieth century: by Irish republican Eamon de Valera, who saw Lincoln's ideal of government "of the people, by the people, for the people" as a model for resisting partition and returning Irish representation to its native soil, but also by British patriots, who presented any division of the United Kingdom as dangerously analogous to Confederate secession. The one political group in Britain that was never much impressed by Lincoln was the Labour Party, particularly after 1945. According to Richard Carwardine, the great social-ist orator Aneurin Bevan never once alluded to Lincoln, whereas Michael Foot, Labour leader during the early 1980s, "regarded him as a conserva-tive figure." Whereas the liberal Nonconformist Welsh communities of the nineteenth and early twentieth century admired Lincoln for his moral stand on slavery, Welsh socialists of a later period were less happy with what they took to be Lincoln's relative lack of interest in social equality. Indeed, as Jay Sexton has noted, U.S. international diplomacy around the time of the ses-quicentennial of Lincoln's birth in 1959 succeeded in rebranding him as an epitome of the "self-made man theme" in American culture, not so much an abolitionist or political reformer but a rugged pioneer whose primary virtue lay in the way he overcame personal setbacks and succeeded in hauling him-self up by his own bootstraps.[39]

What all this suggests, as Richard Hofstadter observed in 1948, is how Lincoln was "thoroughly and completely the politician," even to the extent of being able to hold together opposing factions in death as well as life.[40] Matthew Pinsker suggests that over the years Lincoln has been made to "appear too much of a philosopher/poet and not enough of a politician," although of course it was precisely his own skill as a politician that ena-bled him radically to dehistoricize the Declaration of Independence and thus, as Garry Wills perceptively remarked, to reinvent a version of the U.S. Constitution based on its supposed "spirit" rather than its "letter."[41] Moreover, Lincoln's political and poetic skills worked in the same direc-tion, because the impulse to transliterate himself and his conception of federal unity into emblems of universal truth was entirely consistent with his performative skills in oratory, which similarly enabled him throughout his public career to transpose historical contingency into mythic necessity. As Adam Gopnik remarked, Lincoln would make "the proposition that Texas and New Hampshire should be forever bound by a single post office sound like something right out of Genesis."[42] Particularly in his Gettysburg Address, the president drew on biblical echoes ("fourscore and seven years ago") to endow his rhetoric with an apocalyptic dimension.[43] Part of this skill involved a radical egalitarianism, a shrewd sense that political lan-guage worked best when its cadences were simple and memorable; Lincoln's mastery of this evangelical idiom can be seen by contrasting his address at Gettysburg with that of Edward Everett, whose preceding two-hour speech was full of classical references – to the Battle of Marathon, the Ancient Greeks, Persian invasions – but whose efforts thus to elevate the idea of American military sacrifice came out merely as pompous and strained.

Lincoln's idiom of stylistic simplicity was also honed by his taste for the works of Shakespeare, something that went back to his earliest years, with many of the contributors to William Herndon's oral biography attesting to the young Lincoln's interest in Shakespeare. Given that we know how Lincoln later carried around a volume of Shakespeare's plays with him in the White House, it might seem surprising that there are hardly any direct allusions to Shakespeare in Lincoln's writings. Again, however, Lincoln's genius involved in part an art of concealment, the appropriation of Shakespearian language not for ostentatious cultural capital – Lincoln would have loathed the idea of aligning himself in public either with cutthroat princes or with the louche theatrical world of Elizabethan England – but, rather, in the interests of investing his own language with the heavy burden of eternal truth. One of Lincoln's favorite Shakespeare extracts was the "Fear no more the heat o' the sun" dirge from *Cymbeline*, and the tone of fatalism endemic to that poem – "Golden lads and girls all must, / As chimney sweepers come to dust" – is itself reminiscent of the Book of Ecclesiastes, both in its radical simplicity and in its equation of temporal cycles with the inevitable way of the world. One specific Shakespearian derivative is the resonant final phrase in Lincoln's First Inaugural Address invoking "the better angels of our nature."[44] This involves a conscious reworking of Shakespeare's Sonnet 144, which contrasts the "two spirits" of human nature:

> The better angel is a man right fair,
> The worser spirit a woman colour'd ill.
> To win me soon to hell, my female evil
> Tempteth my better angel from my side.

One of Lincoln's few explicit comments on Shakespeare comes in a letter he wrote to the Shakespearian actor James H. Hackett on August 17, 1863, thanking him for sending a copy of his book, *Notes and Comments on Shakespeare*. Lincoln, who had once been to four Shakespeare history plays in one week and who had seen Hackett play the role of Falstaff in *Henry IV, Part One*, subsequently invited him to dinner at the White House, where he quizzed Hackett on various stagecraft issues, such as why the tavern scene's play-within-a-play between Hal and Falstaff was always cut in performance. In his 1863 letter to Hackett, Lincoln admits that while he has not read some of Shakespeare's plays, "others I have gone over perhaps as frequently as any unprofessional reader. Among the latter are *Lear, Richard III, Henry VIII, Hamlet,* and especially *Macbeth*. I think nothing equals *Macbeth*. It is wonderful."[45] Given the president's taste for the brutalities of *realpolitik*, it is hardly a surprise to find him so enthusiastic about *Macbeth*, and indeed during his own last days, as Union armies finally closed down the

Confederate resistance, Lincoln read aloud from *Macbeth* to members of his war cabinet on the presidential yacht. He was, however, taken aback when Hackett allowed this letter on Shakespeare to be published without first asking permission, an event that led to the *New York Herald* satirizing Lincoln as "the latest and greatest of Shakespeare's Commentators" and being particularly sarcastic about the president's suggestion that "the soliloquy in *Hamlet* commencing 'Oh, my offense is rank,' surpasses that commencing 'To be or not to be.'" The *Herald* commented that Lincoln's preference for Claudius's soliloquy over the more famous soliloquy of Hamlet was entirely appropriate for a political manipulator who was, in imitation of the infamous King of Denmark, "like a man to double business bound."[46]

Just as he astutely secularized biblical rhetoric in order to maximize his own political impact, therefore, so Lincoln appropriated the language of Shakespeare in order to invest his political activities with an aura of higher purpose. This was not necessarily a merely cynical strategy on his part, because, as Garry Wills has suggested, such putative displacement of worldly affairs into a realm of the spirit was characteristic of American intellectual life more generally during this period. Lincoln succeeded in extrapolating what Wills called a "transcendental" significance from the American Civil War, and this aligned him intellectually with Whitman and Ralph Waldo Emerson, both of whose work Lincoln read and admired, who were seeking similarly to evoke a version of U.S. identity predicated on the categorical imperatives of higher laws.[47] Lincoln, though, cannily balanced his instinctive attachment to national exceptionalism against a more prudential sense of America's place within a wider world, a world often skeptical toward millennial conceptions of the United States. Typically, the coat Lincoln was wearing when he was assassinated had the legend sewn into its lining, "One Country, One Destiny"; but on his way to Washington some years earlier to assume the presidency, he had more warily placed himself "in the hands of the Almighty, and of this, his almost chosen people."[48] It is that "almost" – itself, almost invisible – that signals the balance between providentialism and politics, universalism and nationalism, on which the success of Lincoln's presidency ultimately rested. It may, as Wills says, have been the rhetoric of Gettysburg that transformed the United States from a "plural" into a "singular" noun, but the transnational dimension to Lincoln's polity always projected itself as an implicit formal principle, a chameleonic recognition of structural doubleness.[49] We see this in what he acknowledged – albeit at times reluctantly – to be the necessity of expanding his horizon beyond the domestic field of a "house divided" to negotiate with Britain and other overseas interests, and also in his admission of the United States as grounded on a skillful rhetoric of partiality and political expediency in addition to the grander claims of human liberty.

NOTES

1 Abraham Lincoln, "Annual Message to Congress" (1862), in Philip Van Doren Stern, ed., *The Life and Writings of Abraham Lincoln* (New York: Modern Library, 1940), 736; "Opinion of the Draft" (1863), in *Life and Writings*, 770; letter to Albert G. Hedges, April 4, 1864, in *Life and Writings*, 807.

2 Shirley Samuels, *Facing America: Iconography and the Civil War* (New York: Oxford University Press, 2004), 34.

3 Lincoln, *Life and Writings*, 232.

4 George B. Forgie, *Patricide in the House Divided: A Psychological Interpretation of Lincoln and His Age* (New York: Norton, 1979), 98, 107.

5 Lincoln, *Life and Writings*, 649.

6 Lincoln, *Life and Writings*, 657; Hugh Brogan, ed., *The American Civil War: Extracts from* The Times, *1860–1865* (London: Times Books, 1975), 86; R. J. M. Blackett, *Divided Hearts: Britain and the American Civil War* (Baton Rouge: Louisiana State University Press, 2001), 226.

7 Walt Whitman, *Leaves of Grass*, Sculley Bradley and Harold W. Blodgett, ed. (New York: Norton, 1973), 330, 337, 333.

8 Craig L. Symonds, *Lincoln and His Admirals: Abraham Lincoln, the U.S. Navy, and the Civil War* (New York: Oxford University Press, 2008), 94.

9 Brogan, *American Civil War*, 61; Blackett, *Divided Hearts*, 163.

10 Symonds, *Lincoln and His Admirals*, 101, x.

11 Blackett, *Divided Hearts*, 152.

12 Blackett, *Divided Hearts*, 4.

13 Mary Ellison, *Support for Secession: Lancashire and the American Civil War* (Chicago: University of Chicago Press, 1972).

14 Blackett, *Divided Hearts*, 177.

15 Howard Temperley, *Britain and America Since Independence* (Basingstoke: Palgrave, 2002), 68; Blackett, *Divided Hearts*, 146.

16 Will Kaufman, *The Civil War in American Culture* (Edinburgh: Edinburgh University Press, 2006), 129.

17 Blackett, *Divided Hearts*, 96, 208.

18 Thomas Carlyle, "Occasional Discourse on the Nigger Question," *Fraser's Magazine* (December 1849): 671.

19 David Simpson, *Romanticism, Nationalism, and the Revolt Against Theory* (Chicago: University of Chicago Press, 1993), 122.

20 Blackett, *Divided Hearts*, 47, 104.

21 Christine Bolt, *Victorian Attitudes to Race* (London: Routledge and Kegan Paul, 1971), 87.

22 Kathleen Biddick, *The Shock of Medievalism* (Durham, NC: Duke University Press, 1998), 8, 11.

23 Thomas Carlyle, "Shooting Niagara: and After?" in *Critical and Miscellaneous Essays*, vol. III (London: Chapman and Hall, 1869), 592.

24 Carlyle, "Shooting Niagara," 593, 594, 607, 598.

25 T. Peter Park, "John Stuart Mill, Thomas Carlyle, and the U.S. Civil War," *The Historian* 54.1 (Sept. 1991): 103.

26 Anthony Trollope, *North America*, 2 vols. (1862; rpt. London: Dawson, 1968), I, 1.

27 Ibid., II, 50.

28 Ibid., I, 10.
29 Ephraim Douglass Adams, *Great Britain and the American Civil War*, 2 vols. (New York: Russell and Russell, 1958), I, 78; Park, "John Stuart Mill," 95.
30 Trollope, *North America*, I, 223.
31 Ibid., II, 231.
32 Ibid., II, 227.
33 Ibid., I, 298.
34 R. H. Super, *Trollope and the Post Office* (Ann Arbor: University of Michigan Press, 1981), 41.
35 James Bryce, *The American Commonwealth*, 2 vols., 3rd ed. (New York: Macmillan, 1896), I, 206, 66; Don E. Fehrenbacher, *Lincoln in Text and Context: Collected Essays* (Stanford: Stanford University Press, 1987), 140.
36 Blackett, *Divided Hearts*, 216.
37 Fehrenbacher, *Lincoln in Text and Context*, 203.
38 "Interchange: The Global Lincoln," *Journal of American History* 96.2 (Sept. 2009): 474.
39 "Interchange," 493–494, 486, 483.
40 Richard Hofstadter, *The American Political Tradition and the Men Who Made It* (New York: Knopf, 1948), 94.
41 Matthew Pinsker, "Lincoln Studies at the Bicentennial: A Round Table. Lincoln Theme 2.0," *Journal of American History* 96.2 (Sept. 2009): 430; Garry Wills, *Lincoln at Gettysburg: The Words That Remade America* (New York: Simon and Schuster, 1992), 38.
42 Adam Gopnik, "Angels and Ages: Lincoln's Language and Its Legacy," *New Yorker*, May 28, 2007, 32.
43 Lincoln, *Life and Writings*, 788.
44 Lincoln, *Life and Writings*, 657.
45 Lincoln, *Life and Writings*, 775.
46 Lincoln, *Life and Writings*, 775; John C. Briggs, "Steeped in Shakespeare," The Claremont Institute for the Study of Statesmanship and Political Philosophy, February 17, 2009: http://www.claremont.org/publications/crb/id.1605/article.detail.asp
47 Wills, *Lincoln at Gettysburg*, 37.
48 Mark E. Neely, Jr., "Lincoln, Slavery, and the Nation," *Journal of American History* 96.2 (Sept. 2009): 458; Dorothy Ross, "Lincoln and the Ethics of Emancipation: Universalism, Nationalism, Exceptionalism," *Journal of American History* 96.2 (Sept. 2009): 396.
49 Wills, *Lincoln at Gettysburg*, 145.

10

BETSY ERKKILA

Lincoln in International Memory

> In *giving* freedom to the *slave*, we *assure* freedom to the *free* – honorable
> alike in what we give, and what we preserve. We shall nobly save, or
> meanly lose, the last best hope of earth.
> Abraham Lincoln, Message to Congress, December 1, 1862

On November 29, 1864, the International Workingmen's Association, a fed-
eration of European workers, trade unionists, and social reformers founded
in London, wrote to Abraham Lincoln. "We congratulate the American
people upon your reelection by a large majority," the address began, drawing attention to the importance of the popular vote in sounding the death
knell to slavery in the American republic. "If resistance to the Slave Power
was the reserved watchword of your first election, the triumphant war cry of
your reelection is, Death to Slavery."[1] Written in English by Karl Marx and
signed in London on behalf of the International Workingmen's Association
by some fifty-seven members from Great Britain, France, Italy, Poland, and
Switzerland, the letter envisions the Civil War not as an isolated national or
internecine struggle but in epic terms as a "titanic American strife" in which
"the star-spangled banner" will also determine "the destiny" of European
workers.

Lincoln's speeches had consistently envisioned the Union war as part of a
world historical struggle for the people and democracy: "We cannot escape
history," he said of the logic of emancipation in an address to Congress in
1862, "We know how to save the Union. The world knows we know how
to save it."[2] The International Workingmen viewed the American Civil War
in similarly historical and global terms. However, for them it was a war for
black and white free labor. They presented the "Armed Revolt" of "300,000
slaveholders" in the very place where "the idea of one great Democratic
Republic had first sprung up, whence the first Declaration of the Rights of
Man was issued, and the first impulse given to the European revolution of
the eighteenth century" as a "counterrevolution" that sought to solve the
"problem of 'the relation of labor to capital'" by proclaiming "property in
man 'the cornerstone of the new edifice.'"[3]

For "the working classes of Europe" the American war was their war:
They looked on "the slaveholders' rebellion" as "a general holy crusade of

property against labor." The workers in effect articulated an international class struggle between labor and capital. "Let us re-adopt the Declaration of Independence," Lincoln said in his famous speech at Peoria in 1854, in words that would become the moral compass of his life: "Let north and south – let all Americans – let all lovers of liberty everywhere – join in the great and good work."[4] Like Lincoln, Marx redefined the Declaration of Independence as the announcement of a political break and the inauguration of a social revolution. Echoing the sacrificial language of Lincoln's Gettysburg Address, of blood shed for "a new birth of freedom – and that government of the people, by the people, for the people, shall not perish from the earth,"[5] Marx described the active engagement and suffering of European labor during the war:

> For the men of labor, with their hopes for the future, even their past conquests were at stake in that tremendous conflict on the other side of the Atlantic. Everywhere they bore therefore patiently the hardships imposed upon them by the cotton crisis, opposed enthusiastically the proslavery intervention – importunities of their betters – and, from most parts of Europe, contributed their quota of blood to the good cause.

European workers shared Lincoln's belief in the right to enjoy the fruits of one's own labor as the essence of liberty and the foundation of the American republic. Even before Lincoln issued the Emancipation Proclamation in 1863, they identified with the American struggle as an antislavery struggle on behalf of the working classes worldwide. "The workingmen feel sure," they wrote, "that as the American War of Independence initiated a new era of ascendancy for the middle class, so the American Antislavery War will do for the working classes."[6]

The workers' address concluded with a *salut et fraternité* to Lincoln as the working-class hero and leader of a struggle for liberation and "reconstruction" that would continue into the future and beyond the United States to an entire "social world": "They consider it an earnest of the epoch to come, that it fell to the lot of Abraham Lincoln, the single-minded son of the working class, to lead his country through the matchless struggle for the rescue of an enchained race and the reconstruction of a social world."[7]

Given the perspective of the Workingmen's address, it might seem highly unlikely that Lincoln, generally regarded as an embodiment of fundamentally American values, would respond to an address written by the author of the *Communist Manifesto*. However, much to Marx's delight, Lincoln did respond, in language that echoes the internationalist language and vision: "So far as the sentiments expressed by it are personal," Lincoln wrote through his ambassador in England, "they are accepted by him with a sincere and anxious desire that he may be able to prove himself not unworthy of the confidence which has been recently extended to him by his fellow citizens and by so many of the friends of humanity and progress throughout the world." But Lincoln did not stop at what concerns him personally. He went on to affirm the common "cause" of human rights, freedom, and happiness that the United States shared with European workers in its war against insurgent slave masters: "Nations do not exist for themselves alone, but to promote the welfare and happiness of mankind by benevolent intercourse and example. It is in this relation that the United States regard their cause in the present conflict with slavery-maintaining insurgents as the cause of human nature, and they derive new encouragement to persevere from the testimony of the workingmen of Europe that the national attitude is favored with their enlightened approval and sympathy."[8]

This key exchange between the First International and Lincoln draws attention to dimensions of Lincoln the international president that have fallen out of the public record because historians and biographers have focused so singly on Lincoln in national memory.[9] While Lincoln was being ridiculed and undermined by government leaders and the press in Great Britain, France, Germany, Spain, Italy, and other European countries, he was hailed by radicals, socialists, and democrats throughout Europe as a working-class leader in the fight for democracy among workers and the oppressed throughout the world. He was admired by Karl Marx, who closely followed Lincoln's every word and action over many years as a foreign correspondent for the New York *Daily Tribune* in the 1850s and early 1860s and for *Die Presse* during the Civil War. From as early as his 1838 Lyceum Address about America as a democratic experiment in the eyes of the world, Lincoln also cultivated an international language and vision that is as much a product of the Old World as it is a product of the Declaration of Independence, itself shaped by the natural and universal human rights discourse of the revolutionary Enlightenment and the transatlantic world.

To understand Lincoln's place in international memory, it is important to begin with the context of the revolutionary transatlantic, in relation to the American and European revolutions of the eighteenth century and the Revolutions of 1848 in Europe. Marx's writings on Lincoln and the Civil War in Europe can illuminate the different functions Lincoln's image, language, and vision served in the years before his assassination. The concluding discussion of the massive outpouring of European sympathy that followed Lincoln's assassination shows us Lincoln in international memory and the transatlantic origins of Lincoln's visionary language.

The International Turn: Lincoln and the Revolutions of 1848

Lincoln never went to Europe, but as an American politician and especially as president, he envisioned himself as a historical actor on the stage of the world. During his term in Congress in 1847–1848, in response to the U.S. invasion of Mexico, the extension of slavery into the territories, and the European Revolutions of 1848, he began to fashion an international language of human liberty and the right of all people everywhere to rise up and "revolutionize." On January 12, 1848, Lincoln delivered a speech to the House of Representatives protesting President Polk's invasion of Mexico and defending the "sacred right" of popular revolution: "Any people anywhere," he said, "have the *right* to rise up, and shake off the existing government, and form a new one that suits them better. This is a most valuable, – a most sacred right – a right, which we hope and believe, is to liberate the world."[10] On the same day that Lincoln delivered this speech, the people of Palermo rose up against Ferdinand II, the tyrannical king of Naples and Sicily, a revolution that inspired a popular uprising in France that overthrew King Louis Philippe and led to the outbreak of revolutions throughout Europe. Lincoln's speech on the right to "revolutionize" as a means "to liberate the world" suggests the extent to which he – like his compatriots Walt Whitman, Margaret Fuller, and Harriet Beecher Stowe – was in touch with the revolutionary ferment of his times on both sides of the Atlantic.[11]

Lincoln's first public act in support of the revolutions in Europe occurred in September 1849 when he helped to write a series of resolutions adopted by Springfield citizens in support of the Hungarian freedom struggle, one of the most long-lasting European revolutions led by Lajos Kossuth against the oppressive Hapsburg regime. The resolutions express "highest admiration" for the "glorious" Hungarian "struggle for liberty" and urge the U.S. government to recognize Hungary as an independent republic.[12] Although Lincoln may not have been the single author of these resolutions, his simultaneously legalistic, visionary, and international voice – and a glimpse of his future policy as president – is more audible in a further set of resolutions Lincoln proposed in 1852, when Kossuth, the popular Hungarian freedom fighter, was touring the United States in search of possible U.S. intervention in the Hungarian revolution. Lincoln's resolutions urge "non-intervention" by any government "as a sacred principle of the international law" at the same time that they reaffirm "the right of any people … to revolutionize, their existing form of government"; they "recognize in Governor Kossuth of Hungary the most worthy and distinguished representative of the cause of civil and religious liberty on the continent of Europe"; they announce that "the sympathies" of the United States "should be exerted in favor of the people of every nation struggling to be free"; in the course of doing "honor to Kossuth and Hungary," they "pour out the tribute of our praise and approbation to the patriotic efforts of the Irish, the Germans, and the French, who have unsuccessfully fought to establish in their several governments the supremacy of the people"; and they conclude by censuring the British government for "her treatment of Ireland" and for joining "the despots of Europe in suppressing every effort of the people to establish free governments, based upon the principles of true religious and civil liberty."[13] Although Lincoln did not know it at the time, the resolutions accurately predict the British government's later response to both Lincoln and his own freedom struggle against the South.

The Revolutions of 1848 were short-lived: By the end of 1849, the old regime had returned in force. But what Harriet Beecher Stowe called the "earthquake" of 1848 would continue to convulse the United States with shockwaves that spurred the antislavery struggle, labor radicalism, and the outbreak of the Civil War. Many republicans and radicals from the Revolutions of 1848 sought refuge in the United States, including some 10,000 German "48ers," thousands of whom became actively involved in the antislavery movement, the formation of the Republican Party, and the election of Lincoln.[14] Of the 400,000 foreign-born persons who served in the Union army – more than a quarter of the Union ranks – the Germans contributed the largest number. More than 5,000 German-Americans served as officers in the Union army, all of whom were exiled radicals from the Revolutions of 1848 who knew Marx and, in some cases, Lincoln personally.[15]

Most Lincoln biographers and historians of the Civil War pass over the relationship between Lincoln and Marx in seemingly embarrassed silence, reading both Lincoln and Civil War as primarily national affairs.[16] But like Lincoln, Marx recognized the prehistory of the Civil War in both the American Revolution and the European Revolutions of 1848. In fact, in his Workingmen's address to Lincoln, Marx interprets the Civil War as a kind of deferred Revolution of 1848, attributing the failure of the Revolutions of 1848 to the failure of white American labor to find common cause with either European or black slave laborers. "The workingmen, the true political powers of the North, allowed slavery to defile their own republic," Marx wrote in words that echo Lincoln's response to the Kansas-Nebraska Act in 1854: "They were unable to attain the true freedom of labor, or to support their European brethren in their struggle for emancipation, but this barrier to progress has been swept off by the red sea of Civil War." In Marx's view this "red sea" might usher in a new era of ascendancy for the working classes, a proletarian revolution that could even be achieved peacefully through the ballot box in countries such as the United States, England, and Holland.[17]

Marx, Lincoln, and the Antislavery War

Karl Marx had a lifelong fascination with the United States. He considered the United States the most advanced bourgeois democracy in the modern world. As a political exile living in Brussels in 1845, he even considered emigrating to the United States – perhaps to Texas. Marx did not emigrate, but he corresponded with many German friends and radicals who did, including the first American Marxist leader, Joseph Weydemeyer, who fought in the 1848 Revolution in Germany and later served as a major-general in the Union army during the Civil War.[18] Marx's interest in the United States intensified when, as an impoverished exile from the Revolutions of 1848 living in London in 1851, he was hired as a foreign correspondent by the New York *Tribune*, the largest and most influential American newspaper and Marx's main source of livelihood between 1851 and 1862. Like Lincoln in his 1854 speech in Peoria – "Our republican robe is soiled," he said; "Let us re-adopt the Declaration of Independence" – Marx interpreted political events of the fifties and sixties as a "return" from "the aberrations which United States history, under the slaveowners' pressure, had undergone for half a century ... to the true principles of its development."[19]

After the outbreak of what Marx called "the American Antislavery War," Abraham Lincoln, the "average man of good will" who was elected to lead this struggle, became a "household name" and much-admired presence in the Marx home. Interest was so intense that even Marx's daughter, Eleanor, who was only six when the war broke out, felt moved to write letters of advice to Lincoln. "American battle reports and Blue Books" replaced "Marryat and Scott," she recalled: "For days I brooded over English Government reports, over American maps.... I had the unshakable conviction that Abraham Lincoln could not succeed without my advice, and so I wrote him long letters, which Mohr ["Moor," Marx's family nickname] had to read and take to the post office."[20]

Marx's own "letters" about Lincoln and the Civil War appeared more publicly in articles published in the *Tribune* in 1861 and *Die Presse*, an influential Viennese newspaper, between 1861 and 1862. Rarely cited by biographers and historians, Marx's shrewd analyses of Lincoln and the Civil War are historically accurate, politically savvy, and uncannily prophetic. Although the British government professed neutrality, government officials, the upper class, and the press predicted Confederate victory and secretly waited for an opportunity to intervene on the side of the Confederacy; or if that failed, to invade Mexico with Napoleon III, the reactionary king of France. Splintering the United States into competing states would assist British and French imperial designs in the New and Old World.

What particularly fascinated Marx about Lincoln was the fact that he was the first American president to rise from the working class. At first Marx was struck by Lincoln's "personal insignificance" compared to William Seward and John Frémont. But as he watched Lincoln slowly wean himself from the control of the "loyal" slaveholders under the growing pressure from the Northwest and the Northeast for the abolition of slavery, he grew to admire Lincoln's cool – his ability to deliver a "coup" in "the most unpretentious way." "President Lincoln never ventures a step forward before the turn of circumstances," Marx wrote of Lincoln's removal of George McClellan as commander-in-chief of the Union army. "But once 'Old Abe' has convinced himself that such a turning point has arrived, he surprises friend and foe alike by a sudden operation carried out as quietly as possible."[21]

At a time when President Lincoln was being burlesqued by the London *Times* as a "respectable buffoon," Marx wrote a character sketch acclaiming Lincoln's uniquely democratic manner and style:

> The figure of Lincoln is *sui generis* in the annals of history. No initiative, no idealistic eloquence, no buskin, no historic drapery. He always presents the most important act in the most insignificant form possible.... Hesitant, resistant, unwilling, he sings the bravura aria of his role as though he begged pardon for the circumstances that force him 'to be a lion.' The most awesome decrees, which will always remain historically remarkable, that he hurls at the enemy all resemble, and are intended to resemble, the trite summons that one lawyer sends to an opposing lawyer.

This same legalistic, "pettifogging," and "undraped" style is evident even in the Emancipation Proclamation, Marx notes, "the most significant document in American history since the founding of the Union and one which tears up the old American Constitution."[22]

A bit of a bourgeois himself when it came to questions of class, Marx acknowledged "what is aesthetically repulsive, logically inadequate, officially burlesque, and politically contradictory in Lincoln's actions and policies." As "the offspring" of "the electoral system" rather than "a people's revolution," Lincoln was in fact "a plebian," "an average man of good will" who rose from rail-splitter to congressman in Illinois. It is this very ordinariness that makes Lincoln a figure of world historical significance. "Never has the New World scored a greater victory than in the demonstration that with its political and social organization, average men of good will suffice to do that which in the Old World would have required heroes to do!"[23]

For Marx, then, Lincoln was a new kind of democratic hero: "Nowadays, when the most insignificant event on this side of the Atlantic Ocean takes on an air of melodrama, is it entirely without significance that in the New World what is significant should appear in a workaday coat?" he asked. As early as 1862, when the English government and press still thought – or hoped – that the Confederacy would win the war, Marx proposed that "in the history of the United States and humanity, Lincoln will take his place directly next to Washington!"[24]

Lincoln and the Civil War in Europe

The ruling classes in Europe were very far from sharing Marx's assessment of Lincoln. The British government's official relations with Lincoln were strained from the outset by what John Stuart Mill called "the general frenzy" and "rush of nearly the whole upper and middle classes of my own country, even those who passed for Liberals, into a furious pro-Southern partisanship." This hostility to Lincoln is evident even in the print world where the British preferred the more gentlemanly image of Jefferson Davis to the off-putting democratic image of Lincoln as backwoods rail-splitter, bargeman, and small-town lawyer. "I think all who see them will agree that Jefferson Davis bears out one's idea of what an able administrator should look like better than Abraham Lincoln," said one conservative member of Parliament in 1861; "We cannot help seeing that, while Abraham Lincoln is an incapable pretender, Jefferson Davis is a bold, a daring, yet politic statesman."[25]

In Charles Francis Adams's view, this pro-Southern feeling emerged not so much from "genuine sympathy" for the rebels as from fear of the spread of democracy in England should the Union succeed.[26] As Marx and others recognized, however, the British commercial and industrial classes also feared the rise of a fully *United* States as a dominant economic power in the world. This fear escalated to the very brink of war when on November 8, 1861, two Confederate envoys sent to England and France to urge recognition of the Confederacy were intercepted by a Union warship while aboard the British mail steamer the *Trent* and were arrested. Many in England interpreted the arrest as an order from Lincoln and an act of war. "Abraham Lincoln, whose accession to power was generally welcomed on this side of the Atlantic, has proved himself a feeble, confused, and little-minded mediocrity," the London *Morning Chronicle* wrote. While Lincoln and William Steward, "the firebrand at his elbow," "stagger on at the head of affairs," wrote the *Chronicle* fomenting the public cry for war, "their only chance of fame consists in the probability that the navies of England will blow out of the water their blockading squadrons, and teach them how to respect the flag of a mightier supremacy beyond the Atlantic."[27]

Lincoln put an end to the affair by quietly releasing the envoys, but not before the British government had sent some 18,000 additional troops to Canada in preparation for an invasion of the United States. Truth to tell, some in England, including the London *Times*, the largest and most influential British journal in the world, sought to fan the flames of war, especially after the Union blockade prevented shipments of cotton to England and Europe, which angered the industrial and manufacturing classes and led to unemployment, impoverishment, and famine among the cotton weavers in England. "It has been said how much better it would be, not for the United States, but for us, if these states should be divided," said John Bright, a representative to Parliament, labor activist, and eloquent spokesperson in defense of Lincoln and the Union cause. Urging British neutrality, Bright noted that in the London *Times*, "the most powerful representative of English opinion, at least of the richer classes ... there has not been, since Mr. Lincoln took office, one fair, and honorable and friendly article on American affairs in its columns."[28]

Ironically, as Bright, Marx, and other spokesmen for the working class noted, it was the workers of England, especially those most affected by the cotton shortage in Manchester and Lancashire, who were most uncompromising in their support of Lincoln, the Union, and the struggle to abolish slavery.[29] Against the putatively neutral British government and the pro-Confederacy ruling classes, the agitation of the working class became the most powerful force in keeping England from intervening in the American struggle through all-out war, breaking the blockade, mediation, or invasion of Mexico with the aid of France, Spain, and possibly Russia.[30]

The support of the English working class for Lincoln and the sense of common cause they felt with the antislavery struggle in the United States are particularly evident in a letter sent to Lincoln on the eve of the Emancipation Proclamation. At a time when the Manchester mills had been closed due to the cotton shortage, the unemployed and long-suffering workers gathered to express their "warm and earnest sympathy" with President Lincoln in turning "the victory of the free North" into a war that "will strike off the fetters of the slave" by offering "unconditional freedom for the slaves of the rebel States" under the terms of the Emancipation Proclamation. "We joyfully honor you, as the President, and the Congress with you," the Manchester workers wrote, "for many decisive steps toward practically exemplifying your belief in the words of your great founders: 'All men are created equal.'"

The workers' letter was finally a call to finish the work of revolution that anticipates the providential and visionary language of the Gettysburg

(November 20, 1863) and Second Inaugural Address (March 4, 1864). "We implore you, for your own honor and welfare, not to faint in your providential mission," the workers wrote:

> While your enthusiasm is aflame, and the tide of events runs high, let the work be finished effectually.... The vast progress you have made in the short space of twenty months fills us with hope that every stain on your freedom will shortly be removed, and that the erasure of that foul blot upon civilization and Christianity – chattel slavery – during your Presidency will cause the name of Abraham Lincoln to be honored and revered by posterity.

The workers concluded by avowing their identification with the American freedom struggle: "Our interests ... are identified with yours. We are truly one people, though locally separate.... Accept our high admiration of your firmness in upholding the proclamation of freedom."[31]

The Manchester workers transformed the Declaration of Independence, the Emancipation Proclamation, and the Civil War, which are commonly interpreted in primarily national and American terms, into historical and revolutionary acts that form part of a more universal struggle for freedom and equality worldwide. As such, the workers' letter suggests the more transatlantic impact of the Emancipation Proclamation: first in putting an end to European ambitions to intervene in support of the Confederacy and slavery; second in further inspiring not only workers but liberals and even some conservatives in Europe to support Lincoln once the Union war became a war against slavery; and finally in inspiring the future agitation of both black and white workers for similar reforms in England and throughout Europe.[32]

Even before Lincoln's Gettysburg Address represented the Civil War as a trial whether a nation "dedicated to the proposition that all men are created equal ... can long endure," Europeans who admired Lincoln viewed him as the leader of a struggle to preserve the most advanced democratic republic in the world against slavery as the most debased form of human subjection in history. Oddly, however, European sentiment was intensely Southern. "The fashion in Europe is to admire the South and predict its victory," wrote Prosper Mérimée in a letter to the nephew of Robert E. Lee, comparing the southern "revolution" to the French Revolution of 1848 without "its terrifying grandeur."

The reasons for this support for the South varied. In France, under the Second Empire, Napoleon III maintained a public position of neutrality but schemed throughout the war for a Southern victory that would advance his own imperial designs, especially in Mexico. Even after Lincoln's Emancipation Proclamation turned the Union war into an antislavery struggle, Napoleon III told his councilors: "If the north is victorious, I shall be happy; if the South is victorious, I shall be enchanted!" And his councilors continued to work for southern victory, including a plan to cede Texas back to Europe in exchange for Confederate support, even if it meant war with the United States: "France would not object, perhaps even wish for it, in order at least to be able to interfere with armed force in favor of the South," wrote a Vienna newspaper of the Confederate-French dealings.[33]

As the French abolitionist Count Agénor de Gasparin was the first to recognize, the South depended on European intervention to win the war, and thus Europe played a more central role in determining the outcome of the war than is commonly known. "The real centre of the American question is to be found in Europe," Gasparin wrote; "it is at Paris and London, not at Washington and Richmond that the essential resolutions are taken on which depend the future of the United States." Critical of the fact that "Europe leaped with joy at the thought of rending the United States in twain" and thus eliminating a future rival and bully on the world stage, Gasparin embraced "the future entrance of the United States into the concert of great powers" and praised Americans for the election of Lincoln: "What an immense step America has just taken! Between the presidency of Mr. Buchanan and that of Mr. Lincoln, there is the distance of a social revolution."[34]

Gasparin's high opinion of Lincoln was not shared by many in France. When Prince Napoleon, the cousin Napoleon III, met President Lincoln at the White House on August 3, 1861, he was so put off by his shabby dress and lack of social grace that he "became bored" and left after ten minutes. "What a difference between this sad representative of the great republic and its early founders!" the prince wrote:

> This is a compromise President who was elected simply because people could not agree on some more prominent figure. I fear that the level of human values has fallen considerably. Mr. Lincoln is a worthy enough man, a lawyer from Illinois, and a one-time carpenter.... But he's a poor specimen of a President, and they tell me here that he is the commonest they have had thus far.[35]

When the princes of Orléans, the Comte de Paris and his brother, the Duc de Chartres, fought in the Civil War under General George McClellan, in support of "a young and liberal nation defending its institutions and its very existence," King Leopold of Belgium expressed his royal horror in a letter to his niece Queen Victoria: "They have a chance of being shot for Abraham Lincoln and the most rank Radicalism. I don't think that step will please in France, where Radicalism is at a discount fortunately."[36]

Even liberals who sympathized with republicanism and the antislavery cause, such as Maurice Sand, the son of the celebrated French novelist Georges Sand, had trouble with Lincoln as the face of American freedom.

When he met Lincoln as part of the party that accompanied Prince Napoleon on his visit in 1861, he was struck by "his big hairy hands" holding "a pair of white gloves which had never been worn and never would be worn," "a beard trimmed in the American style – which would make Jove himself look vulgar – a long lock of hair combed across his forehead and hanging down on the other side like a weeping willow, a kindly expression not without subtlety – such is 'Honest Abe.'" Sand's condescending portrait verges on disgust and caricature as he details Lincoln's awkwardness. "The worthy man, quite evidently, was filled with the best intentions. But neither in his speech nor in his manner was this symbol of freedom free."[37] To Sand, Lincoln was vulgar and, as Marx noted, Europeans liked their republican heroes gallant and full of fiery eloquence.

The antirepublican sentiment of the French government was nowhere more evident than in the Corps Législatif's response on April 15, 1865, to news of the fall of Richmond: The cry from the floor was *tant pis* [too bad]. Nevertheless, Eugène Pelletan, the leader of the opposition to the Second Empire, proposed to amend an address from the crown, which contained no allusion to "what concerns America," by sending a "heartfelt felicitation" to the United States. "The slaveholding rebellion is stricken to the earth, and the American republic is reinstated in its majestic unity," Pelletan declared. "Under the fire of the enemy" for four years, Lincoln protected his "executive authority" not through "arbitrary power" but an appeal to law. "This page of American history is the most illustrious page in the nineteenth century," Pelletan said. "President Lincoln has been fully aware that he held the destinies of the New World in his hands, and he has shown himself equal to the emergency; he has abolished slavery, and he has founded a second time the glorious American republic."[38] The amendment failed by a vote of 195–24, a margin that indicates the narrowness of French support for either the "glorious American republic" or its refounding by Lincoln as the protector of republican liberty. But as a purely symbolic political gesture, Pelletan's republican amendment to the Emperor's speech reveals the ways Lincoln would continue to circulate *sub rosa* in the European liberal and working-class imaginary as a symbol of the republican ideal of "liberty and equality."

Two of the most moving French responses came toward the close of the war. The first was written by Marquis Adolphe de Chambrun, an ardent supporter of the Union, who departed for the United States in 1864, where he played a kind of double role as informal observer for the French Foreign Ministry and intimate member of Mary Todd Lincoln's inner circle. His letters to his wife between 1864 and 1865 were written with a psychological depth that self-consciously rejected the democratic caricature that marked other French responses to Lincoln: "His face denotes an immense force of resistance and extreme melancholy," he wrote of meeting Lincoln for the first time:

> It is plain that this man has suffered deeply. His eyes are superb, large and with a very profound expression when he fixes them on you. It cannot be said that he is awkward; his simplicity is too great for that. He has no pretense to having worldly ways and is unused to society, but there is nothing shocking in this, quite the contrary. The elevation of his mind is too evident; his heroic sentiments are so apparent that one thinks of nothing else. Nobody could be less of a parvenu. As President of a mighty nation, he remains just the same as he must have appeared while felling trees in Illinois. But I must add that he dominates everyone present and maintains his exalted position without the slightest effort.[39]

Here Chambrun anticipated the more mythic and heroic stature that the president began to assume in Europe only after his assassination.

On their return from Richmond, where there was "no sound of hoofs in the abandoned streets, not a single voice raised in this city of thirty thousand souls," Chambrun recalled that Lincoln read passages from Shakespeare's *Macbeth* aloud: "The lines after the murder of Duncan, when the new king falls a prey to moral torment, were dramatically dwelt on. Now and then he paused to expatiate on how exact a picture Shakespeare here gives of a murderer's mind when, the dark deed achieved, its perpetrator already envies his victim's calm sleep. He read the scene over twice."[40] Lincoln appears to have viewed himself as a murderer, a head of state with blood on his hands, guilt-ridden, haunted, and tragic. Chambrun's uncanny portrait almost foresees the final act of blood violence that would complete the tragedy of president and nation on the stage of the world.

If Chambrun dramatized Lincoln as a tragic Shakespearean literary character, the bishop of Orléans, Monsignor Dupanloup, was one of the first to focus on Lincoln's literary use of language. He was particularly moved by The Second Inaugural Address: "I have read this document with deep religious emotion and with profoundly sympathetic admiration," he wrote. Whereas the Catholic bishop hoped that "this lamentable civil war" would end, the providential language of Lincoln's address appears to have helped him see its momentous historical significance: "It will have demonstrated the amazing energy of a great people; it will have given the death blow to the odious institution of slavery; it will have caused the grandiose idea of expiation to prevail over the spirit of profit." He found Lincoln's religious language striking in comparison with political speech in Europe: "How momentous to hear the leader of a powerful nation speaking the words of a Christian, so rarely heard here in Europe, announcing the end of slavery and showing the way to this fusion of Justice and of Mercy which is mentioned in the Holy Scriptures." Given the suspicion about Lincoln's religious beliefs in the United States, how momentous that a Catholic Bishop in France would be the first to pay tribute to the global significance of Lincoln's Second Inaugural Address as a "noble page in the history of great men."[41]

Whereas in France these tributes to Lincoln circulated in private correspondence, in Spain, which established a conservative constitutional monarchy under the reign of Queen Isabelle II, Lincoln and democracy became part of a fiercely waged public battle among reactionaries, liberals, and progressives. "In the model republic of what *were* the United States," wrote the reactionary *Pensamiento Español* in a September 1862 editorial, "we see more and more clearly of how little account is a society constituted without God, merely for the sake of men." The destructive "blood and mire" of the Civil War and "their wild ways of annihilating each other" were in fact a cautionary tale about the dangers of "the flaming theories of democracy" and a "model republic" founded on "rebellion" and "atheism" and "populated by the dregs of all the nations in the world."[42]

This reactionary response was countered by an upsurge of Spanish liberal and progressive support for Lincoln, especially after the Emancipation Proclamation. As Laboulaye had argued as early as August 1862, the South could not succeed without the aid of Europe, and one impediment to this was slavery: "This is the feeling of Europe, and the knowledge of this feeling will hold back more than one government." Lincoln's Emancipation Proclamation, issued at the very moment when Spain was contemplating following France in recognizing Southern independence, put an end to European intervention in the war and Spanish (and French) ambitions in the New World.[43] As in France, it also inspired liberals and progressives who sought to reform or overthrow Spanish monarchy to rally around Lincoln as the heroic leader of a worldwide struggle against slavery. "The good, the honorable of all countries are with you and with the people you lead victorious in noble strife," wrote the Democratic Party of Barcelona in a letter dated December 6, 1864. They congratulated "the citizen Abraham Lincoln" on his reelection, which "proves that the President's proclamation for the abolition of slavery well expressed the noble aspiration of the people of the United States." "Persevere, illustrious President, in your work," they declared; "and when the solemn hour of your complete triumph shall sound, let the abolition of slavery in the United States be the signal for the abolition of all slavery among mankind."[44] For other "citizens" of Spain, whose voices had been silenced by the return of military and monarchical oppression, the triumph of Lincoln and an American republic founded on the will of the people assumed particular significance as a beacon of hope for the future of democracy in Europe. "Now, when unfortunate Spain is plunged in a frightful reaction," wrote the citizens of Eclhe, Spain, in an address to Lincoln that enumerates the loss of freedom of speech, freedom of the press, and free inquiry "the honest and brave Spanish people" have suffered; "now, it is highly consolatory for us who have faith and hope in the future, and who do not doubt the justice of God, to see that liberty does not succumb, that progress goes on and makes its daily journey." Echoing Lincoln's own language of democratic trial and sacrifice in the Gettysburg Address and his providential reading of the war in his Second Inaugural Address, the citizens of Spain hail "the destruction of barbarian slavery" as the triumph of democratic governance, the American people, and President Lincoln. They assert that the "President of the republic, called by Providence ... will live always in the memory of coming generations."[45] Written before Lincoln's assassination led to his international and not merely national sanctification as an emancipator in the history of mankind, the address suggests the ways the president's own providential reading of the war would come to shape the way he himself would be remembered internationally.

Lincoln and National Unification

Unlike France and Spain, where political sympathizers celebrated Lincoln as an international emancipator and liberator, the Italian and German states, which were both engaged in major wars of unification during Lincoln's presidency, showed more interest in Lincoln as national unifier. The Kingdom of Italy was officially proclaimed on March 17, 1861, the same month Lincoln was inaugurated as president of the United States. In early 1862, the American minister to Italy reported that Bettino Ricasoli, the prime minister of a newly reunited Italy, expressed "the strongest possible interest in the success of the constitutional authorities in crushing the rebellion."[46] Two years later, Lincoln sent a note to the Italian king and people thanking them for their unwavering friendship and support in the American struggle to preserve national unity: "I am free to confess that the United States have in the course of the last three years, encountered vicissitudes and been involved in controversies which have tried the friendship and even the forbearance of other nations, but at no stage of this unhappy fraternal war, in which we are only endeavoring to save and strengthen the foundations of our national unity, has the King or the people of Italy faltered in addressing to us the language of respect, confidence, and friendship."[47] Lincoln's Italian missive also bears an implicit criticism of the apparent breakdown in the "language" of respect and friendship shown by other European powers at a time of "fraternal war."

Giuseppe Mazzini and Giuseppe Garibaldi, who were well-known in Europe and the Americas as veterans of the Revolutions of 1848 in Italy and as national heroes in the struggle for Italian unification, both identified with and admired Lincoln as the leader of what Garibaldi called "this Holy Battle."[48] Garibaldi even named a grandson after Lincoln: "The name of LINCOLN, like that of Christ, makes the beginning of a glorious era in the history of humanity, and I am proud to perpetuate in my family the name of the great emancipator," he wrote to the American minister in Turin in March 1865. After the Union victory, Mazzini said of the importance of the American struggle in Italy: "You have done more for us in four years, than fifty years of teaching, preaching, and writing from all your European brothers have been able to do."[49]

Early in the war, as the leader of a dissolving American union, Lincoln may also have figured negatively as an emblem of the dangers of both democracy and disunion against which the newly united Kingdom of Italy defined itself. This more negative Italian image of Lincoln is suggested by a mysterious 1861 lithograph, published in Amsterdam, in which small portraits of Lincoln and Jefferson Davis appear beneath a more dominant portrait of the Italian nationalist and prime minister, Bettino Ricasoli.[50] As the only known print of Lincoln with a contemporary foreign leader, the portrait may have been "a mere introduction of three new heads of government."[51] Given the placement and size of the portrait of Ricasola, however, it seems more likely that it was intended to celebrate Ricasola as the head of a newly unified Italy against the diminished stature of Lincoln and Davis as leaders of newly disunited states.

In fact, by mid-1861 Lincoln had so little confidence in his generals that he offered Garibaldi a command in (or perhaps the command of) the Union army. This "honorable proposition" to Garibaldi, a hero of the Revolutions of 1848, who had captured the world's imagination through his daring in the Italian struggle for unification, appears to have been made through U.S. agents in Europe early in the war. By the summer of 1861 Garibaldi was corresponding with U.S. diplomats in Europe, presenting himself as an "adoptive citizen" of the American republic and asking if "the emancipation of Negroes" was part of "this agitation" or not. "If His Majesty King Victor Emmanuel believes he has no need of my services," he wrote the U.S. minister in Belgium in August, 1861, "then provided that the conditions upon which the American Government intends to accept me are these which your messenger has verbally indicated to me, you will have me immediately at your disposal."[52]

The "conditions" of the offer remain unclear, but the correspondence indicates that Garibaldi thought Lincoln would offer him his own position as "Commander-in-Chief of the Army of the United States" and commit fully to a war for the emancipation of slaves. "I will go thither with my friends," Garibaldi wrote to the U.S. minister in Italy in October 1862, "and we will make an appeal to all the democrats in Europe to join us in fighting this Holy battle. But in this appeal it will be necessary to proclaim to them the principle which animates us – the enfranchisement of the slaves, the triumph of universal reason."[53] Lincoln appears to have been unwilling either to relinquish command of the Union army or to commit to a war for what Garibaldi called "universal freedom." The negotiation with the Italian liberator and former general of the red shirts ended there. But those who had fought with Garibaldi and other Garibaldinis in New York formed the 39th New York Infantry Regiment, which fought on the Union side wearing red shirts and bearing the same flag that was used during the Revolutions of 1848–1849 in Italy.[54]

At about the same time that Lincoln was preparing to fire General McClellan for his failure – or refusal – to achieve a definitive Union victory over the rebel South, Bismarck, as prime minister of Prussia in 1862, undertook his own military campaign to unify the German states under Prussian authority. Compared to England and France, the Germans remained relatively unaffected by the war. Bismarck even claimed (perhaps ironically) not to know what the North and South were fighting about.[55] The official position of the Prussian government was neutral, but the king and his ministers, especially Bismarck, made it clear that they supported the rightful authority of Lincoln and the North. "From the inauguration of Lincoln to his death," Prussia "never failed ... to cultivate the most friendly relations with the United States of America," the American minister in Berlin, George Bancroft, later wrote; "it came out more clearly during the ministry of Count Bismarck who maintained unreservedly the view that the North was right."[56] The German people also contributed several hundred million dollars to a fund-raising campaign in Europe for Lincoln's government in 1863, much more than any other European nation. "It was reported to me that Lincoln could not keep the war going if he did not receive financial aid from Germany," Bismarck recalled. "His Commissioner stated that they had been rebuffed in London & Paris. We wished the Union restored. The North seemed to me to be morally right, but, quite apart from that, we desired a strong prosperous and united Nation on the other side of the Atlantic."[57] More strategic than moral or ideological, Bismarck's support for Lincoln's aggressive drive to reunite the warring American states was grounded in a broader vision of the rise of a newly reunited America and a newly united Kleindeutchland as a means of shifting the former balance of power away from British and French imperial dominance in the transatlantic world.

American historians have usually insisted on the fundamental difference between Lincoln the democrat and Bismarck the autocrat: "The Gettysburg Address would have been as foreign to Bismarck as a policy of 'blood and iron' would have been to Lincoln," David Potter wrote. However, the analogies between Lincoln and Bismarck and the lessons of total war they bequeathed to each other suggest a darker side to Lincoln's national and international legacy as national unifier and the thinness of the line between legitimate and illegitimate exercises of authority and violence in the name of national survival then and now.

As Carl N. Degler has importantly argued, the Gettysburg Address "may not have been a Bismarkian document, but Lincoln's unrelenting prosecution of the war came closer to Bismarck's 'blood and iron' than Americans like to remember."[58] The Civil War produced more wounded, amputated, and dead bodies than had ever been witnessed in European history; and even Europeans who sympathized with Lincoln expressed horror and disgust at the oceans of blood. "Men and angels must weep as they behold the things that are being done," wrote the English novelist Anthony Trollope. "No sight so sad has come upon the earth in our days."[59] Lincoln's poetic words in the Gettysburg Address sought to justify and mythologize the incredible slaughter of the war as "a new birth of freedom" and a national and international "testing" whether "a new nation, conceived in Liberty, and dedicated to the proposition that all men are created equal" might survive. Beneath the poetry, however, was the stark reality of massive blood carnage, the aggressive use of military force even against civilians, and the suspension of constitutional rights and civil liberty, all in the name of preserving the union. Lincoln may even have taught Bismarck a thing or two about the use of "blood and iron" to build a nation. In 1870, Philip H. Sheridan, known for his unrelenting "scorched earth" campaign against the civilian population in Virginia in 1864, went to France in the midst of the Franco-Prussian War to advise Bismarck on the need to pursue a war of all-out annihilation in the Siege of Paris: "The people must be left nothing but their eyes to weep over the war," he said.[60] Without the example of the "American Federal Union of 1787" and Lincoln's successful defense of it in "the ordeal by fire of 1861–65," observes historian John Hawgood, "neither of these great powers, for better or for worse, might have come into existence."[61]

Lincoln in International Memory

Lincoln's assassination by John Wilkes Booth on the night of April 14, 1865, while he was watching a play at Ford's Theatre in Washington, D.C., dramatically changed his stature in the European and international mind.

Berated and ridiculed by many while he was living, after his violent death even some who had reviled him as president began to transform him into a legendary martyr and saint of international fame. "Whatever may have been done in the United States," wrote Norman Judd, the U.S. minister in Berlin, after Lincoln's assassination, "Mr. Lincoln is being canonized in Europe. A like unanimity of eulogy by sovereigns, parliaments, corporate bodies, by the people, and by all public journals, was never before witnessed on this continent. The most truthful and eloquent testimonials are now given by some of those that belied him most while living."[62]

In England, the most dramatic change came from the *Punch* cartoonist, John Tenniel, whose *Britannia Sympathizes with Columbia* paid tribute to the American president he had consistently mocked in cartoons published throughout the war. The engraving appeared along with a poem in which the *Punch* editor, Tom Taylor, turned his satirist's pen against himself for four years of "self-complacent British" sneering against Lincoln:

> *You*, lay a wreath on murdered Lincoln's bier,
>> *You* who with mocking pencil wont to trace,
> Broad for the self-complacent British sneer,
>> His length of shambling limb, his furrowed face,
> His gaunt, gnarled hands, his unkempt, bristling hair,
>
>> His garb uncouth, his bearing ill at ease.
> ...
> Yes, he had lived to shame me from my sneer,
>> To lame my pencil, and confute my pen;
> To make me own this hind of princes peer,
>> This rail-splitter a true-born king of men.

Taylor, the author of *Our American Cousin*, the comedy about a boorish American meeting his aristocratic relatives in England that Lincoln was watching the night he was assassinated, aptly captures the ways Lincoln grew in Europe's esteem from being caricatured as an uncouth, incompetent, and laughable American buffoon to being apotheosized as a "true-born king of men" and "martyr" to the cause of liberty, civilization, and humanity worldwide. His "character" had "steadily and visibly gained upon the minds and hearts, not of his countrymen alone, but also of the world," observed the London *Daily News*.[63]

Kings, queens, emperors, and legislative bodies throughout Europe sent formal expressions of sympathy to the American government or its consuls in Europe. But the most overwhelming response came from European laborers and shopkeepers. For them, Lincoln's assassination unleashed a passionate overflow of powerful working-class feeling and sentiment expressed in letters sent by town meetings, workingmen's associations, Masonic lodges, religious organizations, emancipation societies, and other public gatherings throughout Europe and its colonies, including the "creoles of Guadeloupe, of African descent," "natives" of the African Gold coast, and "the colored people of Bermuda."[64] If the Revolutions of 1848 had failed in Europe, the struggle of liberty against slavery had triumphed in America; and as the victorious leader of this struggle, Lincoln, especially after the blood sacrifice of his death, was hailed as the luminous symbol of hope, regeneration, and the ultimate triumph of the oppressed over centuries of authoritarian power in Europe.

"A people who wish to be united, free, and independent have long bent their eyes upon events in the great republic, whence they expect a new light to radiate upon the world, with a new era of democratic civilization," wrote the Italians of Abrazzo to the people of the United States. "Your history is the same as ours," they affirm. "From Camillus and Cincinnatus to Franklin and Washington, from Lincoln and Seward to Garibaldi and Mazzini, the tradition of the great struggle between good and evil, liberty and slavery, civilization and barbarism, national autonomy and the rule of foreign despots, has ever been the same." Signed by some 230 people in a small village in the Apennines, the letter is representative of hundreds of missives that express similarly ardent popular will for liberty, equality, and forms of republican governance that had been repressed in Europe.

Sent to Americans or through American consuls in Europe, these collective expressions of grief read like one long plaint of oppressed Europeans seeking redress at the tomb of Lincoln, who "gave his life to save the integrity of the Union and the grandeur of his country, to rescue the colored man from slavery, to give to all men liberty and equality." By identifying with Americans as brothers, by mourning their common loss of Lincoln as a blood sacrifice for the redemption of liberty and equality for all oppressed people, ordinary Europeans found a common voice, a figure of republican redemption, and a hope for the future that enabled them to resist the stultifying regimes of monarchy, hierarchy, privilege, and impoverishment in which they lived their daily lives. "His blood spilt in America by the base assassin's hand will fertilize the continent of Europe," wrote the masons of Harmony Lodge in France "To their Brethren in America."[65]

In country after country, "the humblest associations" rallied around Lincoln as "the saviour of his country" (Sunday School Union of Stockport); "the glory of a free people" (Mechanics' Society of Sissa); the personification of "the cause of liberty and human fraternity" and "the most illustrious of martyrs" (Freemasons of Ghent); the "most virtuous republican"

(Workingmen's Society of Bologna); "the son of a laborer, and himself a laborer [who] took up the fight for the rights of free labor and carried it to a triumphant termination" (Berlin Workingmen's Club); the "champion of human freedom" (Citizens of Canzo); "the glorious father of a whole world's regeneration" (Leon Lewis, England); "a friend of humanity, citizen of the whole world, and martyr to the holy principle of liberty and the rights of man" (Italian Emigration Society); and "the living incarnation of the principles of equality and fraternity, the embodiment of true patriotism, of honest intentions, of firmness and integrity," whose death, "like Christ ... may be the cause of the complete triumph of the humane and holy principle of true liberty [which] will resurrect with more beauty and effulgence, and reflect its genial rays over Europe with beneficent effects" (Mechanics Mutual Aid Society of Bresia).[66]

This secular *cum* religious hagiography of Lincoln as republican liberator and savior expressed something more than sorrow at his assassination: It also served as mass political protest against the unyielding force of despotism in Europe. One letter of condolence, signed by representatives of "all the classes of Caen" takes a clear shot at Louis Bonaparte Napoleon, who overthrew the French republic in 1852 by declaring himself Emperor Napoleon III. Impressed by the simple transition of constitutional power observed by Grant and Sherman following Lincoln's death, they write: "Among us, a powerful general, commanding nearly a million soldiers, would have profited by that crime to proclaim that it was necessary to save the republic by a dictatorship, and he would at last have destroyed it for the profit of personal ambition." Expressing the sorrow of heart brought to "all lovers liberty" by the news of Lincoln's death, the Mechanics of Sissa wrote: "The champion of true liberty, the glory of a free people, is no more; but his name and memory will shed a refulgent light over the benighted world, and may arouse the spirit of progress in the darkness of Europe."

Others want more than Lincoln's memory: They want American intervention. "We, maidens, spouses, and mothers of suffering Italy," wrote the Ladies Society of Bologna, "are waiting hopefully for the time when America, restored to ... her rightful station among the great nations of the earth, will come to our aid and relieve us from foreign oppression." In sharing their grief with the American people, the Berlin Workingmen's Club was more ambiguous but uncannily prophetic in anticipating a day when the "fight for the rights of free labor" that Lincoln carried "to a triumphant termination" would spread to Europe. "In giving expression of our deep sympathy in the death of Lincoln," the Berlin workers also "feel compelled" to express their "hopes and wishes ... that the freedom ... sealed with the blood of one of the noblest men will only the more fully prevail, and that the star-spangled banner may wave in triumph wherever it is unfurled, in battling for the cause of freedom and civilization."[67]

The multitude of political sympathies and desires expressed in these "private" letters may have stood in for more open and public manifestations of political sympathy with the United States that were prohibited throughout Europe. According to Bigelow, thousands of French flocked to the American consul to express "their sorrow and sympathy," but fearful that these republican well-wishers might turn violent, the French police intervened. "Unfortunately," Bigelow wrote, "their feelings were so demonstrative in some instances as to provoke the intervention of the police.... I am sorry to hear that some have been sent to prison in consequence of an intemperate expression of their feelings."[68]

Blocked, silenced, or arrested for more public manifestations of sympathy, workers and other republican sympathizers throughout Europe found more symbolic forms of action. "The mass of people cannot sign addresses," wrote one Frenchman in a letter to the editor of *Le Temps* in Paris. He suggested that "the people of Paris" wear "some sign of mourning" such as "a piece of crape, or a simple black ribbon – on the arm" as a means of "publicly lamenting the fate of the former workman – almost one of themselves, who was the greatest and the purest minded among the successors of Washington!" Inspired by "fraternal feeling," the silk weavers of Lyons who were hardest hit by the industrial crisis caused by the war, honored the "glorious name" of Lincoln as "the pledge of alliance between the American republic and the democracy of Europe" by sending a silk banner inscribed in gold and woven by themselves:

SOUSCRIPTION POPULAR: A LA REPUBLIQE DES ETAS UNIS OFFERT EN MEMOIRE D'ABRAHAM LINCOLN, LYONS, 1865

Workingmen's associations throughout Italy draped banners and flags "in token of condolence for the memory of the illustrious martyr of liberty" and "those that mourn under the yoke of oppression." Some inscribed "the name of Lincoln beside those of Garibaldi and Mazzini in the list of honorary members"; and the municipality of Fermo, "wishing, by a public demonstration, to do honor to that great name" as the liberator of "humanity at large," named a new street in the south side of the city "Abraham Lincoln."[69]

One form of collective commemoration took place in France, where some forty thousand Frenchmen, "anxious to manifest their sympathies for the American Union," contributed to a campaign to coin a gold medal in honor of Lincoln to send to Mary Todd Lincoln. Although the French government tried to stop the popular subscription campaign, it was successfully realized. "Tell Mrs. Lincoln that in this little box is the heart of France," wrote the French opposition leader Eugène Pelletan, when he delivered the medal to John Bigelow. One side shows a profile of Lincoln encircled by the inscription: "Dedicated by the French Democracy to Lincoln, twice elected President of the United States." The reverse portrays an allegorical figure and a tomb inscribed, "Lincoln, an honest man; abolished slavery, saved the republic, without veiling the Statue of Liberty. He was assassinated the 14th of April, 1865." This inscription is underwritten by the French revolutionary motto: "Liberty Equality Fraternity." The letter to Mrs. Lincoln that accompanied the commemorative coin was signed by twenty republican opponents of the French Empire, including Victor Hugo, Jules Michelet, and the socialist Louis Blanc, who wrote: "If France had the freedom enjoyed by republican America, not thousands, but millions among us would have been counted as admirers of Lincoln, and believers in the opinions for which he devoted his life, and which his death consecrated."[70]

The visual counterpart of these tributes to Lincoln as an international hero is a striking French print by C. Schultz titled *Fraternité Universelle*, which was published in Paris in 1865. Portraying Lincoln as part of an international pantheon of "martyrs" from history and mythology, including Socrates as the "martyr of freedom of thought," Gutenberg as "the universal propagator of human thought," Franklin as the representative of "success through hard work," and Washington, joining hands with Lincoln who joins hands with a black man and his child, as "the recent martyr of equality, the emancipator of slavery in the United States," the print celebrates major milestones in the progress of human freedom at the same time that it projects an international vision of brotherhood among individuals and nations. *Fraternité Universelle* reveals "the provincial nature of American popular prints," where "American printmakers rarely thought in terms of an international pantheon." In visual as in print representations in the United States, Lincoln has been memorialized within a more exclusively American national frame.

And yet, as this chapter has sought to elucidate, reading "Our Lincoln" from the other side of the Atlantic reveals understudied perspectives not only on Lincoln and the Civil War but on the transnational origins of some of the dominant rhetorics and myths that have shaped American history and culture. As Lincoln surely knew, "let us re-adopt the Declaration of Independence" cannot be read as an exclusively national turn because the Declaration was addressed not to the American colonists only but to the world; and its language was drawn from an Enlightenment and transatlantic discourse of natural rights and rule by the people. As the exclamation points following the terms "Liberty! Egalité! Fraternité!" on the medal sent to Mary Todd Lincoln suggest, when workers, republicans, and radicals in Europe speak this language, they are not imitating either Jefferson or Lincoln, they are speaking, reaffirming, and in some cases reinventing a democratic language and struggle that is theirs as well as ours.

Lincoln consistently framed his addresses on the American war as part of a broader historical struggle for liberty, equality, and rights. If he referred to America as "the last best hope of earth" in his address on the Emancipation Proclamation or to the Civil War as a struggle over the proposition that "government of the people, by the people, for the people, shall not perish," he was not inventing an exceptionally American fantasy. As Timothy M. Roberts has argued, Lincoln's words echo Mazzini, who may have used them first in 1833 to describe the uprising of Young Italy as a revolution "in the name of the people, for the people, and by the people."[71] Like those who celebrated Lincoln as a Christ-like liberator, working-class hero, and martyr of humanity in Britain, France, Spain, Italy, and Germany, Lincoln gave voice to a vision and a mythology of America that was as much the creation of Europe – and in many cases the oppressed workers of Europe – as it was a self-serving American ideology.

"Your history is the same as ours," write the people of Europe. "You are our children," claim the English. "We are your brothers and sisters," proclaim the French. "We share a common father in Columbus," declare the Italians. European workers and republicans cooperate in the mythic construction of the Civil War as a war for freedom of the laboring classes and democracy worldwide. In their many paeans to Lincoln as a man of the people, a common laborer who rose to be the president of the United States, the savior of democracy, and the liberator of oppressed humanity, we see the ways the European imagination participated in the creation of the American dream and such fundamental American mythologies as the self-made man, the rise from common laborer to "true-born king of men," the American republic as the beacon of "a new era of democratic civilization," and the "star-spangled banner" as savior of the world.

Rather than reading slavery as a "peculiarly" American problem, European workers and radicals saw the mounting crisis over slavery in the late 1840s as part of a broader transatlantic struggle over freedom and labor in the European Revolutions of 1848. Understanding the Civil War not only as a second American Revolution but, like the republican uprisings throughout Europe in the sixties and seventies, a deferred 1848, underscores the direct line between the Revolutions of 1848 and the Civil War, in which, as we have seen, Lincoln literally filled the ranks of the Union army with refugees from the Revolutions of 1848, republican, socialist, and otherwise. This transatlantic perspective enables us to understand the furor over Lincoln's image and the Civil War in Europe, and the impact that Lincoln's victory and the victory of both liberal democracy and constitutional union had on such political reforms in Europe as the British Reform Act of 1867, the North German Constitution of 1867, the overthrow of Napoleon and the declaration of the Third Republic in France in 1870, and the liberal uprisings in Italy and Spain.

As the multiple and conflicting responses to Lincoln in Europe suggest, his image like his ambiguous words could be used to support contradictory actions from radical to conservative, liberation to control. One sees this in Bismarck's admiration for Lincoln as a leader willing to curtail civil liberties and constitutional rights as necessary measures in a time of war; and the model Lincoln may have provided for Garibaldi, who broke with the radical communal vision of Mazzini in order to unify Italy under a constitutional monarchy. At the same time, nineteenth-century Europe reveals a potentially more radical and international Lincoln, one identified with the laboring classes and with socialist and communist radicals throughout Europe, including Marx in England, Louis Blanc in France, and Mazzini in Italy. The power of this more radical figure is suggested in the role played by the working classes in preventing the governments of England, France, and Spain from intervening in the Civil War. But for the ardent support of European workers, even against their own economic self-interest, the Civil War might have had a very different end; and Lincoln might have bequeathed a darker legacy to the world as the loser rather than the noble savior of "the last best hope of earth."

NOTES

1 Karl Marx, *On America and the Civil War*, Saul K. Padover, ed. (New York: McGraw-Hill Book Company, 1973), 236.
2 Abraham Lincoln, *The Collected Works of Abraham Lincoln*, Roy Basler, ed. (New Brunswick, NJ: Rutgers University Press, 1953), 5:537.
3 Marx, *America*, 236–237.
4 Lincoln, *Collected Works*, 2:276.
5 Lincoln, *Collected Works*, 7:23.
6 Marx, *America*, 237.
7 Ibid.
8 Marx, *America*, 239, 239–240.
9 See Merrill D. Peterson, *Lincoln in National Memory* (New York: Oxford University Press, 1994); and Eric Foner, *Our Lincoln: New Perspectives on Lincoln and His World* (New York: W. W. Norton and Company, 2008).
10 Lincoln, *Collected Works*, 1:438. Emphasis in the original.
11 See Larry J. Reynolds, *European Revolutions and the American Literary Renaissance* (New Haven, CT: Yale University Press, 1988).
12 Lincoln, *Collected Works*, 1:62.

13   Lincoln, *Collected Works*, 2:115–116.

14   John Hawgood, "The Civil War in Central Europe," in Harold Hyman, ed., *Heard Round the World: The Impact Abroad of the Civil War* (New York: Alfred A. Knopf, 1969).

15   Saul K. Padover, "Introduction: Karl Marx on America and the Civil War," in Karl Marx, *America*, xxiv.

16   For a recent exception to this, see Al Benson, Jr., and Walter D. Kennedy, *Red Republicans and Lincoln's Marxists: Marxism in the Civil War* (iUniverse: 2007), an ill-informed book by two pro-Confederacy "enthusiasts."

17   Padover, "Introduction," xiv–xv.

18   Alexander Trachtenberg, "Editor's Preface," in Karl Marx and Frederick Engels, *Letters to Americans, 1845–1895: A Selection*, ed. Alexander Trachtenberg, trans. Leonard E. Mins (New York: International Publishers, 1953), 3–6.

19   Lincoln, *Collected Works*, 2:276; Marx, *America*, 56.

20   Cited in Padover, "Introduction," xxii.

21   Marx, *America*, 171.

22   London *Times* cited in Marx, *America*, 213; Marx, *America*, 221–222.

23   Marx, *America*, 222.

24   Ibid.

25   Alexander J. Beresford-Hope, *A Popular View of the American Civil War* (London: J. Ridgway, 1861).

26   Letter of Charles Francis Adams to William Seward 1864, cited in Ephraim D. Adams, *Great Britain and the American Civil War*, 2 vols. (Harlow: Longmans, Green, and Company, 1925), 1:300.

27   *Morning Chronicle*, November 28, 1861, in Belle Sideman and Lillian Friedman, eds., *Europe Looks at the Civil War* (New York: Orion, 1960), 101.

28   John Bright, *A Friendly Voice from England on American Affairs* (New York: William C. Bryant and Company, 1862).

29   "Letter From the Working Men of Manchester to President Lincoln," *Manchester Guardian*, reprinted in Belle Becker Sideman and Lillian Friedman, eds., *Europe Looks at the Civil War: An Anthology* (New York: The Orion Press, 1960), 198–201.

30   On Lincoln and the British working classes, see Marx's essays for the New York *Daily Tribune* and *Die Presse*, in *America*.

31   "Letter from the Working Men of Manchester to President Lincoln," Sideman and Friedman, *Europe Looks at the Civil War*, 198–201.

32   For a discussion of the Civil War in Europe, see especially essays collected in Hyman, *Heard Round the World*, and Sideman and Friedman, *Europe Looks at the Civil War*; and Donaldson Jordan and Edwin J. Pratt, *Europe and the American Civil War* (Boston: Houghton Mifflin Company, 1931).

33   John Bigelow, *Retrospections of a Busy Life* (New York: Baker and Taylor, 1909); Monsieur B. Theron to Governor F. R. Lubbock of Texas, August 18, 1862; report on Confederate-French dealings, in Sideman and Friedman, *Europe Looks at the Civil War*, 161–162, 162–163.

34   Count Agénor de Gasparin, *America Before Europe*, trans. Mary L. Booth (New York: C. Scribner, 1862), 16, 7, 331.

35   Prince Napoleon, *Voyage Aux Etats-Unis et au Canada*, in Sideman and Friedman, *Europe Looks at the Civil War*, 78.

36 Comte de Paris to François Buloz, July 29, 1862, in Sideman and Friedman, *Europe Looks at the Civil War*, 157.

37 Sideman and Friedman, *Europe Looks at the Civil War*, 58.

38 Bigelow, *Retrospections*.

39 The Marquis Adolphe de Chambrun, *Impressions of Lincoln and the Civil War: A Foreigner's Account*, trans. General Aldebert de Chambrun (New York: Random House, 1952), 21–22.

40 Chambrun, *Impressions*, 77, 83.

41 Letter from the bishop of Orléans, Monsignor Dupanloup to Augustin Cochin, author of *The Abolition of Slavery* (1861), in Sideman and Friedman, *Europe Looks at the Civil War*, 272–273.

42 Edouard Laboulaye, *Journal des Débats* (August 1862), in Sideman and Friedman, *Europe Looks at the Civil War*, 164.

43 For Spanish Minister Leopold O'Donnell's ambition to bring Mexico into a Spanish sphere of influence in the New World, see Jordan and Pratt, *Europe and the American Civil War*, 246.

44 *Diplomatic Correspondence 1865*, in Sideman and Friedman, *Europe Looks at the Civil War*, 267.

45 *Diplomatic Correspondence 1865*, in Sideman and Friedman, *Europe Looks at the Civil War*, 274–275.

46 George Perkins Marsh to William H. Seward, January 13, 1862; cited in Boritt, 175.

47 Lincoln to Joseph Bertinatti, the Italian Chargé d'Affaires, in Lincoln, *Collected Works*, 7:473.

48 Howard R. Marraro, "Lincoln's Offer of a Command to Garibaldi," in Sideman and Friedman, *Europe Looks at the Civil War*, 73.

49 Letter of Giuseppe Garibaldi to Mr. Marsh, March 27, 1865; Giuseppe Mazzini to Mr. Fisher, May 21, 1865; *New York Times*, June 1865; Mazzini cited in Jordan and Pratt, *Europe and the American Civil War*, 266.

50 See Gabor S. Boritt, Mark E. Neely, Jr., and Harold Holzer, "The European Image of Abraham Lincoln," *Winterthur Portfolio*, 21.2/3 (Summer-Autumn 1986): 178.

51 Holzer, Boritt, and Neely, "The European Image," 177.

52 Sideman and Friedman, *Europe Looks at the Civil War*, 70.

53 Ibid., 73.

54 See Alessandro Mastrorocco, "Italians and the American Civil War: When President Lincoln Offered Garibaldi a Command in the Union Army," June 16, 2009: http://www.suite101.com/content/italians-and-the-american-civil-war-a125528

55 John Hawgood, "The Civil War and Central Europe," in Hyman, *Heard Round the World*, 148.

56 Bancroft to Seward, Berlin, February 29, 1869, cited in Otto Zu Stolberg-Wernigerode, *Germany and the United States During the Era of Bismarck* (Reading, PA: Henry Janssen Foundation, 1937), 289.

57 Cited in Hawgood, "The Civil War and Central Europe," in Hyman, *Heard Round the World*, 152.

58 On Lincoln and Bismarck see Carl N. Degler, "The American Civil War and the German Wars of Unification: The Problem of Comparison," in *On the Road to*

Total War: The American Civil War and the German Wars of Unification, 1861–1871, eds. Stig Forster and Jorg Nagler (Cambridge: Cambridge University Press, 1997), 53–75.

59 Anthony Trollope, *North America* (Philadelphia: J. B. Lippincott and Company, 1863), 94–95.

60 Cited in Carl Degler, "The American Civil War," in Forster and Nagler, *On the Road to Total War*, 68.

61 John Hawgood, "The Civil War in Central Europe," in Hyman, *Heard Round the World*, 176.

62 *The Assassination of Abraham Lincoln, Late President of the United States of America … On the Evening of the 14th of April, 1865: Expressions of Condolence and Sympathy Inspired by These Events* (Washington, DC: Government Printing Office, 1867), 648.

63 Ibid., 505.

64 Ibid., 75, 259, 454.

65 Ibid., 575–576, 576, 100.

66 Ibid., 445; 449; 609, 22, 79, 572, 445, 648, 575, 383, 610, 580, 609, 344, 569, 571, 99, 102, 79, 572.

67 Ibid., 71, 609, 574, 648–649.

68 Ibid., 71, 609, 574, 648–649.

69 Ibid., 192, 76, 573, 571, 580, 581.

70 *Histoire de la souscription popular à la medaille Lincoln* (Paris: Librairies International A. Lacroix, 1865).

71 Timothy M. Roberts, "The Relevance of Giuseppe Mazzini's Ideas of Insurgency to the American Crisis of the 1850s," in C. A. Bayly and Eugenio F. Biagini, ed., *Giuseppe Mazzini and the Globalization of Democratic Nationalism, 1830–1920* (New York: Oxford University Press, 2008), 322.

11

ROBERT FANUZZI

Lincoln's Hemispheric Relations

When historians of the mid-nineteenth century United States invoke the category "Civil War diplomacy," they get the chance to present geopolitical scenarios and possibilities that the most fertile and contentious investigations of our sectional conflict cannot provide. The starting point for their research, after all, is the presumption that the conflict between the northern and southern states of the United States was international, bearing directly on the governments of the new Latin American nation-states, those of Europe, and the fate of Spanish, British, and French colonies of the Americas. When the nation's sectional conflict is expanded to this hemispheric, or transhemispheric scale, the history and geography of the United States itself fairly begs to be rewritten. What if Lincoln's foreign policy toward Mexico had failed, for instance, and Confederate diplomacy succeeded in allying Latin America's largest nation against the United States? Lincoln's government would have had to contend against a transnational circum-Caribbean military and economic power that utilized the strategic location of New Orleans not only to dominate commerce in the Gulf of Mexico but to spread the slaveholding economy throughout the America, starting with the prize of Cuba. Because France had invaded and occupied Mexico in 1862, the United States would have found itself at war against not two but three nations, with French troops massing on the Rio Grande border; a beleaguered President Abraham Lincoln might well have realized that the survival of the Union depended on making an equitable peace with these three powers.[1] North America would have emerged from the Civil War in the image of Europe, a continent governed and shaped in the nineteenth century by the principle of balance of power, and the study of Lincoln would have forever been shadowed by scholarly dissections of his disastrous absolutism and poetic indulgences on behalf of a Union that ended up occupying a drastically reduced geographical and geopolitical share of the American hemisphere.

Diplomatic historians of Lincoln's Civil War and Union policy play parlor games like this in dead earnest, often submerging the latent threat to our sense of American nationality and historical inevitability under a narrative recreation of competing foreign policy interventions, characterizations of obscure but pivotal political actors, and quantitative analyses of competing international economic systems. But for historical thinkers who have been following the "hemispheric" turn in American studies over the past decade, the series of counterfactual scenarios and hypothetical possibilities that emerges from historical assessments of Lincoln's Civil War diplomacy contributes to a critical project that aims to historicize, if not resist, the hegemony of the United States over the American hemisphere and open the meaning of "America" itself to competing claims and dialectical articulations.[2] Can reconstructing Lincoln's hemispheric relations do the same, and help us discover buried, alternative Americas? One of the insights we can take from diplomatic history is that both the Civil War and his policy of Union can be understood analytically, to complicate rather than to consolidate the position of the United States, both historically and geographically, in the Americas. A name for strategies and initiatives that proposed one America among many, Lincoln's Union might well serve as the antithesis to that nearly contemporary figure of United States nationalism, Manifest Destiny.

For many scholars, the historical touchstone for hemispheric research inquiries is Jose Marti's essay "Our America," considered as both a document of political resistance and the model for a scholarly practice. An increasingly regarded historical figure with whom Marti is often linked is Maria Amparo Ruiz de Burton, the creole Mexican-Californian author of the novels *The Squatter and the Don* and *Who Would Have Thought It?* Like Marti, Ruiz de Burton, wrote these novels, particularly the satirical *Who Would Have Thought It*, with the intention of "dismantling the colossus," the regnant term throughout nineteenth-century Latin America for the United States, through stylized and hyperbolic portraits of Civil War protagonists that demystify the Union cause.[3] Collectively, these portraits constitute a farcical version or performance of a still unfolding U.S. history that throws into question every presumption of inevitability about the victory of the Union, the righteousness of Lincoln's cause, and the simple binarism of the sectional conflict. Precisely to the extent that these portraits represent a performance, Ruiz de Burton models both a key feature of hemispheric inquiries – their resistance to the consolidation of historical knowledge – and the collateral benefit of diplomatic history – its impartial receptiveness to alternative historical outcomes. As a novelist, she might well have slight advantage over the diplomatic historian in being able to recreate a role for Lincoln both in American history and in the creation of historical knowledge, an activity she cedes to and sees at work in other novelists.

For this reason, Ruiz de Burton routes her critique of both Lincoln's role through a satiric presentation of New England's ideal of sentimental femininity, associated most famously with Harriet Beecher Stowe's novel *Uncle Tom's Cabin*. Ruiz de Burton intuits that Lincoln, as chief executive of the expansionist, imperialist United States, gains his power as the foil or counterpart for the cultural authority of antebellum sentimental fiction's idealized northern housewife, and that only by unmasking this diminutive, powerless creation will she have dismantled the colossus. Without Stowe, in other words, there is no Lincoln; her critique of the Union cause and U.S. policy takes flight from the generative, allegorical encounter between opposites: the six-feet four inch president and the sentimental novelist – the "little woman," as Lincoln famously described Stowe in her White House visit, "who started this big war." From this paradox of power and weakness, liberal contemporaries were able to fashion a redemptive historiography for the Civil War, with abolitionist sentiment goading Lincoln and the nation toward their "better angels"; using the same dynamics of scale, twentieth-century literary critics unspooled an equally redemptive nineteenth-century literary history, with formerly maligned women novelists and reformers installed as protagonists.[4] Ruiz de Burton, however, wrote her novel with the conviction that the history of the nineteenth century is still being written, and that by belittling the authority of the president and magnifying the ambition of the little woman she can write a counternarrative of the Civil War featuring U.S. imperialism, diplomatic incompetence, and resurgent Mexican nationalism. The portrait of the distracted, uninformed Lincoln that emerges from *Who Would Have Thought It* is indeed so unsparing that it is hard not to ascribe to Ruiz de Burton her own desire to meet the president face to face. Compared to the meeting between the president and the sentimental novelist, this one is not even a fair fight.

Ruiz de Burton begins her novel with the presumption of *realpolitik* at work, first in the divided home of the New England Norval family and then in the White House. In her novel, a conspiratorial faction of Northern ministers, bored housewives, and misguided abolitionists runs roughshod over representative government, creating a mockery of the system Lincoln touted as "last best hope on earth." With an exquisite knowledge of government procurement policy, quartermaster follies, and boardroom ego clashes, she presents a portrait of Lincoln that is less frontier caricature than good-government scandal: here is the forgetful chief executive who lets political cronies hijack the government and its treasury for the sake of munitions contracts and longer-term militarization. In between bouts of laughter at Lincoln's ineptitude and homeliness, we see the erosion of civilian government and the emergence of a militaristic caste that will rule the United States with a succession of ex-generals and Civil War officers for most of the nineteenth century. The end of the novel finds the victorious United States committed to a state of permanent war.

The novel's central plotline – the sanctimonious but lascivious Jemima Norval and Rev. Thomas Hackwell scheming to rob a young Mexican girl both of her virtue and her riches – interjects a new historical narrative and geographical dimension into her critique of Lincoln's United States. At once the foil for a nationalist-abolitionist historiography, he now serves as the catalyst for a hemispheric counternarrative. The moral and geographical compass of the United States is also reoriented, with the poles of North and South and the dichotomy of slavery and freedom rotated onto the east-west axis on which the dichotomy of imperialism and national independence lay. The Civil War itself, the mid-century crucible through which the United States defines itself, becomes a mere episode sandwiched between the Mexican War and the Spanish-American War, the two milestones of the century's hemispheric conflict. The lasting effect of a dilatory war fought between two versions of the same imperialism is more effective mobilization against the true enemy of U.S. interests – Latin America.

Ironically, Lincoln was and remains a useful figure for constructing an anti-imperialist political tradition in the United States. As a freshman representative to Congress, he sought to delegitimize President Andrew Polk's prosecution of the Mexican War and expose the official pretension of a "defensive" war by sponsoring what came to be known as "spot resolutions," demanding from the president the exact location in the disputed territory of Texas on which American blood was supposed to have been shed. In his January 1848 speech that brought him national fame and electoral repudiation, Congressman Lincoln all but ridiculed Polk's understanding of territorial rights that had been fixed by international treaties with France, Spain, and Mexico; he also introduced what eventually became the dominant theme in his antislavery rhetoric, the abuse of constitutional power in policies of territorial expansion and extension.[5]

Unimpressed by Lincoln's opposition to the Mexican War, Ruiz de Burton saw in his aversion to outright invasion the pretext for a more insidious form of American power that had taken hold among the ruling class of Mexico and, by extension, the creole leadership of Latin America. In words that would echo throughout Marti's "Our America," the Mexican intellectual tradition, and in contemporary Latin American postcolonial and subaltern theory, Ruiz de Burton would ascribe to one of her most sympathetic characters, a Spanish-Austrian Mexican patriot, fierce suspicion against the "despotic sway" that the United States holds over "the minds of the leading men of Hispano-American republics."[6] In the aftermath of the 1848 Treaty of Guadalupe, which ceded the northern third of Mexico to the United States, Ruiz de Burton's Mexican patriot sees a larger and more lasting threat looming in his own countrymen's enthusiasm for a republican form of representative government – the only form of government that Lincoln had considered capable of stopping an outright invasion and further territorial expansion by the United States, and in whose name he had opposed the Mexican War. So great is the threat of Lincoln's constitutional system that the Mexican patriot prefers a monarchy, installed by the French, to the "American" form of government championed by Mexican liberal reformers. "If not for this terrible, this fatal influence, – which will eventually destroy us," her patriotic character continues, "the Mexicans ... would be proud to hail a prince who ... will cut us loose from the leading strings of the United States."[7] She of course refers to the short-lived monarchy of the Austrian-born Maximilian III, the final thrust of Napoleon III's military campaign against the U.S.-backed constitutional government of Mexico.

In lamenting the "fatal influence" of the United States, Ruiz de Burton's character expresses the long-standing predicament of postcolonial Hispanic-American nations, whose leaders and founders had enthusiastically hailed the American Revolution as a hemispheric model and even claimed common a Creole American patriotism even as they struggled to devise forms of government suited to their respective societies, circumstances, and histories. The story of the 1821 Pan-American Congress, retold to great effect in Anna Brickhouse's *Trans-American Literary Relations*, encapsulates a hemispheric postcolonial history that saw the United States emerge as a new hemispheric power and divisive force among Latin American nations and national movements.[8] This history has special significance for Mexico, whose leaders were faced with the mixed blessing of United States aid and protection even before they had achieved independence from Spain. "'Holy Mary, please help and free me from these people,'" lamented a representative of the insurgent Mexican nationalist movement when faced with the quid pro quo offered by Secretary of State James Monroe in 1811: Adopt our constitution, and we will grant you first diplomatic, military support in your struggle against Spain and then membership in our confederation.[9]

The threat of the U.S. constitutional system emerged in full force after Mexico's Reform War of 1857, with the victors promoting a constitution expressly modeled on that of the United States. Considered by its proponents to be the only reform possible after the disastrous *caudillo* government of Santa Anna and the speediest path to modernization, the constitutional government that emerged in the aftermath of Mexico's own civil war was so friendly to the United States, its economic interests, and its proposed commercial treaties that conservative opponents, losers in the Reform War,

presented an invasion by still another foreign power as the only way to counteract the "despotic sway" of the U.S. constitutional system over Mexico
and the emerging Hispanic nations of the Americas.[10] Simultaneously mock-
ing and ceding the honor of the "best government on earth" to an inept
Lincoln, Ruiz de Burton looks back to France's 1862 invasion of Mexico
and the installation of a Bourbon monarchy by Napoleon III in 1864 as
a belated independence movement for Mexico that would have finally
rejected Monroe's outstanding offer and divided the Americas into two distinct, competing spheres of influence: a Latin America, anchored in French-
occupied Mexico and sustained by the economic policies of the Confederate
States of America, and a United States now reduced to the dimensions of
Lincoln's Union.

In the single chapter that she voices the apologia for a French invasion of
Mexico, Ruiz de Burton uses both diplomatic history and the novelist's art
to create a hemispheric scale for the American Civil War. Lincoln, already
a polarizing figure in the sectional historiography of the United States, is
interpolated as a character in Mexican history, identified with a constitutionalist faction that is bent on ceding the country's economic and political
sovereignty to the United States. The conflict between the Union and the
Confederacy is recast not only as a civil war within Mexico but as a battle
between possible destinies for the Americas, one perpetuating the example
of Britain in North America and progressing through the imperialism of
the United States and the other founded in the Spanish colonization of the
Americas, supported by a belated but no less essential French intervention.

This hemispheric civil war has special purchase within the Latin American
intellectual tradition, denominating not only the competing colonial empires
in the Americas but distinct cultural legacies and modes of social development – a Hispanic and an Anglo-Saxon – that ultimately become the equivalent of racial formations.[11] In *The Idea of Latin America*, Walter Mignolo
historicizes this dialectical model, giving special emphasis to the intellectual
and geopolitical role played by France in the first part of the nineteenth
century. Mignolo follows the career of Chevalier, a French foreign policy
strategist who conjured the title of a "Latin" America to signify at once the
inferiority of a merely Hispanic descent for the Spanish-American leadership of the hemisphere and the special qualification of a common European
or Latinate genealogy for American creoles; as the bearer and signifier of
European civilization, France will assume custody over this "Latinadad" in
America.[12] Chevalier emerges as a character in American Civil War diplomatic history as an advisor to Napoleon III, emboldening the emperor to
base imperial policy on the fiction of a Latin origin; through dual monarch-
ies and transhemispheric migration, Europe's civilization would finally be

realized in Mexico. An anonymous pamphlet that was published in *The New York Times* in 1863 and linked to Chevalier included among the rationales for the French invasion of Mexico "To Protect Latins":

> France must oppose the absorption of Southern America [Mexico, Central America, and South America] by Northern America; she must in like manner oppose the degradation of the Latin race on the other side of the ocean.... Let the certainty of [France's] protection lead [a European] population to Mexico, and the age of its regeneration will not be long in coming to that country, thenceforth filled with new inhabitants, ready for all progress, familiar with the newest discoveries of modern industry, and supported by the intelligent liberalism of the flag of France.[13]

"Latin," already a contested term in Latin American philosophy and post-colonial theory, acquired new meaning in France's "Grand Design" not merely as a counteragent to U.S. imperialism but to Lincoln's policy of Union – a disastrous attempt, in Chevalier's estimation, to suture through war what geography, culture, and economic interests meant to bifurcate and realign. For France and Mexican conservative nationalists, Lincoln's determination to bring the Confederate States into an economic and political system dominated by the northern states of the United States was only the military version of a diplomatic and economic strategy that had already cost Mexico its sovereignty. Let us be clear: A proposed loan package that the Lincoln administration hoped would bolster Mexico's new constitutional government against its European creditors, the looming invasion of France, and the conservative faction in the Reform War included a stipulation that the United States possess a lien on the very public lands that the new government had recently seized from the Catholic Church.[14] Lincoln's support for the constitutional government of Mexico before Napoleon III's invasion might very well have consolidated the racial signifier that would resonate in the Latin American imagination as the antithesis to Latin: Anglo-Saxon greediness.

If Lincoln can play the role of antagonist in the Latinate historiography of the Americas, his administration's support for the constitutional government of Benito Juarez creates a competing model of hemispheric relations based on the proposition of a common American liberal tradition. This proposition, deeply rooted in theories of American exceptionalism and articulated most famously by the founding American studies scholar Herbert Eugene Bolton, yokes the United States and Mexico, or the governments of Lincoln and Juarez, as mutually reinforcing examples of each other's Americanness.[15] That each chief executive fought a civil war against retrograde forces of aristocracy and peonage only intensifies the evidence of a liberal capitalist democratic consensus within the nations. In this parallel version of hemispheric history, the victory of Juarez's army over French forces in the Battle of Puebla – celebrated in the United States as Cinco de Mayo – saves the United States by stalling the progress of Napoleon's Grand Design until the Union army can turn the tide of the Civil War against the Confederacy. When Lincoln orders troops massed in Texas for the invasion of French Mexico as soon as Appomattox is signed, he speeds the fall of Maximilian's monarchy and the return of Juarez's constitutional government. Collaboratively, Lincoln and Juarez complete a hemispheric defense of American sovereignty against European imperialism, although Lincoln was careful never to invoke the Monroe Doctrine for fear of compelling France and Mexico to recognize the Confederacy.[16] The two leaders, one the self-taught frontiersman and the other the Indian, embody complimentary versions of American indigeneity that is ultimately linked to underlying American constitutional principles. Clearly, the pairing of the six-foot-four Lincoln and the four-foot-six Juarez is no less generative than the encounter between the chief executive and the little woman, or the Anglo-Saxon and the Latin American. Their names joined in common defense of their nation's constitutions, Lincoln-Juarez constitutes a pedagogy for understanding a hemispheric "Americanity."[17]

"Lincoln-Juarez" is also the proper name for any number of public schools on the Texas and California border, erected more as symbols of good relations between sovereign states than statements of cultural fusion. The same can be said of the bust of Lincoln placed in Ciudad Juárez, Chihuahua, Mexico by President Johnson (of the Great Society, not the Reconstruction); during the Nixon administration, Mexican leaders reciprocated by placing a bust of Juarez directly across from the Watergate Hotel. The spectacle of these heads of state exchanging busts of Lincoln and Juarez speaks volumes about the role that both formal diplomacy and formalist models of government play in hemispheric formations. The construction of a common American governmentality that suppresses differences in culture or region in the name of legal formalism is indeed one of the legacies of Lincoln's Civil War diplomacy. As much as Napoleon III's invasion of Mexico catalyzed the definition of a Latin American, Lincoln's defense of Jaurez's constitutional government constituted an Americanness that could only define itself negatively – against assimilation with African Americans and Native Americans – and which deliberately skirted issues of ethnic descent in order to emphasize at once the inevitability of contingent diplomatic alliances and the universalism of constitutional government.

The fact that diplomatic historians can find in Lincoln's support for the Juarez government the beginning of U.S. "dollar diplomacy" in Latin America is a reminder that Lincoln's hemispheric relations will always be reconstructed and assessed within the context of still unfolding debates over the course of social and economic development in Latin America.[18] Mexico will always be Janus-faced, in the words of Valdez-Ugalde, confronted with dueling versions of its history; the convergence of Lincoln's and Juarez's civil wars in the 1850s and 1860s, he contends, sets in motion a narrative that begins with U.S. economic investment in Mexico and ends with the loss of economic sovereignty, the passage of NAFTA, and the impoverishment and displacement of millions of impoverished Mexicans across the U.S. border.[19] With Lincoln employing his fellow anti-Mexican War Whig Thomas Corwin to negotiate for investment access, trade rights, infrastructure concessions, and even land cessions for one of Lincoln's most cherished humanitarian causes – the colonization of African Americans – it is hard not to regard the establishment of complimentary constitutional systems as merely the underlying condition for U.S. economic imperialism.

Civil War diplomacy, however, complicates this conclusion, just as the diplomatic history of dueling U.S. and Confederate diplomatic legations in Mexico and immanent French recognition of the Confederacy disturbs our sense of American nationality. Lincoln established hemispheric relations with Mexico and Latin America, I would argue, as logical extensions of the formalist positions that he took against the extension of slaveholding into newly acquired U.S. territories, Mexico's northern provinces included. It is even possible to argue that he came to antislavery positions through the debates and conflict over the disposition of these territories. Let us recall that his invocation of the Constitution as a bar against the expansion of slavery, made famous in his 1858 debates with Stephen Douglass, was intended to place Nebraska and Kansas, the two newest territorial acquisitions, outside the reach of slavery. The speech that announced his return to national politics, his 1854 Peoria, Illinois, address, however, took a much broader hemispheric approach, moving through every territorial acquisition and treaty with foreign powers before concluding that the principle of non-extension established by the Missouri Compromise should be retained.[20] So although it is tempting to reduce the Kansas-Nebraska conflict to a sectionalist battle for wartime spoils, we should also recognize in Lincoln's opposition to the expansion of slavery the germ of a foreign policy toward Latin America. By organizing a national political party and then a government around this principle of non-extension, Lincoln sought to place Mexico and the Caribbean outside the reach of southern states, which were already improvising their own territorial expansion policy before secession through extensive use of "freebooters," or "filibusters." The invasion of Nicaragua by William Walker and the invasion of Cuba by Narciso Lopez provided early rehearsals for the southern states' defiance of the U.S. constitutional system, and to this extent, inspiration for Lincoln's Union policy. Indeed,

Lincoln understood southern slaveholders trafficking their human property into U.S. territory not yet legalized or constituted as sovereign states in exactly the way that he would understand these "foreign" invasions of Latin America: as illegal, extraconstitutional, piratical acts. Kansas and Nebraska, the contested western territory of the United States, would have suffered the same fate as Mexico and the Spanish jewel of the Caribbean, Cuba, and become part of an illegally constituted "Slave Power" if not for the constitutional order of Unionism. Lincoln's Unionism, in other words, was both a domestic and foreign policy, emerging from an antislavery position that specifically sought to regulate both mobile property and commercial traffic within legally proscribed territories.

With the Confederate States of America announcing "southward to destiny," proposing to annex Mexican provinces for slave states, and openly planning for an invasion of Cuba, Lincoln's defense of the Union can be considered a rearguard action designed to counteract the economic and diplomatic integration of southern plantation economies with the European-financed merchant capitalism of Caribbean colonies. Indeed, the Union was less a geospatial designation for the antislavery states of the United States than a set of formal principles for governance that could concatenate various nation-states, political parties, and political constituencies into a legalistic formation of America. Refusing to limit the sovereignty of this Union by naming its territories, Lincoln would declare war on other territories, seeking always to interdict an illegal commerce that would expand the domain of southern states into a Global South. "Southward to Destiny" was indeed the motto of the Confederacy, and so Lincoln had to declare war on New Orleans, the economic capital of an emerging circum-Caribbean power that threatened to link Havana, Vera Cruz, and the ports of France.[21] That this city was also the site from which filibusters carried their slaves, their personalized right of conquest, and their fraudulent form of American democracy to the "banana republics" of the hemisphere was for Lincoln both an injury and insult, his standard of just government being based on the non-extension of slavery.

There is an "Abraham Lincoln" in La Habanera, Cuba. There is also a heroic bust of Abraham Lincoln in Havana. With what politics, policies, and diplomatic histories do we construct the hemispheric relation of Lincoln and the Union to Cuba? That construction, I will suggest, is more troubling than generative, for even though there is a record of Lincoln's opposition to the illegal invasion of Cuba by Confederate agents, his policy against the extension of slavery never allowed him to imagine a liberation narrative for a Spanish colony bound to its slaveholding economy. Without a willingness to make the abolition of slavery a foundation of legitimate popular government in the United States, he could not engage with Cuban abolition-ist-nationalist movements and was left supporting Spanish colonialism. The hemispheric relations we construct through transnational abolitionist polit-ics remain the most complicated, and unfortunately, the most elusive.

NOTES

1 See Thomas David Schoonover, *Dollars Over Dominion: The Triumph of Liberalism in Mexican-United States Relations, 1861–1867* (Baton Rouge: Louisiana University Press, 1978); Schoonover, "Napoleon is Coming! Maximilian is Coming?: The International History of the Civil War in the Caribbean Basin," in Robert E. May, ed., *The Union, the Confederacy, and the Atlantic Rim* (West Lafayette, IN: Purdue University Press, 1995), 101–130; Lester D. Langley, *Struggle for the American Mediterranean: United States-European Rivalry in the Gulf-Caribbean* (Athens: University of Georgia Press, 1976); Alfred Jackson Hanna and Kathryn Abbey Hanna, *Napoleon III and Mexico: American Triumph Over Monarchy* (Chapel Hill: University of North Carolina Press, 1971).

2 Models of hemispheric critical inquiry include Kirsten Silva Gruesz, "America," in Bruce Burgett and Glenn Hendler, eds., *Keywords for American Cultural Studies* (New York: New York University Press, 2007), 16–22; Gruesz, *Ambassadors of Culture: The TransAmerican Origins of Latino Writing* (Princeton, NJ: Princeton University Press, 2002), 11–26; Diana Taylor, "Remapping Genre through Performance: From 'American' to 'Hemispheric' Studies," *PMLA* 122.5 (2007): 1416–1430; Susan Gillman, "*Ramona* in 'Our America,'" in Jeffrey Belknap and Raul Fernandez, eds., *Jose Marti's Our America: From National to Hemispheric Cultural Studies* (Durham, NC: Duke University Press, 1998), 91–109.

3 See Rosaura Sanchez, "Dismantling the Colossus: Marti and Ruiz de Burton on the Formation of Anglo-America," in Belknap and Fernandez, eds., *Jose Marti's Our America*, 115–128. See also Jose David Saldivar, *The Dialectics of Our America: Genealogy, Cultural Critique and Literary History* (Durham, NC: Duke University Press, 1995).

4 See Jane Tompkins, "Sentimental Power: Uncle Tom's Cabin and the Politics of Literary History," in *Sensational Designs: The Cultural Work of American Fiction, 1790–1860* (New York: Oxford University Press, 1985), 122–146.

5 See Abraham Lincoln, "'Spot' Resolutions in the U.S. House of Representatives," in Don E. Fehrenbacher, ed., *Abraham Lincoln: Speeches and Writings, 1832–1858* (New York: Library of America 1989), 158–160.

6 Maria Amparo Ruiz de Burton, *Who Would Have Thought It?* (Houston: Arte Publico Press, 1995), 198.

7 Ibid.

8 Anna Brickhouse, *TransAmerican Literary Relations and the Nineteenth Century Public Sphere* (Cambridge: Cambridge University Press, 2004), 1–9.

9 Bernando Guiterrez de Lara quoted in Francisco Valdes-Ugalde, "Janus and the Northern Colossus: Perceptions of the United States in the Building of the Mexican Nation," *Journal of American History* 86.2 (1999): 568–600.

10 On the Constitutionalist movement in Mexico, see Richard N. Sinkin, *The Mexican Reform, 1855–1876: A Study in Liberal-Nation Building* (Austin: University of Texas Press, 1971).

11 See Jose Vasconcelos, *The Cosmic Race*, trans. Didier T. Jaen (Baltimore: The Johns Hopkins University Press, 1997); Edmundo O'Gorman, *The Invention of America: An Inquiry into the Historical Nature of the New World and the Meaning of its History* (Westport, CT: Greenwood Press, 1972).

12 Walter Mignolo, *The Idea of Latin America* (London: Blackwell, 2005), 58–50 and 79–80.

13 Chevalier quoted in Hana and Hana, *Napoleon III and Mexico*, 61–62.

14 See Schoonover, *Dollars Over Dominion*, 60–77.

15 An overview is found in Ralph Bauer, "Hemispheric Studies," *PMLA* 124.1 (2009): 234–250.

16 See Hana and Hana, *Napoleon III and Mexico*. Also see James M. McPherson, "'The Whole Family of Man': Lincoln and the Last Best Hope Abroad," in *The Union, the Confederacy, and the Atlantic Rim* (West Lafayette: Purdue University Press, 1995), 131–159.

17 On "Americanity," see Annabel Quijano and Immanuel Wallerstein, "Americanity as a Concept, or America in the Modern World System" International Social Science Journal 44. 4 (1992): 549–557.

18 See Schoonover, *Dollars Over Dominion*, xiii–xx.

19 See Valdes-Ugalde, "Janus and the Northern Colossus," 570.

20 See Abraham Lincoln, "Speech at Peoria, October 16, 154," in Roy Basler, ed., *The Collected Works of Abraham Lincoln* (New Brunswick, NJ: Rutgers University Press, 1953), 247–283.

21 On New Orleans, see Kirsten Silva Gruesz, "The Mercurial Space of 'Central America': New Orleans, Honduras, and the Writing of the Banana Republic," in Caroline Levander and Robert S. Levine, eds., *Hemispheric American Studies* (New Brunswick, NJ: Rutgers University Press, 2007), 140–165.

ANNE NORTON

Lincoln on Hallowed Ground

There was a great battle at Gettysburg. Men screamed and died, and their blood soaked into the ground. The wheels of the artillery wagons dented the earth, and gunpowder scorched the trees. There were no monuments then.

When Lincoln came to speak at Gettysburg, the blood had dried and the screams were silent. There is silence now, and the dead have gone into the earth. There are monuments there. There are ghosts. They rose for Lincoln, when he called the dead out of the hallowed ground. When we read the Gettysburg Address we find ourselves on that same hallowed ground. Our ground, our land, is not on earth alone. Our people are not all numbered among the living.

Americans are a people whose homeland is the text. Our allegiance goes not to a land whose boundaries and contours change, but to words: to the words of the Declaration of Independence, the Constitution, and the Gettysburg Address. Those words have made us. It is to those words, those ideals, those promises, those aspirations, that we give our first and most enduring loyalties. The Gettysburg Address has become one of the canonical texts of the American nation. Generations of students, myself among them, were taught to recite it as a kind of republican catechism. In this text, which grounds our nationality, this text that is our American earth, we find ourselves among the dead.

This is, after all, an address given on a battlefield graveyard, a speech that commands us not only to honor the dead, but to submit to them. The dead, Lincoln reminds us, have proven their selfless devotion to the cause of the Union. They possess, in consequence, a moral authority far superior to that of the living. We, the living, are indebted to the dead, those who gave "the last full measure of devotion," those who "here gave their lives that that nation might live."

Our first debt, and that with which the speech begins, is to the dead of the Founding, to the Revolutionary generation.

> Four score and seven years ago our fathers brought forth upon this continent a new nation, conceived in liberty, and dedicated to the proposition that all men are created equal.

The Gettysburg Address begins where the nation does, in the Declaration of Independence. But Lincoln not only revives, he revises the ideals of Jefferson's Declaration. Jefferson had counseled posterity to be wary of the dead. Nowhere does the dead hand of the past lie so heavily on our shoulders as in the Gettysburg Address. Lincoln reminds us that we are met "on a great battlefield of that war." We are met there to honor the dead. "The world will little note nor long remember what we say here," Lincoln said, "but it can never forget what they did here."

Few men could know better than Lincoln how easily men were killed, how readily they were replaced, the numbers of the dead, and the ease with which the world forgot them. A moment earlier in the speech he recalled some words (the words of the Declaration) that had outlived their maker. His would do likewise. The monuments that stand every few feet at Gettysburg, the statues that stand in almost every American town, the parades and Fourth of July speeches, the "Union Stations" that spread with the railroads, the names of schools, streets, and cities, the documentaries and the reenactments have preserved only the names of only a few of the dead. The passion of memory that enthralled the nineteenth century did not succeed in securing the memory of the ordinary soldiers or their officers into our time.[1] Even the names of the great and powerful are lost. This speech given in a graveyard proved the spoken word superior to the unspeaking dead. Lincoln's words called on the living to submit themselves to the rule of the dead. "We cannot dedicate, we cannot consecrate, we cannot hallow, this ground. The brave men, living and dead, who struggled here have consecrated it far above our poor power to add or detract." Lincoln called us to a nation ruled not by words but by the sword, not by the living but the dead. We are called to dedicate ourselves to their cause. "From these honored dead we take increased devotion to that cause for which they gave the last full measure of devotion."

This dedication was no mere rhetorical invocation. For the nation of the Revolution, the words and the will of the living were to rule. "It is the living, and not the dead, who are to be accommodated," Thomas Paine wrote. "I am contending for the rights of the living." The earth belongs to the living, Paine proclaimed, and called on Americans to witness it.[2] Revolution invited the refusal of the past, an escape from history. The old phrases – "This is our custom" or "This is how it has always been" – that licensed the claims of monarchs and aristocrats, that furnished excuses for oppression and submission, would have their power broken. Commitment to the consent of the governed was a commitment to the living: to be governed in and by and as those present in the flesh.

Paine's old opponent, Edmund Burke, had long argued otherwise. Custom, Burke argued, was the distilled wisdom of generations. Life in a community required constant compromises, adaptations, "small and temporary deviation[s]" that shaped a common life.[3] These reflected the requirements of necessity. Custom was thus the accretion of many prudent and practical responses to circumstances reason could not foresee. The limits of a lifetime could not hold this practical knowledge. Wisdom thus required deference to custom. One submitted to the work of men long dead not for the sake of wisdom alone. In doing so, one joined a community whose boundaries reached beyond the living. When Burke argued for conciliation with the colonies he sought to persuade the rebellious colonists and their parliamentary rulers that they were bound within a single cultural community. All were Englishmen, with an English love of liberty. Living and dead were bound in a single people, stretching through time and space. "My hold of the Colonies is in the close affection which grows from common names, from kindred blood, from similar privileges, and equal protection. These are ties, which, though light as air, are as strong as links of iron."[4] Burke's was no sentimental argument. The account of British constitutional history offered in the speech argued for the accretion of custom and memory in institutions and institutional practice.[5] The wisdom of the dead ruled not only in deference to custom but in adherence to precedent in law, in the form of institutions and offices and in the physical boundaries of political jurisdictions.

Lincoln accepted, even welcomed, the governance of the dead, in his commitment to – indeed reverence for – the law. In his address to the Young Men's Lyceum of Springfield, he praised the North as "the land of steady habits" inhabited by men who "desire to abide by the law." Law secured the accomplishments of the founding generation. Lincoln's is not, however, a perfect deference or submission to the will of those who came before. The dead haunted Lincoln. Passages in his 1838 Lyceum Address testify to the reverence and envy with which he regarded the achievements of the Founding generation. They lived in memory, but memory too died. "I do not mean to say, that the scenes of the revolution *are now* or *ever will* be entirely forgotten; but that like every thing else, they must fade upon the memory of the world, and grow more and more dim by the lapse of time." They had lived, triumphed, died, and remained – for awhile – among the living; "in the form of a husband, a father, a son or brother, a *living history* was to be found in every family." Their deeds could be read on their bodies, heard in their words, and read finally as though they were words in books: "In the limbs mangled, in the scars of wounds received, in the midst of the very scenes related – a history, too, that could be read and understood alike by all."[6]

Lincoln lived among the dead in a more profound sense. No critic of Lincoln or the Lincoln myth (I am among them) can doubt that he numbered every death, mourned the loss of each life, and walked, day after day, in the company of men –North and South – he had sent to their deaths. The dead of Gettysburg, Antietam, Chancellorsville, Bull Run, and all the battles of the Civil War haunted him.

The dead haunt the Gettysburg Address in another sense as well. This speech is the inaugural address of America's refounding. The nation that emerged from the Civil War was not the nation of the Founding. Cleansed, perhaps, of the sin of slavery, the nation had been reformed not by Constitutional amendment but by war. The blood that soaked the earth at Gettysburg belonged to the living, to men four generations removed from the Revolution, yet when they died the Revolution died with them. The Civil War marked the death of the first American republic. It was, many thought, a death in a good cause.

One of those who knew and honored that cause was Herman Melville. We know Herman Melville as the author of *Moby Dick*, *Billy Budd*, and *Typee*, but he was also the author of a cycle of poems on the Civil War. For Melville, the Civil War was a "Conflict of Convictions," and he prayed:

> *In this strife of brothers*
> *(God hear their country call)*
> *However it be, whatever betide*
> *Let not the just one fall.*

The North was on the side of the angels. And the South? The South was proof that "Satan's old age is strong and hale." A southern fortress was "the fastness of the Anarch" for Melville: "Richmond goes Babylon's way, Sing and Pray." Melville's language and its rhetoric of place made the North's cause that of order and Christianity. Whether order was the support of Christianity, or Christianity the source of order, the two were inextricably linked, and the North was their agent.

So simple, so profound a war, and yet Melville wrote,

> Who looks at Lee must think of Washington;
> In pain must think, and hide the thought,
> So deep with grievous meaning it is fraught.

The American Revolutionaries had rebelled against the British. They knew that they were traitors and that the punishment for treason would be theirs if they lost. Benjamin Franklin's admonition to his colleagues, urging them to hang together "or assuredly we shall all hang separately," which sounds now like a bit of wry humor, acknowledged a harsh reality. Yet, as Patrick Henry recognized, it also opened all the possibilities of outlawry and rebellion: "If this be treason, make the most of it." The men who founded the nation were, at least for a moment (and perhaps longer) lawless, faithless men, the enemies of order and union. They were Rebels. They had seceded. The South stood not only for Satan but for the willful faith of the Revolution.

As Michael Adams's work demonstrated many years ago, the memory of the Revolution haunted the early years of the Civil War. Generals and soldiers alike were loath to confront the Rebels on the grounds of an earlier rebellion. They shied away from battles too close to Mount Vernon, Arlington, Montpelier, and Monticello. They believed, as the rebellion often insisted, not only that the southerners were more dangerous and more violent, but also that they were closer, in space, heritage, and culture, to the revolutionary founders.[7]

Melville believed that the Founding had failed. The principles of the Founding had proven inadequate to the defects of human nature. We had thought, we Americans, that we could make a nation, a republic, unlike any nation the world had seen. We had thought that we could fashion a new world order, where governments ruled by the consent of the governed. We could not. "The Founders' dream shall flee," Melville wrote,

> Age after Age shall be
> As Age after Age has been
> (From Man's changeless heart their way they win).

The nation of the American Revolution was born in the faith that we could rule ourselves, that "Man was Nature's Roman, never to be scourged," that nations could be conceived and dissolved by the will and words of the people alone, and that we could make a nation with a mere Declaration of Independence and unmake it when we chose. That faith no longer held. The United States was to be as other nations: founded on force rather than the consent of the governed; ruling the people, not to be ruled by them. These were inevitabilities: originating in human nature, revealed in history.

The repudiation – or, if you prefer, the refutation – of the faith of the Revolutionaries represented, Melville recognized, a profound political reversal. The Civil War made us a nation held together, as other nations are, by military force, by conquest.

> But God is in Heaven, and Grant in the Town,
> And Right through might is Law –
> God's way adore.

The insolubility of the antebellum conflict proved the inadequacy of a deistical Founding, a Revolutionary regime that sailed too close to anarchy. God required the imposition of right through might and founded law not in consent but in force of arms and divine warrant.

For Lincoln, as for Melville, the cause of the Union was a just cause, and more, a divine one. For Lincoln, as for Melville, the conflict was of world historical and cosmic significance. "Now we are engaged," Lincoln said, "in a great civil war, testing whether that nation, or any nation, so conceived and so dedicated, can long endure." For Lincoln, as for Melville, the cause of the Union could be, must be, put in the hands of the army. The cause of the Union entailed the abandonment of faith in the consent of the governed. The Union was no longer the nation of the Founders, and no longer adhered, in the strictest sense, to the provisions of the Constitution.

The Civil War began, so it was said at the time, in a dispute over the Constitution. Lincoln thought this Constitutional dispute – the dispute over text and law – might (as he said in his First Inaugural Address) "arguably have been awarded to the South." The war for the Union was not, therefore, a war to defend the Constitution, or even a Constitutional war.

Lincoln was devoted to the Union, but he was no rigorous adherent to constitutional principles. In the course of the Civil War Lincoln suspended habeas corpus without the counsel or consent of Congress, and he did so with an explicit acknowledgment of the possible unconstitutionality of the act. He imposed martial law, imprisoning men for questioning the conduct of the war and for casting aspersions on the character and appearance of the president. Those judges who imposed these arbitrary imprisonments found themselves imprisoned as well. Lincoln closed newspapers and imprisoned their editors, without charges. He imprisoned, again without charges, the entirety of the Maryland state legislature (lest they vote – as they would surely have voted – for secession), and with them the mayor and the chief of police of the city of Baltimore. Areas of the cities of New York and Baltimore were occupied by the Union army (which had been brought up from confronting Lee in the South to confront restive Union citizens in the North). Cannon volleys were fired on rioters. Bounties were placed on draft resisters. Neighbors were encouraged to denounce neighbors, without evidence, to the office of the Secretary of State. Seward, the man who held that office and created that system, boasted to the British ambassador,

> My lord, I can touch a bell on my right hand and order the arrest of a citizen of Ohio. I can touch the bell again and order the arrest of a citizen of New York, and no power on earth, except that of the President, can release them. Can the Queen of England do so much?[8]

There are many ironies here. The Americans had rebelled against the arbitrary rule of the British Empire. They had established a republic. Now their minister boasted to his British rival of the arbitrary power he exercised, a power greater than that of the monarchy the United States had rejected. Seward's pride was not in adherence to the Constitution or republican principles, but in power alone.

During and after the war, long and well-documented accounts were published, detailing these violations of the letter and the principles of the Constitution. The authors of these confidently assured their readers that "the unlawful and oppressive acts of Mr. Lincoln, his advisers and subordinates, during the war between this government and that of the Confederate States will hereafter constitute no insignificant portion of the history of these times." They might have said, with Lincoln, "the world will little note nor long remember what we say here, but it will never forget what they did here." They, like Lincoln, were wrong. These accounts have virtually disappeared from our histories. The thousands who died in the draft riots receive little notice. The political prisons of the Northeast, once notorious on two continents, are forgotten in condemnations of Andersonville. Large leather books detailing prisons and draft riots, never reprinted, lie in our libraries covered with red rot. We smugly condemn the excesses of the military in Latin America and the Middle East, secure in the knowledge that no such thing can happen here. We forget that it already has. Why do we forget this? All nations have selective memories.

Forgetfulness as well as memory (as Burke and Nietzsche so perceptively observed) is essential to both history and national identity, for both depend on a selective construction of the past. The questions then come back in an altered form: Why do we forget *these* facts? And why, when we are reminded of them, do we dismiss them? Why do they seem insignificant, leaving no mark on the course of the war or the grandeur of the character of Abraham Lincoln?

If this defense of the Constitution demanded, indeed depended on, violation of the Constitution and the abrogation of the rights that it secured, if the Constitutional dispute "might arguably have been awarded to the South," then what remained for Lincoln to defend? How could the deaths of the Civil War give us "a new birth of freedom?" What was Lincoln's Constitution?

In his "Address to the Young Men's Lyceum of Springfield, Illinois," Lincoln called the Constitution, which he praised rhapsodically "a legal inheritance," that is, at once law and inheritance. Law and inheritance are principal traits of Lincoln's Constitution, and each trait carries many meanings in it. Law was of profound importance to Lincoln personally. It had removed him from the poverty and ignorance of his family to a position of wealth and prestige, power, and influence. It would give him glory, even immortality, and a kind of posthumous charisma in the office of the presidency and his conduct of the war. Law, in that personal experience that informed Lincoln's understanding, was not merely a source of power and influence, but it was the means by which men were raised up.

Accordance to, and the practice of, the law raised up individual men. Legislation, and obedience to law, raised up nations. Law, in Lincoln's view, secured liberty, union, and order. It was not the artifact, or the product, of these things, but it was their prerequisite. The Constitution, as the first law of the land should thus receive collective veneration. It should become "the political religion of the nation" in which children would receive an early and thorough catechism. "Reverence for the law [would] be breathed by every American mother, to the lisping babe." This was a very different view from that Walt Whitman held. He praised America as a land "where men and women think lightly of the laws." It was a view very different from Patrick Henry's "if this be treason make the most of it." It was a view strangely at odds with the document itself, which invites its own amendment.

Because the law and Constitution were an inheritance, disobedience or even disrespect to these showed irreverence to fathers and indifference to children. The Constitution was, for Lincoln, that which binds us to our past and our posterity, to the dead and the unborn. It was the instrument in which we collectively transcended the limits of a natural lifetime.

Lincoln recognized that it was the written character of the Constitution that enabled it to accomplish this. In his "Second Lecture on Discovery and Invention," Lincoln marked writing as "a world historical invention of the first importance, one of inestimable value." He argued, contrary to Socrates, that "speech has not advanced the condition of the world much." Writing had. It did so because it enables us, in Lincoln's words, to "converse with the dead, the absent, and the unborn." This conversation with the dead gives us memory. It makes us a historical people, binding us to the past. Conversation with the unborn grants us a stake in posterity and imposes on that posterity the obligations of memory. Writing enables us to create a timeless nation, as Lincoln said, "a perpetual Union." It was in writing that we became no longer a people of the flesh but a people of the word. Writing, particularly the living writing of the dead, removed us from earthly things and placed us on the hallowed ground of the scripture.

Lincoln's faith in writing and the written law was, however, neither perfect nor continuous, and it gave way to other, more profound commitments. When Lincoln speaks and writes of the Constitution, he does not urge us to honor unambiguously the particular provisions of the document – some of which he explicitly disagreed with. Rather he has his eye on the constitution of an ideal nation, in the minds and hearts of the people, the covenant made by scripture with flesh and written, as scripture has it, "on their inmost parts." This covenantal constitution enables us to partake of the glories of the past and the triumphs of the future, but it also obliges us to participate in the sins and shortcomings of our ancestors and those of our posterity.

Given this understanding of the Constitution, it is not adherence to the provisions of the document that is decisive, but the preservation of a historical community. This view of the Constitution is itself an inheritance forming a historical community. It belongs to the Puritans. Lincoln had inherited this from the Puritans through the Whigs, a lineage he acknowledged proudly even after the Whig party had disappeared.

The Puritan view of the Constitution as covenant, like Lincoln's, created links to the dead and the unborn. Like Lincoln's, it formed a sacred union. Like Lincoln's, it was not the creation of liberty or the expression of union, but a prerequisite for these. Because it was an inheritance, it was not an occasion for pride, but an occasion for gratitude. It was not the evidence and security of the freedom of the living, but the imposition of a duty to the dead and the unborn. It made America the New Israel; its inhabitants became a Chosen People in a Promised Land. In this Puritan vision, the Constitution became the culmination of a series of covenants: The covenants with Abraham and Noah, the covenant of the New Testament, the Magna Carta, the Declaration of Rights, and the Mayflower Compact. Each had made the community larger; each had extended it from the sacred to the secular. This conception made politics a deeply religious experience: The achievement of public liberty and private virtue were seen as essentially linked. It was a progressive history, whether secular or sacred: realizing God's will, or (in its Hegelian form) the rule of mind, in the world.

Most importantly, this history was incomplete. It bound the living with the dead and the unborn in a common endeavor. It gave them a common end and a common will. Most importantly, it enabled the living to surpass the accomplishments of the dead, and it enabled the sons to transcend the achievements of the fathers.

The religious understanding of the constitution held by Lincoln obliges us to consider the religious Lincoln. The attribution of religiosity to Lincoln might seem to be contradicted by Lincoln's neglect of the institutions and ceremonies of organized religion and by speculations of his contemporaries that he was an agnostic. It is, however, not Lincoln the private man but Lincoln the statesman and Lincoln the myth with whom we are concerned here. We can never wholly know his private beliefs, for we have no access to the minds and hearts of men. Rather we should consider the man of our histories, our legends, and our myths. It is the legendary president who has ideal authority here. The private man is dead; the statesmen and the myth grow stronger.

People of Lincoln's time read only Lincoln's speech. The Lincoln of that speech had made and would make other speeches. After the assassination, we read not only Lincoln's speech but the speech's Lincoln. In his death Lincoln became one with the martyrs he had praised. He was the man who gave "the last full measure of devotion" to the cause of the Union.

The covenant of the New Testament had been sealed by the death of the representative, by the death of the Son of man. Lincoln was identified with Jesus throughout high and popular culture, in the years immediately after the assassination, and in the histories and myths that preserve that event in memory.[9] The identification was perhaps made most explicitly in one of Melville's poems, which played on the fact that Lincoln was assassinated on Good Friday, a distinction he owed to the favor, or the stupidity, of John Wilkes Booth. Lincoln became a secular avatar of Jesus Christ. He became the shepherd who gives up his life for the sheep, the savior (in this case, of the Union) and the redeemer.

This is the most important aspect of the identification of Lincoln as savior and redeemer. Lincoln became the redeemer of a broken covenant, the restorer of that *corpus mysticum* the body politic. He redeemed a people born in original sin. Americans were a people whose founding was marred by the sin of slavery. It was from that sin that Lincoln redeemed them.

In redeeming the nation from the sin of slavery, Lincoln was able to surpass the deeds of the fathers. This surpassing of the Founding Fathers, like the Christian myth of redemption, is ambiguous. Lincoln, like Jesus, founds a new covenant with his death, but, again like Jesus, he comes "in fulfillment of the scriptures." Lincoln was seen not as opposing the Constitution but as fulfilling its as yet unrealized promise.

The reading of Lincoln as martyr, or (more precisely) as the martyred redeemer, is not merely the recognition of a death on behalf of the people. It is also a recognition of Lincoln's representative function. Lincoln was representative in life and in death. As president, he was representative of the nation, of government, and, as Tocqueville noted, of party. However, it is in death that his role as representative becomes most important. He was representative in sacrificing himself on behalf of the people, and, finally, he was representative of the sacrifices made by the people themselves: of those who died in the conflict to preserve the Union, Southerners as well as Northerners.

The Christian myth, and our imposition of that myth on Lincoln, reveals the relation of representation to authority. In it the representative becomes an author. Jesus, in Christian myth, serves as the representative of God to man, and of man to God. Through his representation, he becomes the author of the new covenant.

Lincoln, in his role as representative, became authoritative. He authored a new understanding of presidential rule, an understanding subsequently imitated by presidents as diverse as Wilson, Roosevelt, and Nixon. He authored a new America, comprising newly enfranchised black citizens and newly disenfranchised rebels, with new laws and new Constitutional amendments. He authored a new vision of America, a new founding, particularly in the Second Inaugural Address and the Gettysburg Address. In these speeches, he gave a new account of the meaning of the war and of the place of the war in American history. The history seen in the Second Inaugural is a tragic history.

We think of the Civil War in Lincoln's words, as the conflict that ensured that "government of the people, by the people, and for the people shall not perish from the earth." We think of Lincoln as the man who sought to end the conflict (in the words of the Second Inaugural Address) "with malice toward none, with charity for all." Yet in that same Inaugural Address, Lincoln said,

> If God wills that it shall continue until all the wealth piled up by the bondsman's two hundred and fifty years of unrequited toil shall be sunk, and until every drop of blood drawn by the lash shall be repaid by another drawn by the sword, as it was said three thousand years ago, so still it must be said "The judgments of the Lord are true and righteous altogether."

There is no charity here.

We think of our Constitution as securing peace, precluding violence, abjuring force, and above all, as founded in the consent of the governed. If we accept Lincoln as the savior of the constitutional order, the redeemer of the Union, and the maker of a new birth of freedom, then we must either acknowledge that our constitutional order is founded not only on the consent but also on the conquest of the governed or recognize that Lincoln set the Constitution aside. With the weight of recent years heavy on us, we should be loathe to license further suspensions of rights or mark conquest as a legitimate title to rule. Nor should we deny that citizens of the Confederacy returned to the Union not as citizens but as conquered subjects. If we recognize that Lincoln set the Constitution aside, whether we accept or condemn those acts, we are able to regard his actions as alien. The refusal of the consent of the governed is to be no governmental principle. These acts are not to shape our people; they are not to constitute the nation.[10]

We think of Lincoln as the Great Emancipator, yet it takes little learning to discover that Lincoln was at best a late and uncertain believer in black equality. He had hoped that black leaders would lead their people back to Africa and encouraged them to do so. We think of the Civil War as a war "dedicated to the proposition that all men are created equal" yet we know that – despite the Fourteenth Amendment – racial inequality persists in America: from the nineteenth century to our own time. Why then do we continue to believe the promise that closes the Gettysburg Address?

> That this nation, under God, shall have a new birth of freedom; and that government of the people, by the people, and for the people shall not perish from the earth.

The answer is in a poem by Langston Hughes – and in the Gettysburg Address itself.

> A long time ago, but not too long ago, a man said:
> ALL MEN ARE CREATED EQUAL –
> ENDOWED BY THEIR CREATOR
> WITH CERTAIN UNALIENABLE RIGHTS –
> AMONG THESE LIFE, LIBERTY
> AND THE PURSUIT OF HAPPINESS.
> His name was Jefferson. There were slaves then,
> But in their hearts the slaves believed him, too,
> And silently took for granted
> That what he said was also meant for them.[11]

In this poem, Hughes offers a decisive refutation of originalism's facile faith. The words that ground our nationality, that have become our ground, our homeland, our American earth, are greater than their authors, greater indeed, than the intentions of their authors – and they are willfully so. The Declaration aims not at preservation but at overcoming. The Constitution – written (and so, to be read and spoken) in the present tense, providing for its own amendment, looking to a greater future – aimed at the same overcoming. We were not to be as we had been. We are not to be as we were. We are not to be as we are. We are called to our own overcoming.

The following stanza in "Freedom's Plow" is followed immediately by the recollection of Lincoln, moving, as the Gettysburg Address does, between the Declaration and the Civil War.

> It was a long time ago,
> But not so long ago at that, Lincoln said:
> NO MAN IS GOOD ENOUGH
> TO GOVERN ANOTHER MAN
> WITHOUT THAT OTHER'S CONSENT.
> There were slaves then, too,
> But in their hearts the slaves knew
> What he said must be meant for every human being –
> Else it had no meaning for anyone.[12]

Lincoln opens the Gettysburg Address with an invocation of the Declaration. For him, as for the people, the Declaration marks the beginning of the nation. The Declaration is the North Star of the Gettysburg Address. Lincoln takes his bearings from it and in so doing marks a course out of subjection and into freedom. Our adherence to the principles of the Declaration is not, as the opening of the speech suggests, simply filial piety to the Founding Fathers. It is not, in the end, even reverence to the honored dead. "It is rather for us to be here dedicated to the great task remaining before us." The dead who haunt this speech direct the living to turn away from death: "That this nation shall have a new birth of freedom; and that this government of the people, by the people, for the people, shall not perish from the earth." The Declaration affirms Paine's principle that the earth belongs to the living. They are endowed with rights. They cannot be governed without their consent. They may institute governments to secure these rights and alter them when they choose. The culmination of the speech affirms these rights.

Lincoln turns away from the dead. It is we the living who have an unfinished task remaining before us. It is we the living who will ensure the new birth of freedom.

In the end, the cause returns to us. "Keep your hand on the plow."[13]

NOTES

1 Drew Faust, *This Republic of Suffering: Death and the American Civil War* (New York: Vintage, 2009); Kelly McMichael, *Sacred Memories: The Civil War Monument Movement in Texas* (Austin: Texas Historical Association, 2009); Donald McLaughlin, *Crossroads of the Conflict: Defining Moments for the Blue and Gray: A Guide to the Monuments of Gettysburg* (Outskirts Press, 2008); *The Memory of the Civil War in American Culture*, Alice Fahs and Joan Waugh, eds. (Durham, NC: University of North Carolina Press, 2004).

2 Thomas Paine, *The Rights of Man*, in *Common Sense, The Rights of Man, and Other Essential Writings of Thomas Paine* (New York: Penguin, 1984), 128, 129.

3 Edmund Burke, *Reflections on the Revolution in France* (London: Methuen, 1905), 37, 24.

4 Edmund Burke, "Speech on Moving His Resolution for Conciliation with the Colonies," from *Select Works of Edmund Burke* (Indianapolis: Liberty Fund, 1999), paragraph 530, Online Library of Liberty: http://oll.libertyfund.org/.

5 Ibid., 201–206.

6 Abraham Lincoln, "Lyceum Address" or "The Perpetuation of Our Political Institutions: Address Before the Young Men's Lyceum of Springfield, Illinois," January 27, 1838, Abraham Lincoln Online: http://showcase.netins.net/web/creative/lincoln/speeches/lyceum.htm.

7 Michael C. C. Adams, *Our Masters the Rebels: A Speculation on Union Military Failure in the East 1861–1865* (Cambridge, MA: Harvard University Press, 1978).

8 John Marshall, *American Bastille: A History* (Philadelphia: Thomas Hartley, 1883), frontispiece.

9 See Michael Rogin, "The President's Two Bodies" in *Ronald Reagan: The Movie and Other Episodes in Political Demonology* (Berkeley: University of California Press, 1988).

10 Bruce Ackerman, *Before the Next Attack: Preserving Civil Liberties in an Age of Terrorism* (New Haven, CT: Yale University Press, 2007) See also Sanford Levinson, *Our Undemocratic Constitution* (New York: Oxford University Press, 2008).

11 "Freedom's Plow," in Arnold Rampersad, ed., *The Collected Poems of Langston Hughes* (New York: Knopf, 1994), 265–266.

12 Ibid., 266.

13 Ibid., 268.

GUIDE TO FURTHER READING

This guide is intended as a starting place for the many excellent historical and biographical works on Abraham Lincoln; it also provides access to the historical, cultural, and literary contexts of the Civil War and the nineteenth-century United States. Such a guide must be selective because the bicentennial of Lincoln's birth produced an astonishing increase in the number of available books as well as special issues of journals, such as the *Journal of American History*, devoted to scholarship on Abraham Lincoln, excellent scholarly work that cannot be fully covered in this small space. Readers might want to consult online archives such as "The Valley of the Shadow" (University of Virginia: http://valley.lib.virginia.edu/) or "Southern Cultures" (University of North Carolina, Chapel Hill: http://www.southerncultures. org/content). Sites such as the "Making of America" (Cornell University: http:// digital.library.cornell.edu/m/moa/) enable browsing of nineteenth-century books and magazines.

Critical Books on Lincoln

Boritt, Gabor. *The Gettysburg Gospel: The Lincoln Speech That Defined America.* New York: Simon and Schuster, 2006.

Bray, Robert. *Reading With Lincoln.* Carbondale: Southern Illinois University Press, 2010.

Briggs, John Channing. *Lincoln's Speeches Reconsidered.* Baltimore: Johns Hopkins University Press, 2005.

Diggins, John Patrick. *On Hallowed Ground: Abraham Lincoln and the Foundations of American History.* New Haven: Yale University Press, 2000.

Farber, Daniel. *Lincoln's Constitution.* Chicago: University of Chicago Press, 2003.

Foner, Eric. *The Fiery Trial: Abraham Lincoln and American Slavery.* New York: Norton, 2010.

Foner, Eric, ed. *Our Lincoln: New Perspectives on Lincoln and His World.* New York: W. W. Norton & Company, 2008.

Goodwin, Doris Kearns. *Team of Rivals: The Political Genius of Abraham Lincoln.* New York: Simon and Schuster, 2005.

Guelzo, Allen. *Lincoln and Douglas: The Debates That Defined America.* New York: Simon and Schuster, 2008.

Holzer, Harold, Gabor S. Boritt, and Mark E. Neely, Jr., eds. *The Lincoln Image: Abraham Lincoln and the Popular Print.* New York: The Scribner Press, 1984.

Holzer, Harold, and Sara Vaughn Gabbard, eds. *Lincoln and Freedom: Slavery, Emancipation, and the Thirteenth Amendment.* Carbondale: Southern Illinois University Press, 2007.

Holzer, Harold, John Simon, and Dawn Vogel, eds. *Lincoln Revisited: New Insights from the Lincoln Forum.* New York: Fordham University Press, 2007.

Kunhardt, Philip B., III, Peter Kunhardt, and Peter W. Kunhardt, Jr. *Looking for Lincoln: The Making of an American Icon.* New York: Alfred A. Knopf, 2008.

Lander, James. *Lincoln and Darwin: Shared Views of Race, Science, and Religion.* Carbondale: University of Illinois Press, 2010.

McPherson, James. *Abraham Lincoln and the Second American Revolution.* New York: Oxford University Press, 1991.

Meserve, Frederick Hill. *The Photographs of Abraham Lincoln.* New York: Harcourt, Brace and Company, 1944.

Neely, Mark E., Jr. *The Fate of Liberty: Abraham Lincoln and Civil Liberties.* New York: Oxford University Press, 1992.

Nichols, David A. *Lincoln and the Indians.* Urbana: University of Illinois Press, 1999.

Oakes, James. *The Radical and the Republican: Frederick Douglass and Abraham Lincoln.* New York: W. W. Norton, 2008.

Peterson, Merrill D. *Lincoln in National Memory.* New York: Oxford University Press, 1994.

Schwartz, Barry. *Abraham Lincoln and the Forge of American Memory.* Chicago: University of Chicago Press, 2000.

Tackach, James. *Lincoln's Moral Vision: The Second Inaugural Address.* Jackson: University Press of Mississippi, 2002.

Thomas, John L., ed. *Abraham Lincoln and the American Political Tradition.* Amherst: University of Massachusetts Press, 1986.

White, Ronald C. *Lincoln's Greatest Speech: The Second Inaugural.* New York: Simon and Schuster, 2002.

Wills, Gary. *Lincoln at Gettysburg: The Words that Remade America.* New York: Simon & Schuster, 1992.

Wilson, Douglas L. *Lincoln's Sword: The Presidency and the Power of Words.* New York: Vintage, 2006.

Winger, Stewart. *Lincoln, Religion, and Romantic Cultural Politics.* DeKalb: Northern Illinois University Press, 2003.

Critical Books on the Civil War

Ayers, Edward. *In the Presence of Mine Enemies: War in the Heart of America, 1859–1863.* New York: Norton, 2003.

Blight, David W. *Race and Reunion: The Civil War in American Memory.* Cambridge: Harvard University Press, 2001.

Faust, Drew Gilpin. *This Republic of Suffering: Death and the American Civil War.* New York: Knopf, 2008.

Foreman, Amanda. *A World on Fire: Britain's Crucial Role in the American Civil War.* New York: Random House, 2010.

Gallagher, Gary. *The Union War.* Cambridge, MA: Harvard University Press, 2011.

Gannon, Barbara. *The Won Cause: Black and White Comradeship in the Grand Army of the Republic.* Chapel Hill: University of North Carolina, 2011.

Manning, Chandra. *What This Cruel War Was Over: Soldiers, Slavery, and the Civil War*. New York: Vintage, 2008.

Marten, James. *Sing Not War: The Lives of Union and Confederate Veterans in Gilded Age America*. Chapel Hill: University of North Carolina, 2011.

McCurry, Stephanie. *Confederate Reckoning: Power and Politics in the Civil War*. Cambridge: Harvard University Press, 2010.

McPherson, James. *Battle Cry of Freedom: The Civil War Era*. New York: Oxford University Press, 2003.

Rable, George. *God's Almost Chosen People: A Religious History of the American Civil War*. Chapel Hill: University of North Carolina Press, 2010.

Samuels, Shirley. *Facing America: Iconography and the Civil War*. New York: Oxford University Press, 2004.

Silber, Nina. *The Romance of Reunion: Northerners and the South, 1865–1900*. Chapel Hill: University of North Carolina Press, 1993.

Weeks, Jim. *Gettysburg: Memory, Market, and American Shrine*. Princeton: Princeton University Press, 2003.

Critical Books on Nineteenth-Century American Culture

Castiglia, Christopher. *Interior States: Institutional Consciousness and the Inner Life of Democracy in the United States*. Durham: Duke University Press, 2008.

Castronovo, Russ. *Necro Citizenship: Death, Eroticism, and the Public Sphere in the Nineteenth Century United States*. Durham: Duke University Press, 2001.

Cavitch, Max. *American Elegy: The Poetry of Mourning from the Puritans to Whitman*. Minneapolis: University of Minnesota Press, 2007.

Dain, Bruce. *A Hideous Monster of the Mind: American Race Theory in the Early Republic*. Cambridge: Harvard University Press, 2002.

Dudden, Faye. *Fighting Chance: The Struggle Over Woman Suffrage and Black Suffrage in Reconstruction America*. New York: Oxford University Press, 2011.

Fahs, Alice. *The Imagined Civil War: Popular Literature of the North and South, 1861–1865*. Chapel Hill: University of North Carolina, 2002.

Finseth, Ian. *Shades of Green: Visions of Nature in the Literature of American Slavery, 1770–1860*. Athens: University of Georgia Press, 2009.

Isenberg, Nancy. *Sex and Citizenship in Antebellum America*. Chapel Hill: University of North Carolina, 1998.

Jehlen, Myra. *American Incarnation: The Individual, the Nation, the Continent*. Cambridge: Harvard University Press, 1986.

Lott, Eric. *Love and Theft: Blackface Minstrelsy and the American Working Class*. New York: Oxford University Press, 1995.

Norton, Anne. *Alternative Americas: A Reading of Antebellum Political Culture*. Chicago: University of Chicago, 1986.

Rogers, Molly. *Delia's Tears: Race, Science, and Photography in Nineteenth-Century America*. New Haven: Yale University Press, 2010.

Rubin, Louis D. *The Edge of the Swamp: A Study in the Literature and Society of the Old South*. Baton Rouge: Louisiana State University Press, 1989.

Smith Rosenberg, Carroll. *This Violent Empire: The Birth of an American National Identity*. Chapel Hill: University of North Carolina Press, 2010.

Smith, Shawn Michelle. *American Archives: Gender, Race, and Class in Visual Culture*. Princeton: Princeton University Press, 1999.

Stoll, Steven. *Larding the Lean Earth: Soil and Society in Nineteenth-Century America*. New York: Hill and Wang, 2002.

Sweet, Timothy. *Traces of War: Poetry, Photography, and the Crisis of the Union*. Baltimore: The Johns Hopkins University Press, 1990.

Trachtenberg, Alan. *Lincoln's Smile and Other Enigmas*. New York: Hill and Wang, 2007.

Wilson, Ivy. *Specters of Democracy: Blackness and the Aesthetics of Politics in the Antebellum U.S.* New York: Oxford University Press, 2011.

Young, Elizabeth. *Disarming the Nation: Women's Writing and the American Civil War*. Chicago: University of Chicago Press, 1999.

Biographies

Baker, Jean Harvey. *Mary Todd Lincoln: A Biography*. New York: W. W. Norton, 2008.

Burlingame, Michael. *Abraham Lincoln: A Life*. Baltimore: The Johns Hopkins University Press, 2008.

Carwardine, Richard. *Lincoln: A Life of Purpose and Power*. New York: Alfred A. Knopf, 2006.

Donald, David Herbert. *Lincoln*. New York: Simon & Schuster, 1996.

Fleischner, Jennifer. *Mrs. Lincoln and Mrs. Keckley: The Remarkable Story of the Friendship Between a First Lady and a Former Slave*. New York: Broadway, 2003.

Kaplan, Fred. *Lincoln: The Biography of a Writer*. New York: Harper Collins, 2008.

McPherson, James M. *Abraham Lincoln*. New York: Oxford University Press, 2009.

Oates, Stephen B. *With Malice Toward None: A Life of Abraham Lincoln*. New York: Harper Perennial, 1994.

Stauffer, John. *Giants: The Parallel Lives of Frederick Douglass and Abraham Lincoln*. New York: Twelve, 2008.

Primary Texts from the Nineteenth Century

Chesnut, Mary. *Mary Chesnut's Civil War*, C. Vann Woodward, ed. New Haven: Yale University Press, 1981.

Douglass, Frederick. *Narrative of the Life of Frederick Douglass, an American Slave, Written by Himself*. 1845 [repr. Library of America, 1993].

Hawthorne, Nathaniel. "Chiefly about War-Matters." *Atlantic Monthly* 10 (July 1862): 43–61.

Keckley, Elizabeth. *Behind the Scenes; Or, Thirty Years a Slave, and Four Years in the White House*. New York: G. W. Carleton, 1868.

Lincoln, Abraham. *The Collected Works of Abraham Lincoln*. 9 vols. Roy P. Basler, ed. New Brunswick: Rutgers University Press, 1953–1955.

Speeches and Writings, 1832–1858, Don E. Fehrenbacher, ed. New York: Library of America, 1989.

Speeches and Writings, 1859–1865, Don E. Fehrenbacher, ed. New York: Library of America, 1989.

Richardson, James D., ed. *The Messages and Papers of Jefferson Davis and the Confederacy*. 2 vols. 1905. New York: Chelsea House-Robert Hector, 1966.

Timrod, Henry. *The Collected Poems of Henry Timrod*. Edd Winfield Parks and Aileen Wells Parks, ed. Athens: University of Georgia Press, 1965.

Walker, David. *Appeal in Four Articles; Together with a Preamble, To the Colored Citizens of the World, But in Particular, and Very Expressly, To Those of the United States of America, Third and Last Edition*. Boston: David Walker, 1830.

INDEX